AMERICA'S SUPERSTAR

A DEEPER DIVE

DAVID SOREN

Cover images Shutterstock.com

www.innovativeinkpublishing.com
Send all inquiries to:
4050 Westmark Drive
Dubuque, IA 52004-1840

Published in the United States of America

About the Author

Dr. David Soren is a world renowned archaeologist who has been credited with making one of the top 75 discoveries in the history of world archaeology: finding the source of the Great Mediterranean Earthquake of A.D. 365 on the island of Cyprus and detailing the events that led to the rise of Christianity and the fall of Roman paganism on the island (Source: Oxford University Press).

He is a fellow of Great Britain's Royal Institute of International Affairs and of the Johns Hopkins School of Advanced International Studies as well as a Fellow of the American Academy in Rome and the author of more than 25 books on archaeology. His archaeological excavations have discovered the lost sacred spings of the emperor Augustus in Tuscany and he has explained the decline of the Roman Empire in Italy through his discovery of a burial ground of infants believed to have died from a malaria epidemic in A.D. 450.

At the University of Arizona where he is Regents Professor of Classics and Anthropology, he regularly teaches as many as 1000 students per year. After finishing his most recent book on the pandemic that stopped Attila the Hun from daring to attack Rome, he decided to turn to something different: an archaeologist looking at the life and art of Taylor Swift.

Converted to becoming a Swiftie by his own students, Dr. Soren became fascinated by how much students could learn from studying Taylor's lyrics and self-created videos and Eras Tour presentations and his new book invites Swifties to do a deeper dive and learn the implications of Swift's work in Surrealism and the Paranoiac-Critical Method, Steampunk Culture, Retro-Futurism, Art Deco, Expressionist-Cubism, Caligarism, Star Wars, Plato and Neo-Platonism, Aristotle's Poetics and numerous other topics.

Soren, who has designed and produced multi-million dollar exhibitions for the American Museum of Natural History in New York City (and a Star Wars show with the film's original production designer Harry Lange at the Hayden Planetarium), is a major fan of Swift's visionary and lyrical talents and in this textbook, written in clear non-jargony prose especially for Swifties, and featuring 150 illustrations, he hopes to share why he finds Swift's work so engaging and such a stepping stone to advanced intellectual engagement. He also shares his thoughts on what her next career steps might possibly be.

Introduction

Before you begin reading this volume, there are a few things you need to know. First, it is written by a Swiftie (albeit an elderly one) specifically for Swifties who want to go a little deeper into some of the reasons why Taylor Alison Swift is such an extraordinary and enduring world-wide phenomenon. Secondly, I didn't want to produce a book that said the same things as so many other books and articles that you can find: the story of her life from childhood to the Eras Tour, her scholarly literary parallels and influences, her business acumen, her fashions, her girlfriends and squads, her boyfriends, and assorted positive and negative gossip.

I thought it would be a better idea to try to analyze in detail some of her body of work and determine what it is that she does that is unique and what has produced such an incredible international following for her. I even dared to offer some suggestions about how she might be thinking about her creative process. Finally I offer some background on how her work has mirrored and affected a good deal of my life.

There are some drawbacks to the book so I want to state them right away up front. It is <u>un-official</u> and <u>unauthorized</u> which means that we can't get access to some of the Eras Tour images that we would like to have which show the set design and innovations specially developed for the tour and which help to give detail to her life and creative processes. However, fortunately, there are some definite pluses to consider. If you view the videos that I discuss you will find that just about everything in the text is rather easily viewable online either in video form or in fan videos taken of the Eras Tour or in the official Eras Tour movies.

To help illustrate the points we make in the text we have included about 150 photographs, among them many we've been able to obtain of Taylor herself but also many other images that hopefully add clarity to what you are reading about or simply are intended to make the reading more fun. The text tries to be a serious but plain clear language study of Taylor's work and an attempt to get inside her mind to the extent that we can (or think we can!) to reveal how she works her magic. To this end you will see a large number of footnotes which will refer you to short articles, videos and books which underline and compliment the ideas expressed in our text.

Thus you could read a chapter and then get on your computer and find a host of articles providing details and imagery for things we discuss in the book. There are so many articles in the footnotes that you can have a whole other book of things you can read that will give more background about the subjects discussed. We tried to form a bridge between the super esoteric articles and books that are coming from distinguished college professors and the tabloid books that show up at the supermarket in hopes of getting you to do that impulse buy for that Swiftie you know or have raised. Instead it is our hope that this book will help you go a little deeper into perceiving her body of work and her amazing talents.

When we discuss specific Taylor Swift videos we encourage you to first view the complete official video or the Eras Tour version of it in order to enhance your understanding of our text. Some of the fan-shot Eras Tour videos are a bit rough to view but they show some of the backgrounds she has used and some of the LED images shown on the actual stage floor, panels and backscreen. We have listed some of them for your convenience but we cannot show any screen shots from them.

I should also confess at the start that I am a professional practicing research archaeologist and university professor who is guilty of writing books and giving lectures on a variety of esoteric subjects, from the origin of malaria in the ancient Roman world to spa bathing and health immersion under the Roman emperor Augustus leading to the granting of remission of taxes for doctors in the Roman empire. I've also held forth on the beginnings of Christianity and its relation to ancient earthquake destruction on the island of Cyprus and I've published a reconstruction of an Umbrian Roman villa featuring architectural innovations we hadn't heretofore known that the Romans could do. For many years I have been attempting to explain the devastation of fifth century A.D. Rome as evidenced by a *Plasmodium falciparum* malaria pandemic.

In between writing books and articles on those diverse topics, for relaxation, I write books on the entertainment business including a history of American vaudeville from the 19th century to the present and a biography of Vera-Ellen, the marvelous dancer who was such a standout with the great Fred Astaire and Gene Kelly. I also helped actor/dancer Russ Tamblyn of *West Side Story* fame with his recent autobiography, producing the first draft of it for him to substantially revise and augment.

However, I decided to turn my focus onto Taylor Swift for this book because I think she is one of the most well-known and yet complex and mysterious creators of entertainment that I have ever encountered. Her interviews whether serious and scholarly or just plain fun on popular talk shows are masterful examples of how to adjust to or play to an audience whether the interviewer is highly sophisticated such as Martin McDonagh (*Variety* 2022) or just out for fun such as David Letterman (Letterman 2014). The lyrics of her songs are often so beautiful that they bring tears to countless fans, myself among them…and offer insight, hope and consolation. And her melodies can be so haunting they seem not to have been written by humans (I'm thinking now of the bridge to *This Love* or *Cowboy Like Me*) but rather to have been dropped onto this world from outer space, so simple yet uniquely beautiful are they. And she has literally saved huge numbers of people from suicide including people I actually know (Johnson 2023) plus she has had large numbers of people propose marriage to each other during her songs, sometimes right in front of her (Vargas 2023). Her business acumen is astounding (Milano 2024) and her instincts toward music writing and production (Penn and Trust 2024), set design (McLaughlin 2024) and fashion (Taylor Swift Style 2024) are already legendary.

People across the world realize that the Eras Tour constitutes a milestone in American popular entertainment that will likely not be soon forgotten and may never be equaled. Certainly, if you were fortunate enough to see it live, you marveled at the phenomenon: the screaming, the jumping up and down and the ever-flowing tears and bodies quite literally trembling all over with sheer excitement, the singing along and acting out of every word by the superfans, her astonishing physical and vocal endurance, the magnificent staging, the myriad costume changes, the discipline of her background singers and her dancers, and her phenomenal memory for every lyric and chord and dance move. We can marvel at the visual beauty of the music that we thought we knew as it takes shape and emerges more clearly in our minds through the staging and presentation and often becomes different from what we had originally imagined. We see the harmony of the fans making and sharing friendship bracelets, the feeling of good will resembling to me a cleaner, neater Hippie movement in San Francisco in the 1960s, and above all the remarkable way in which Taylor held 80,000 people or more in the palm of her hand riveted on her every gesture and comment for 3 ½ hours. I'm lucky if my students can survive a 50 minute class of mine without requiring life support.

The beauty of it all comes through on film too but not quite with the transformative immediacy and delirium of being there and having the strong sense that you are literally watching an historical movement and moment unfold before your eyes. The ending of it on December 9th, 2024 produced a sadness to many across the entire world that was palpable.

This book is called *America's Superstar: A Deeper Dive* in reference to the sudden dive Taylor takes from and through the stage during each performance. When it first happened in Glendale, Arizona at State Farm Stadium with the first Eras Tour fans, they didn't know what to expect and gasped audibly as she seemed to plunge through the stage and then swim underwater, finally emerging at the far side of the stadium. And many fans have asked what is the meaning of that strange shock that we Arizonans in Glendale got that first night.

Clearly, as in the old time show biz tradition, Taylor wants her performances to surprise and entertain and the surprise dive certainly shocked and astounded, then quickly became an iconic part of her Eras Tour. In addition there is a surreal aspect to the dive which is pure fantasy and couldn't really happen in real life and yet somehow it did right before your eyes. I take it as an invitation to an evening of magic, the magic of coming together to enjoy a wondrous experience and a trip that emerges from Taylor's fertile mind.

Writing this work was a delightful, relaxing and fun experience for me as it helped me to understand and appreciate even more the unique talent of Taylor Swift. Much of it is based on lectures given in my various classes on popular culture and on conversations with Swifties including my principal physician, a physical therapy receptionist, many students, a medical secretary and so on. Some have even helped me to get medical appointments I couldn't have otherwise gotten scheduled (!) and in fact my publisher Angela Lampe was there in Glendale with her daughters at the first Eras Tour concert and actually saw the first dive and felt the shocked reaction to it by the audience around her.

As an archaeologist I am used to studying ancient sites around the Mediterranean and having to make sense of things that happened thousands of years ago. These days in archaeology we use theoretical constructs to help us put things together such as Identity Theory as studied by scholars such as the brilliant Emma Blake at the University of Arizona in which instead of trying to make huge generalizations such as who were the ancient Greeks or Romans, we look at cultures more individually and see what makes each one what it is. We study the efforts of individual people or sub-groups to learn more about who they were rather than starting with overall generalizations about societies and peoples as if their thoughts were all unified all the time.

The reason for this new approach to breaking down ancient societies into their component parts is that in our own culture we tend nowadays to be so fragmented that we are interested in things such as what is Black Lives Matter, LGBTQ+, MAGA, Proud Boys etc. etc. and it is hard to talk anymore about one unified culture. Rather we focus on the diverse and often antithetical fragments that make up the national dialogue these days. And new advancements in science such as bio-archaeology make it possible for us to know more about ancient individuals and sub-groups so that we don't have to think of Romans or Greeks back then or now as all unified and we start to color in all the varied aspects of the cultures of ancient peoples.

I tried to use this approach in this book in order to avoid pigeon-holing Taylor as the media so often does as "the *Fortnight* singer" or defining her through her dating history or what she chooses to wear each day. Instead of considering her monolithically as if she just fits into one slot, I have taken some of her lyrics and her visual creations as well as her actions (a great number of them humanitarian and generous) and attempted to show her as a complex multi-faceted individual who can lead the student of her work into some remarkable areas (this is why she is used so much as a teaching tool all across the world and dozens of new classes in Taylor are springing up in diverse disciplines all the time) (Attridge 2024). In addition I've tried to illustrate as best I can what I am discussing and I've tried not to use genre-specific words so that those Swifties who want to come along on this trip with me can understand clearly what I am discussing and not have to worry about highly technical jargon associated with a particular discipline. That's it. You're ready to start.

I hope you like the book.

NOTES

Attridge, Margaret, "You Can Study Taylor Swift at These Colleges," *Best Colleges* 6-25-2024 https://www.bestcolleges.com/news/these-colleges-have-taylor-swift-classes/

Johnson, Brittany, "An Oddly Specific List of 19 Taylor Swift Songs to Listen to If You're a Trauma Survivor," *The Mighty* 10-22-2023 https://themighty.com/topic/trauma/taylor-swift-songs-trauma-survivor/

Letterman, "Taylor Swift Loves New York, Not Lousy Boyfriends," *Letterman* 10-28-2014 https://www.youtube.com/watch?v=ozrrUio3AB0

McLaughlin, Katherine, "The Eras Tour Stage: See the Intricate World-Building of Every Set in Taylor Swift's Most Ambitious Shows Ever," *AD* 5-10-2024 https://www.architecturaldigest.com/story/the-eras-tour-set-design

Milano, Brett, "Taylor's Version of copyright: At a Harvard Law School event, an expert in digital exploitation of intellectual property says Taylor Swift singlehandedly shifted composition copyright considerations," *Harvard Law Today* 4-3-2024 https://hls.harvard.edu/today/how-taylor-swift-changed-the-copyright-game-by-remaking-her-own-music/

Penn, David and Gary Trust, "Taylor Swift's Songwriting and Production Analyzed: 13 Secrets to Her Chart Success," *Billboard* 4-30-2024 https://www.billboard.com/lists/taylor-swift-songwriting-production-analyzed/differences-between-swifts-earlier-and-recent-eras/

Taylor Swift Style, "The Original Taylor Swift Fashion Blog," *Tumblr* (Taylor Swift Style. Com) 12-13-2024 https://taylorswiftstyle.com/

Vargas, Chanel, "A Surprising Amount of Fans Are Getting Engaged on Taylor Swift's Eras Tour," *PS* 6-2-2023 https://www.popsugar.com/love/taylor-swift-eras-tour-marriage-proposals-49191292

Variety, "Taylor Swift & Martin McDonagh," | *Directors on Directors* 12-12-2022 https://www.youtube.com/watch?v=x8zfsf4azLo

Contents

Preface

Guest Authors:
Dave Hahn
Gerardo Quintero Bernal
Sydney Early
Liz Rossi
Arielle Sare

Artist:
Barbara Bernal

This book is dedicated to my wife of 58 years Noelle Soren, who has been my inspiration and guiding light. As I tell her first thing every morning, I never thought I would marry anyone so beautiful and amazing.

I also would like to thank Angela Lampe of Innovative Ink Publishing for greenlighting this volume.

Finally I would like to thank all of the Swifties who have helped me to create this work. You all help to keep me young and I hope my insights can find their way into your hearts as yours have entered mine.

Why Do Swifties Cry?

By David Soren

In my classes at the University of Arizona I teach about 1000 students a year including undergraduates, Master's level students and Ph.D.s and among them are about 75 who often openly refer to themselves as Swifties. Since at the time of this writing I am 79 years old and still teaching I might be forgiven for not having known much about Taylor Swift or current country or popular music. Since my Swifties first urged me to include her in my popular culture class in 2022, I set out to learn more.

My elderly neighbors describe her rather vaguely as "that country music singing 'girl' who writes songs about the guys she breaks up with" and the later middle-aged fellow down the street described her as "the one who writes songs for eight year old girls." Until about three years ago that was all I "knew" about Taylor Swift. I am old enough though to remember the beginnings of Elvis (Presley, not Costello) and certainly The Beatles and in my youth I had less generally well remembered favorites such as The Kinks, Loreena McKennitt (who became a personal friend and who let me produce one of her first American concerts in our Social Studies auditorium at the University of Arizona in 1991), Kylie Minogue, The Dixie Chicks (now The Chicks, whose first large general public formal theatre concert I produced in Tucson at the University of Arizona in 1994) and even The Bangles, but I had stopped listening to pop and country by 2022 as I got older and contemporary popular music didn't hold much appeal for me.

When I told my students in 2022 my total knowledge of Taylor Swift, they were appalled and decided to educate me and I immediately learned some basic things. She was no longer a country singer and wasn't exactly a pop singer either but she wrote and sang all kinds of music (variously reported to me as country, country pop, pop rock, synth pop, folk, electro folk, indy folk, electro pop, rap (very little), R&B and straight indie) (Swiftipedia 2024). Whatever it is, that music seemed to deeply affect the Swiftie students whom I knew and they were just as likely to be 20 as 8 years old so I set out to do a deeper dive into the Taylor Swift international phenomenon. There had to be some there there I thought and I was determined to find out what that there there there was and if I liked it…or not.

I wanted to see how much her music and especially her lyrics related to them, with the "them" being primarily females in their teens and younger as well as many many transgender youths in my classes, plus a sprinkling of the general male population.

Featureflash Photo Agency/Shutterstock.com

But there were also a surprising number of older and even senior Swifties, including of all people the former *I Dream of Jeannie* tv star Barbara Eden who was 92 years old when she spoke of being a Swiftie. And 79 year old David Letterman has spoken out repeatedly on her behalf. And I noticed above all that my Swifties seemed to cry a lot when they talked about her and her music and her life. Cry and cry and cry! (Pierides 2024).

I initially watched a remarkable performance of Taylor from 2012 when she was guesting on shows such as David Letterman and was already a major star despite being only 21 years old. She sang a song called *Begin Again* which was a slow song with a slight country flavor but which impressed me as more of a throwback pop song that had been lightly countrified with a slide-bar guitar played by Grant Mickelson (Leon 2012) in the background (Swift 2012)

It was a song about Taylor herself who had emerged from a love affair that had been bumpy and had then found a new relationship (reportedly with Conor Kennedy) who rekindled her belief in love and the lyrics reflected that. The song told about her depression concerning love and how it just breaks her and burns her and finally ends. And then finally on a Wednesday in a café she sees a new love starting and it transforms her and revives her.

This was performed in front of a live audience which was full of young girls hanging on Taylor's every word, many of them visibly shaking and deeply emotional as she got to the point in the song where she had cast off her earlier lover and found

FIGURE 2: Taylor Swift at age 21 at the September 6, 2012 MTV Video Music Awards at Staples Center, Los Angeles (Picture: Paul Smith).

FIGURE 3: Hyannisport Massachusetts, Saturday July 28, 2012. Conor Kennedy and Taylor Swift. Conor is the 18 year old son of Robert F. Kennedy Jr.

love again with a new boy on a Wednesday (often days and times are recorded by Taylor as well as significant places) in a café." Each time that the song came around to these words something happened that I'd never seen before. The audience erupted in cheers *DURING* the song as if to register their personal approval that Taylor herself had rekindled her belief in love with this new boy, so closely did they identify with her. The fans were taking the song *personally* as if it were happening to *them* and many of them were crying (Hopper 2023). And as I enlarged the size of the video of the performance it seemed that the fans were extremely emotional as the song came round to this part especially. I thought that this was something truly extraordinary. This singer/composer was able to relate to her audience in such a personal way that they totally interacted with her. This was someone who wrote music about her own life that these young ladies understood in a primal visceral way and they were clearly gravitating to Taylor for her wisdom about what they were going through in their own lives and most especially about love and boys.

I asked my own Swifties about this and they told me that Taylor was "special" and when they listened to her songs they felt they were in the presence of someone who was speaking honestly and truthfully to them about their own lives as nobody had before, even and sometimes especially including their own parents (Puri 2023).

But what was there that was unique about Taylor's lyrics that spoke so directly to them? I have a really high-brow answer for this and if you will indulge me for a while I think you will believe that I am right when we get to the end of this digression. At least I hope so.

At first, I think Taylor began her career by simply writing down what was happening in her life because she was considered something of an outcast in school and had few friends and few invitations to make more of them

She kept writing poetry and music about her difficult boyfriend relationships, the scary first day of junior high or middle school, surviving getting a crush on a guy and not being able to tell him, being bullied, being an outcast, being told to stay out of the bathroom because she would infect it, and other problems and occasional pleasures of youth (CLRN Team 2025). This was her emotional diary and way of recording her personal life from the age of 11 on and when she recorded and released her initial album at age 16 she was amazed that other girls and outsiders in society could relate to it because they had been going through the same things and thought they too were the only ones to do so.

FIGURE 4: Wyomissing Area School District is a highly rated, public school district located in Wyomissing, PA. Taylor Swift attended WASD from the ages 9 to 14.

Eventually, perhaps by the time she had graduated from a home-schooled high school equivalency she began to figure out that there was actually a reason why she was connecting so amazingly with young girls and women. She knew they were seeing themselves through her songs but a fuller realization of what she was doing may have happened to her a little later on during the time between 2017 and 2023 when she was living with (and confined by the pandemic with) Joe

FIGURE 5: Taylor Swift promoting her first album at age 17 at the American Music Awards, Nokia Theatre, Los Angeles. November 19, 2007. Picture: Paul Smith.

Alwyn, the handsome, introverted actor, composer, pianist, and literary scholar, and grandson of one of the most intellectual and important English composers of classical music, William Alwyn. But Taylor herself, electing not to go to college due to her overwhelming success in the music business, still had a strong desire for learning, especially about antiques (Horton 2023) and great authors and books (Buonocore 2024) and gradually I think she became more deeply aware of how she was able to work her magic on the world's populace.

In order to understand this more fully we need to go back to ancient Greece, and to Athens in fact where we find the most famous *savant* of the time was a man named Aristotle who lived from 384 to 322 BCE and who held forth on a wide variety of subjects including philosophy in an intellectual park known as the *Lyceum* in the eastern area of Athens. It was a gathering

FIGURE 6: Joe Alwyn attends the '*The Favourite*' film photocall during the 75th Venice Film Festival on August 30, 2018 in Venice, Italy.

FIGURE 7: Bust of Aristotle. Roman copy of a lost Greek original. It was found in Athens during the preparation for the building of the new Acropolis Museum.

place for friends and for pursuing athletics including running and general exercising and it was a religious center. There was also a library there started by Aristotle honoring his great mentor Plato. Aristotelian scholars these days spend their entire lifetimes researching the vast array of scholarly works available to us about Aristotle whose mind embraced virtually every aspect of existence that one could imagine in the fourth century BCE.

Among the numerous topics that Aristotle discussed and wrote about extensively was something called the *Poetics* (*Περὶ ποιητικῆς*) only a part of which survives and in it he has some particular theories about why the concept of theatrical performance which had been developed right there in Athens had been so successful and why some playwrights were more effective than others at creating emotion in an audience.

FIGURE 8: Aerial photo of iconic Acropolis hill in Athens with the Greek temple known as the Parthenon on top, the famous Theater of Dionysus at the bottom center and traces of the Odeon or music hall of Pericles at the lower right with the red coverings.

Aristotle was living after the golden age of Greek tragedies written by such famous playwrights as Aeschylus, Sophocles and Euripides, and Aristotle attributed the enduring success of these men and others to a few concepts, one of which he termed *mimesis* or *μίμησις* which translates roughly as a simulated representation or an imitation of something (Edlund 2019).

Following up on the teachings of Plato, Aristotle differed somewhat from his mentor and commented on how an artistic work such as a Greek tragedy might be put together: Aristotle saw it in four distinct but related parts. First came the basic idea, which leads to the formation of what you want to present. The second part is what the thing you are creating is made of, which includes all of its parts or actual ingredients, what you might call your outline of all that makes up your play but which only exists in a rough form. Third is the actual process of taking the basic idea and the rough ingredients or kernels of your thought and creating it. Finally comes what you hope to achieve: the work of art or the actual presentation. That fourth part is what is called teleological which means it reaches your goal or telos (τέλος in Ancient Greek) or final result and if you achieve your effort well your creation may endure as a masterwork.

In presenting this four part system Aristotle is telling us that we are mimetic beings which means that art seeks to imitate something of life and so life itself is the kernel that we reflect upon and polish and hope to mimic in some

FIGURE 9: Relief sculpture depicting Plato and Aristotle arguing by the Early Renaissance artist Andrea Pisano (14th Century). The sculpture adorns the external wall of Florence Cathedral, Italy.

way by attempting to make a work of true art, an art which reflects and represents reality and causes the audience to identify with what you are attempting to depict. Now read that again (please!) and make sure you grasp it because it's important for our discussion here. In other words, if you achieve this *mimesis* or effective creative representation of reality , the audience will relate to it and find something in it to hold dear.

If the audience can truly identify with your story in all of its detail the audience member may achieve a kind of bond with it and experience your outcome (τέλος) with you and you will be a true creative mastermind. In a work of real excellence the identification with your story as it relates to the audience member's real life story may be so well conceived that it can cause you to experience the playwright's own experience as if it were your own sand you will become deeply touched by it.

Viacheslav Lopatin/Shutterstock.com

FIGURE 10: Central section of the famous wall fresco in the Vatican Museum in Rome by the Renaissance artist Raphael from 1511, known as *The School of Athens*, featuring philosophers Plato and Aristotle in the center debating Realism vs. Idealism

Thus you may achieve what the Greeks watching their own tragedies in a theater called *catharsis* (*κάθαρσις*) which is quite literally in the Aristotelian vocabulary a cleansing of emotions which might be achieved by tears, or a strong identification with the plight of a character, or pity, grief, love and so forth, i.e. anything that wrings you out emotionally because of the playwright's ability to achieve *mimesis* in his or her composition. This *catharsis* can even affect you physically as the word also means literally a purging or cleaning out of the digestive system so that you are even physically drained.

So an ancient Greek drama for Aristotle has to be (and this is critically important) two different things: <u>distant</u> and <u>recognizable</u>. The story has to be someone else's story but the story is recognizable enough to you as something you can also relate to. For example, a person is asked to obey a law but another person disagrees with the law because she thinks the law is wrong. Do you disobey it or not? It's someone else's story but you can relate to it strongly if it is well enough presented because you might have been in a similar situation sometime where you debated doing something illegal because you felt justified in doing it. In fact this is the plot of the 5th century B.C. Greek playwright Sophocles' *Antigone*.

If you can select and show pieces of real life that your audience can focus on and you present the characters effectively you may elicit *empathy* which is originally an Ancient Greek word *ἐμπάθεια* meaning to identify sympathetically with the thoughts or feelings or even actions of another individual or other individuals. So it is not just telling a story but artfully and even poetically representing it to evoke the direct feelings of others.

Now, what does this have to do with Taylor Swift you may ask if you managed to make it this far into my hypothesis? Well, this is exactly what she does. In song after song, Taylor provides stories, often colored with times and places and sometimes even specific locations (Black Dog Café, Cornelia Street, The Lakes in England, etc.), which are drawn directly from her life experiences or from the experiences of people she knows which have affected her (e.g. *Ronan*) or occasionally (during the pandemic particularly and her more recent work) from her dreams and fantasies. These personal stories so artfully told are basically examples of mimesis whereby her lyrical scenarios remind us of a situation that may have happened more or less to us: looking in the mirror and sighing about your looks or your life, having a boyfriend who was shorter than you and who didn't like it when you wore high heels and who didn't like your taste in music or your hobbies, who was late for everything that you wanted to do, who left you watching their relationship break slowly apart for eight months and finally end, leaving you feeling depressed.

These things are the minutiae of daily life that Taylor constantly observes and they often aren't things that are especially dramatic or newsworthy about each of us but they are the things that live inside our head and pick our lives apart slowly and painfully so of course we understand the *mimesis* of her lyrics. And to it I would add the warm and delicately emotional delivery of her lyrics almost in a speaking tone as if she is confessing to you her personal problems and deepest darkest anxieties and the background music and singing

blackboard1965/Shutterstock.com

FIGURE 11: A postage stamp from Greece in 1998 showing a bust of Sophocles, the ancient Greek writer of tragedyy.

and even her breathing within a song caress the words as well. It is the mood of the song which can be full of rage (*Who's Afraid of Little Old Me*) or rapturous pounding excitement (*Welcome to New York*) or eerie scratchiness on the edge of horror mixed with an oddly countrified rocking background (*Right Where You Left Me*). Mood is an essential part of her mimesis as well as that of a successful ancient Greek tragedy.

In the song *Begin Again*, which we cited earlier, the negative part of the song where Taylor breaks up with her boyfriend and is depressed and languishing in depression is countered by a positive encounter with a new boy at a local café, something that apparently happened in her real life. That relationship didn't ultimately work out either but that is not important here because what is being brought out is the contrast between the poor behavior of the former boyfriend and the much better behavior of the new one.

Much is made of the fact that when Taylor sits down when taken out presumably on a date for lunch or dinner the new boy holds the chair for her. This kind of nicety means a lot to Taylor and young ladies can identify with such actions, including a boy going around and opening up a car door for her which is mentioned in several other of her songs such as *So High School*.   These are a key part of what Taylor appreciates in a boyfriend i.e. matters of traditional etiquette that show good upbringing and refinement and many Swifties can identify with this even in an age of the independent woman. It's just something nice for Taylor to observe in a guy.

There is also an appreciation by the new beau of her humor in the song and that she can be funny which many people know about Taylor (Anhalt 2024), but her previous boyfriend, the song tells us, didn't "get" her and wasn't quite connecting on her wavelength. She notices the way the new guy throws back his head and laughs and I particularly like the way, early in their dating history, she is walking with him back to her car and she is thinking about bringing him up to her place. So many young ladies have to wrestle with that thought—is he trustworthy, is that a mistake to do so soon and will he turn into a neanderthal?

But the new boy interrupts the minor tension of the moment by talking about movies he watches with his family at Christmas and it turns the delicate situation into a holiday family moment and she wants to talk about that to her listeners and they find it empathetic. It's sweet, it's wholesome and it's something young ladies actually face in a romantic relation-ship as it initially unfolds. It is that most delicate of moments—the end of a relationship and the beginning of a new one and the comparison between the two relationships- that make

Taylor (and ourselves) realize that "what's past is past". That's a moment when I myself cry when I listen to *Begin Again*, just because of the beauty and delicacy of the mimesis. Nobody else can write popular music like that these days. She is our Irving Berlin who was an amazing lyricist and composer of the early to middle 20th century. Just listen to the lyrics of his song *What'll I Do?*, written shortly after the family of his fiancé, the beautiful Irish Catholic heiress Ellen McKay, had spirited her off to Europe to get her away from the self-made Jewish immigrant Berlin and prevent their marriage, and you will feel the same tug on your heartstrings or the tears that are welling up right now at this moment as I write this. And by the way Irving Berlin eventually married his great love in spite of all her family's efforts to keep them apart and they stayed together for 63 years and four children!

Taylor is also our modern version of Aristotle from his *Poetics* and she makes us long to experience the romantic conclusion of the song which we actually do several times within it so we have multiple catharses that bring forth cheering from the crowd each time they hear it. The song begins with her slow and deep depression over eight months and comes to a definitive ending (the *telos*) in which all the problems of her life (and ours vicariously) are resolved happily. With her, we experience a catharsis and are built up to it several times. We've been taken through high drama and depression and are filled with empathy for the Taylor in the story because we so strongly identify with it and now finally, it seems, everything will be all right and we can enjoy a catharsis or two or three. You can do this with song after song with Taylor and the writing is always carefully designed to evoke sympathy and understanding but you should stop right now and listen to the Letterman session so that you can see exactly what I have been writing about here. It is a perfect example of the magic of Taylor Swift and as the camera pans over the audience the feelings aroused- mimesis, empathy, catharsis- are palpable. Don't miss it! (Swift 2012).

This brings me to another connection of Taylor Swift to Aristotle which will also take a few minutes to explain. In the *Tortured Poets Department* song *So High School*, there is a pretty direct description of her boyfriend Travis Kelce. She had written the song *Fifteen* way back in 2008 after leaving Pennsylvania and moving to Hendersonville, Tennessee just northeast of Nashville where she started as a freshman in high school. In her song about being 15 she wrote that she would do more in her life than dating the boy from the football team which at that time she had no chance of dating.

But Taylor would learn from that song years later another tenet of Greek tragedy which is irony or εἰρωνεία in which one might say something that one thinks will happen and, un-

FIGURE 12: August 22 2024 Travis Kelce is an American professional football player who is a tight end for the Kansas City Chiefs of the National Football League NFL.

expectedly, the very opposite does. Taylor is shrugging off not getting the guy on the high school football team and fifteen years later she ends up going with a *professional superstar potential hall of fame* football player. It's ironic that when Taylor performed the song as part of her Eras Tour recently she had to laugh as she sang that part of her old song! (Cox 2024). And her devoted Swiftie crowd all got the joke.

We also find in *So High School,* her song about Travis Kelce, another reference to a male showing courtesy to his date by opening the car door for her ("isn't that sweet"). But this is followed by him pulling her to the back seat (!) to make out and the statement that "no one has ever had me like you." So it's pretty clear that this is a much more grown-up lyric than that of the song *15* all those years before back in 2008.

One passage from *So High School* strongly stands out as important for this discussion and it hasn't been extensively analyzed to the best of my knowledge; this is the section where Taylor says that she is feeling again like a high school kid and plays games like truth or dare, a reference to a 2016 podcast question Travis Kelce answered about whom he would "kiss, marry or kill" among three famous female celebrities: Taylor, Ariana Grande or Katy Perry (Viswanath 2024). Next in the lyrics we get the game of spin the bottle which we used to do as teens back in the 1960s and if the coke bottle pointed to someone you were interested in you kissed them or, if you were same sex, you shook hands.

The passage continues by saying that her love interest knows how to ball, a dual reference to his football prowess but also a surprisingly coarse sexual innuendo that is in keeping with the rest of the song's rather graphic words! She then says out of the blue "I know Aristotle" which seems a stunning contrast to the low-brow comments preceding and following (Swift 2024):

FIGURE 13: Group of teenagers lying on the floor and playing spin the bottle.

> "Truth, dare, spin bottles
> You know how to ball
> I know Aristotle".

What does she mean by this? I think the coarse juxtaposition is to contrast the highly intellectual cachet of Aristotle with the silly high school games of kids and of course the raw physical attractiveness of her current relationship.

Taylor appears to be telling us that what is needed now in this relationship is sheer sensual attractiveness with her mate and fun and she can handle the intellectual stuff of her life herself because she understands what Aristotle is saying about entertainment, and how one needs to know about mimesis, telos, catharsis and empathy and how to create poetry and "theater" in her music to make it work for her public. She has had a super serious boyfriend and she wants someone who isn't afraid to be her "arm candy" (Hatcher 2024) when they step out in public. She can handle the mechanics and the private intellectual side of creating important works of art but the pandemic is over and Travis is attentive, funny and sexy and doesn't need to hide from the public eye as her previous boyfriend, a more private and intellectual sort, did (Jones 2024). Taylor knows what she needs to know to create her magic and Aristotle had laid it all out in ancient Athens as early as circa 350 BCE!

In addition to Taylor's remarkable ability to check all the necessary Aristotelian boxes in her songs, fans have also taken to keeping individual quotes from her songs which have become sayings that can be used to guide people's lives in positive ways and allow one to see a different and better viewpoint from the one you have or to reinforce feelings you already have. Huge numbers of people have been helped by her music, lyrics and personal actions as a role model especially to women and to those of marginalized groups of all kinds in our society. I can mention a few of these that I find personally useful when I get depressed about various things:

- "Don't you worry your pretty little mind. People throw rocks at things that shine," From the song *Ours*.
- "Today is never too late to be brand new." From *Innocent*.
- "Karma's a relaxing thought." From *Karma*.
- "Stood on the cliffside screaming "Give me a reason….
- My best laid plan
  Your sleight of hand
  My barren land
  I am ash from your fire" From <u>Hoax</u>
- "Someday I'll be big enough so you can't hit me" from *Mean*
- And of course "Shake it off". From *Shake It Off*.

FIGURE 14: **Shake It Off Light Installation, Vancouver Art Gallery North Plaza, British Columbia, Canada, 11- 28 2024.**

They have become like homilies that people use when facing adversity or they may provide a little boost to getting through a bad day or understanding the hard hits to the soul that one gets from living through each day (Conroy 2023).

Of course not all of Taylor's lyrics are based on her own life experience and especially during the pandemic she produced some songs that came out of her head as fantasies. But they too often carried the Aristotelian imprint for he did not insist that the mimesis be real but only that it seemed to be real and that producing the effect from your mind was an art.

And this brings me to the Swift song that reduces me to tears just thinking about it and which to this moment I cannot hear without breaking out in tears. It is the song *Seven* from the Folklore album, co-written with Aaron Dessner, about an abused, miserable child who was played with and looked after by a young girl, presumably but not even necessarily Taylor, when they were seven.

The connection to my own life through this song is so strong and the memories it produces so difficult and so real that I can hardly bear to hear it, even now more than 70 years after the events in my life that it seems to describe actually happened. I will tell you about these events and why the song hit me so hard that I can totally understand now how other Swifties feel about her music and lyrics that shaped and in some cases even saved their own lives. And we don't even know if the events of this song ever really happened to her in her life or only in her mind.

My mother and I lived on Abbotsford Avenue in Philadelphia, not far from Wayne Avenue which had movie theaters I loved such as the New Lyric and the Wayne Avenue Playhouse. I went to school near there at what was then Edwin H. Fitler Elementary which was a gigantic (it seemed) squarish Gothic stone building built in 1898 and named for a former Philadelphia mayor! My mother was thinking of filing for divorce and had a boyfriend on the side. My real father eventually abandoned us and my only memory of him is him taking me into a very white bathroom upstairs in our row house on Abbotsford and twisting my fingers painfully and asking my mother if that's how she wanted me punished, so that to this day I have a thing about white bathrooms. My mother took up with a postal worker mail sorter who drank heavily and at times would smash up the place and beat me. I learned to cover up so I got the strikes from his fists over my back but one time I wasn't fast enough at opening the garage door for his car and he got out of it and came through the front of our garage just as I opened up the vertical door for him. At this moment he punched me in the face and I did a 180 degree flip over a sawhorse which unfortunately had been placed right behind me.

He also hit my mother and kept her basically a prisoner in the home keeping out visitors and she told me once he had detached both of her retinas.

Consequently, I couldn't wait to get to elementary school each day where I could work hard and be praised for it by wonderful teachers and it began my love affair with learning which became for me an escape. My love for archaeology meant a further and more remote escape from daily life and was fueled by a spate of archaeology movies at the *New Lyric Theater* Saturday matinees such as *Journey to the Lost City*, *The Mole People*, *Curucu-Beast of the Amazon*, *The Snow Creature* and *Man-Beast*. They were all terrible movies of course but I loved them and what they represented to me and I dreamed of becoming an archaeologist so I could wear khaki pants and a pith helmet and trudge off to great adventure at the far side of the world (and eventually many years later I did!).

On our block in our part of Germantown in Philadelphia lived a red-headed girl with freckles who was a few years older than I was. She was named Camay, after the famous now I think discontinued "soap of beautiful women." Or she might have been named Camée, a lovely French word meaning a cameo or a gem or shell carved in relief, especially one in which the raised design and the background consists of layers of contrasting colors. In any case Camay was a princess to me, living in a row house about 15 houses up the street from mine. She loved to come out and look after the little children on the block and mother them, asking how you were and what you liked and what you were going to do this weekend. No matter how depressed or horribly treated or ignored at home or, worse, constantly blamed for everything that was wrong and made to sit on the "bad boy chair" with a paper dunce cap on my head in the kitchen and told how stupid I was, I would get to go outside for blocks of time periodically where I might hope to meet Camay and we would talk and she would fuss over me and tell me everything would be fine.

FIGURE 15: A variety of vintage cameo brooches made from carved shell in intricate detail.

I am sure if she is still alive somewhere now she would never remember me or any of what transpired and I know she never knew how much she meant to me and how much her quiet understanding showed me to be hopeful for a better future someday with some real hope of escape if only I could learn patience. She was quite the young little caregiver and must have eventually made a wonderful mother to children. Taylor's song *Seven* made me think of myself as the seven year old boy and Camay as the young albeit imaginary Taylor talking about escaping and the boy having problems that she was trying to take him away from. My problems were just loneliness and constant depression and sometimes physical fear and bullying at home ("Someday I'll be big enough so you can't hit me", I thought, and "Shake It Off", Camay would say or words to that effect). Not everything in the song *Seven* parallels my own life but the *mimesis* is such that the song was a trigger to bring those past joys and horrors rushing back into my brain like days filled with a thousand sharp knives interrupted by moments of bliss with Camay.

As I listened in the song about the brief time Taylor and the abused boy spent together when they were seven and how they planned to run away together to India and how they played and made up fairy stories and how she loved him even though she could now at age 30 no longer remember his name or knew what had happened to him, it began to make me cry— about the lost innocence of my youth, how I never really got to be a child, about one's inability to stop the pain that adults who never should have had or even been entrusted with children have caused, about the need to find and sustain hope somehow, about finding friendship when it is most needed, about my unforgivable failing to keep track of my princess over time, and the blurring in my mind of what I actually had experienced with Camay and even exactly what she looked like or said, and about the need to thank her I will never fulfill. It's all there in that song. It's not totally my life but enough is in it to strike deep into every fibre of my being.

For a moment I was seven again and the feeling was overwhelming, the emotions so intense all swirling around and mixing together at once. This is truly the magic of what Taylor Swift and no other popular singer I have ever heard can do. And she does it with the lyrics, the tone of the melody, the timbre and subtly intense feeling in her mood-setting voice and the careful attitude of the arrangements to caress that voice, all made with her accomplices the professional producers of her music such as Aaron Dessner and Jack Antonoff, her remarkable backing vocalists who seem to even breathe when she breathes and her musicians, all of whom tend to stay with her for years and years as almost a family unit.

FIGURE 16: Jack Antonoff at the MTV Video Music Awards 2017 at The Forum on August 27, 2017 in Inglewood, California.

FIGURE 17: Taylor Swift performs at the 2019 Jingle Ball at Madison Square Garden.

You're not done, my university Swifties told me. Taylor's critics have said all she does is write stupid breakup songs for young teens. She does write many breakup songs and explores every nuance of a breakup but it's because she writes about everything that happens to her in real life and casts it out onto a public that can identify with it. Now it's time for you to stop reading here and listen to the song *Ronan*, which is about a mother who lost her child to neuroblastoma cancer at age 4. It doesn't sound like a song I'd want to hear, I said to my Swiftie advisers. Was it a hit?

It was done privately they said and never put on her album *Red* the first time she released it in 2012 but it was released finally when she re-recorded Taylor's Version of the album in 2021. Kelly Clarkson, the famous singer, had alerted her to a legal loophole whereby Taylor could re-record and retake ownership of her earlier songs and when she re-issued *Red* she included many of the songs that were never released in that album the first time and *Ronan* was one of them (Saunders 2023). And by the way, each album she re-recorded sold better than they had even the first time they were issued and this is what the term Taylor's Version means when you see it on one of her albums. If *Seven* had me crying *Ronan* had me completely sobbing. It has to be one of the most beautiful poems ever set to music and Taylor offered it as a gift to the deceased boy's mother Maya Thompson who was so pleased to have this treasured memento of her son.

Ronan was a special song inspired because of Taylor happening on to a blog created by the distraught mother writing to her deceased son, yet hoping to keep his memory alive. You have to be a pretty hardened person not to break down after hearing this song which was only performed extremely rarely, at first in 2012 for a *Stand Up to Cancer* tv special, raising money for cancer prevention, a cause Taylor had long supported. Maya became upset when she learned that Taylor had lost control of her own music when Scott Borchetta and Big Machine Records sold her work without her permission (legally, they point out repeatedly, they didn't need permission). In order to preserve control Taylor added it to the re-release of the *Red* album (Taylor's Version) in 2021 and the song is once again in Taylor's possession (Ahlgrim 2021). The profits from the new release went to help children with cancer and to support Maya's own fund. The chorus of the song suggests that in a more fair world little Ronan would be free to be with his family to live happily ever after:

Christina Aiko Photography/Shutterstock.com

FIGURE 18: Multiple editions of 1989 Taylor's Version by Taylor Swift for sale on a special kiosk inside a Target Store on Halloween in San Diego in 2023.

> "Come on, baby, with me
> We're gonna fly away from here
> You were my best four years"

In the song sung from the mother's point of view, Taylor wishes to have the power to make all things right in the world, if she only could (Mitchell 2021).

In her music Taylor functions for many as a kind of positive nurturing force whose power is manifest but who is also vulnerable and prey to perceived moral frailties and evildoers. She has repeatedly stepped in to try and make right of wrong, sometimes reading a young person's blog about his or her failure to afford a higher education and stepping in to provide funding for the person (Fink 2019). When she learned that homeless people were being moved out of the way of her upcoming concert venue in Edinburgh, she provided a large sum to a food bank there to help them and she has kept a careful watch on this problem of clearing out homeless to help at a number of her Eras Tour venues (PerezHilton 2024). She frequently invited fans to her home early in her career for special dinners and previews, parties and conversations (Duboff 2014). She inspires people with her music and lyrics but there is even the chance that she may show up on your doorstep bringing Christmas gifts of Taylor Swift merchandise (Barnes 2017). David Letterman compared her to Mother Theresa and said he himself would never invite a fan to his home ever (Letterman 2014).

FIGURE 19: Taylor Swift and her idols Faith Hill and Tim McGraw at the EIF's Women's Cancer Research Fund's *An Unforgettable Evening Benefit*, Beverly Wilshire Four Seasons Hotel, Beverly Hills, California 1-27-2010.

To my mind she functions to many Swifties like a Greek goddess who inspires and arrives *deus ex machina*, which was a way of lowering a god or goddess by a hoist down onto the stage of a theater in ancient Greece to resolve the tragic plot of the story and save the protagonists from disaster or fate. In ancient Greek it is *ἀπὸ μηχανῆς θεός* or literally a god (or goddess) from a machine. It was designed to be a major special effect that would support the idea that the inscrutable gods were able to work wonders in a community (Maio 2024).

In Brazil a young Swifty died during a Taylor Swift concert due to an extreme heat wave. Taylor visited the parents and consoled them and helped them financially to deal with the death of their daughter (Nanji 2023). In case after case people who are lucky enough to meet her report on her kindness, generosity and overall sweetness and this is especially true of staff and employees of restaurants, construction crews and security guards associated with her concerts and tours, and her troops (Saunders 2025). When I hear *Seven* or *Ronan* or hear about her philanthropic work, her gentleness and kindness to fans, her reaching out to those in need and especially when I view the sensitivity of her lyrics and the production of her music, it makes me understand why she does know Aristotle in a special way. You are becoming a Swiftie, my students say-- and they are right. I now know what makes Swifties cry.

NOTES

Ahlgrim, Callie, "The mom whose story inspired Taylor Swift's 'Ronan' says it's 'unbearable to think about' anyone else owning the rights to the song," *Business Insider* 11-12-2021 https://www.businessinsider.com/taylor-swift-ronan-true-story-mom-maya-thompson-interview-2021-11?op=1

Anhalt, Bobby, "Hilarious Taylor Swift Interview Moments That Are Hard To Shake Off," *Ranker* 7-3-2024 https://www.ranker.com/list/funniest-taylor-swift-interviews/bobby-anhalt

Barnes, Stephanie, "Taylor Swift casually dropped by a superfan's home to deliver a package," *Hello Giggles* 10-12-2017 https://hellogiggles.com/taylor-swift-casually-delivered-package-to-fan/

Bruce, Amanda and Tom Russell, "Caspar the Friendly Ghost: 13 Facts About His Sad Backstory," *Screen Rant* 10-23-2024 https://screenrant.com/casper-friendly-ghosts-sad-facts-backstory-movie/

Buonocore, Julianne, "Top 25 Favorite Taylor Swift Book Recommendations," *The Literary Lifestyle* 10-8-2024 https://theliterarylifestyle.com/taylor-swift-book-recommendations/

CLRN Team, "Was Taylor Swift Bullied in School," *California Learning Resource* Network 1-3-2025 https://www.clrn.org/was-taylor-swift-bullied-in-school/

Conroy, Kayla and Ava Slocum, "34 Taylor Swift Lyrics to Live By," *Girl's Life* 12-13-2023 https://www.girlslife.com/trending/celebs/42542/34-taylor-swift-lyrics-to-live-by

Cox, Nicki, "Giddy Taylor Swift giggles over lyric about 'dating the boy on the football team' amid Travis Kelce romance," *Page Six* 6-3-2024 https://pagesix.com/2024/06/03/entertainment/taylor-swift-giggles-over-lyric-about-dating-the-boy-on-the-football-team/

Curchin, L.A., "Breaking the Vapor Barrier: What Made the Delphic Oracle Work?," *University of Waterloo, Canada.* (no date) https://uwlabyrinth.uwaterloo.ca/labyrinth_archives/breaking_the_vapour_barrier/

Daly, Rhian, "'You Don't Own Me': The Story Behind Lesley Gore's Empowering Hit," *UDiscoverMusic* 3-20-2024 https://www.udiscovermusic.com/stories/lesley-gore-you-dont-own-me-feature/

Duboff, Josh, "Taylor Swift Invited Hundreds of Fans Into Her Home for Cookies and Dancing," *Vanity Fair* 10-17-2014 https://www.vanityfair.com/hollywood/2014/10/taylor-swift-1989-secret-sessions-video

Edlund, John R., "Aristotle's Poetics in the Classroom," *Teaching Text Rhetorically* 2-16-2019 https://textrhet.com/about/

Fink, Jenni, "Taylor Swift Donated to Fan's College Fund—These 6 Celebrities Also Helped Finance People's Educations," *Newsweek* 8-13-2019 https://www.newsweek.com/taylor-swift-fan-college-fund-celebrities-paying-education-1454136

Hatcher, Kirsty and Dave Quinn, "Travis Kelce Says He Doesn't Mind Being Taylor Swift's Arm Candy: 'It's the Life I Chose,'" *People* 9-5-2024 https://people.com/travis-kelce-says-he-doesnt-mind-being-girlfriend-taylor-swift-arm-candy-8706796

Hopper, Alex, "The Meaning Behind Taylor Swift's Ode to Starting Over, "Begin Again,"" *American Songwriter* 12-20-2023 https://americansongwriter.com/the-meaning-behind-taylor-swifts-ode-to-starting-over-begin-again/

Horton, Maggie, "All the Places Taylor Swift Has Been Spotted Buying Antiques," *Country Living* 7-15-2023 https://www.countryliving.com/life/entertainment/a44506547/taylor-swift-antiques-shops

Jones, Sara, "'Shocked' Taylor Swift was 'blown away' by Travis Kelce-hosted Eras Tour surprise party: 'Meant so much,'" *Page Six* 12-20-2024 https://pagesix.com/2024/12/20/celebrity-news/shocked-taylor-swift-was-blown-away-by-travis-kelce-hosted-eras-tour-surprise-party-meant-so-much/

Leon, A., "Happy Birthday to the Agency's most organized guitar player, Grant Mickelson!" *The Swift Agency* 4-30-2012 https://theswiftagency.com/2012/04/30/happy-birthday-to-the-agencys-most-organized-guitar-player-grant-mickelson/

Letterman, David, "Taylor Swift Loves New York, Not Lousy Boyfriends," *Letterman* 10-28-2014 https://www.youtube.com/watch?v=ozrrUio3AB0

Maio, Alyssa, "Deus ex Machina — Meaning, Definition & Examples," *studiobinder* 12-10-2024 https://www.studiobinder.com/blog/deus-ex-machina-meaning-definition/

Mitchell, Molli, "The Touching Meaning Behind Taylor Swift's 'Ronan,'" *Newsweek* 11-15-2021 https://www.newsweek.com/taylor-swift-ronan-song-meaning-true-story-maya-thompson-red-taylors-version-1649201

Nanji, Noor, "Taylor Swift 'devastated' as fan dies before show," *BBC* 11-18-2023 https://www.bbc.com/news/entertainment-arts-67461445

PerezHilton, "Taylor Swift Gave A HUGE Donation To Edinburgh Food Banks After Learning Of Homeless Population!," *PerezHilton* 2024 https://perezhilton.com/taylor-swift-donation-edinburgh-food-banks-homeless-population/

Pierides, Maria, "Taylor Swift Fans Are Emotional As The Singer Breaks Down Crying On Stage In Toronto: 'We Are Also Sobbing,'" *SHEFINDS* 11-26-2024 https://www.shefinds.com/collections/taylor-swift-breaks-down-tears-toronto-eras-tour-fans-sobbing/

Puri, Upasana, "Why are Young Girls drawn to Taylor Swift? An Era of Femininity," *Medium* 9-21-2023 https://medium.com/@upasana.puri/why-are-young-girls-drawn-to-taylor-swift-an-era-of-femininity-45ef6c774de1

Saunders, Angel, "Kelly Clarkson Says Taylor Swift Sent Her a 'Cute' Gift After *1989* Re-Release: 'She's So Nice,'" *People* 11-10-2023 https://people.com/kelly-clarkson-explains-why-taylor-swift-sends-gifts-8400468

Saunders, Angel, "Taylor Swift Doubled Back to Tip Workers as She Exited 2025 Grammys," *People* 2-12-2025 https://people.com/taylor-swift-tips-workers-as-she-exits-grammy-afterparty-10788154

Swift, Taylor, "Taylor-Swift -Begin Again (Live from New York City)," 2012 https://www.youtube.com/watch?v=cQ5tlnGg4wc

Swift, Taylor, *So High School* 2024 (lyrics) https://www.songfacts.com/lyrics/taylor-swift/so-high-school

Swiftipedia, "Musical Genres of Taylor Swift's Albums," *Swiftipedia* 2024 https://taylorswift.fandom.com/wiki/Musical_Genres_of_Taylor_Swift%27s_Albums

Viswanath, Jake, "Taylor Swift's "So High School" Will Make You Miss Your Teen Days," *Bustle* 4-19-2024 https://www.bustle.com/entertainment/taylor-swift-so-high-school-lyrics-meaning

The Swifties Weigh In: A Deeper Look at Taylor Swift's Lyrics

By Sydney Early

(Sydney Early is a 16 year old student in the tenth grade at BASIS Tucson North in Tucson, Arizona. When she graduates in two years she intends on majoring in musical theatre. Her hobbies consist of musical theatre, singing and dancing, playing guitar and the piano, and soccer. She hopes to one day be an actress on Broadway, though her broader plan is to ultimately be an entertainer. She wants to make her own music that will impact and move even the toughest of listeners the way it does herself).

The well known pop star Taylor Swift is both loved and hated for her notorious music. Many members of Taylor's fan base will describe her music as relatable, catchy, or modern, but I enjoy listening to her music on a deeper level. Not only is Taylor's music uplifting and easy to listen to, but it also holds some incredibly powerful hidden messages. Many of Taylor's songs have a broad theme of heartbreak, primarily that caused by ending a relationship.

However, listening to her music more closely, each of her songs has a more subtle, and even more powerful, meaning. Some of my personal favorites examples of this are *Back to December, Message in a Bottle, The Very First Night, Never Grow Up, You Belong With Me, Teardrops on my Guitar*, and *Slut!*.

Back to December on the surface level sounds like a girl who regrets breaking up with her boyfriend and feels the repercussions of it, but the song is really trying to relay the importance of acknowledging one's mistakes and making the most of them. When Taylor sings that she is swallowing her pride and apologizing and that she keeps returning to December in her mind before she was so cruel to her lover that one night. She wishes she could make everything all right.

This teaches listeners that everyone makes mistakes, both large and small, and that those mistakes cannot be taken back, and rather should be accepted and be used to become a better person.

Another one of Taylor's songs *Message in a Bottle* may seem like it is about a girl who is madly in love with a boy and wants to be with him, but really it portrays the longing to be wanted and noticed by someone. When Taylor sings in this song about how her love interest is so far away and she is depressed and lonely and can do nothing more than just put a message in a bottle to reach out to her love, she admits to feeling hopeless and terrified with nothing more she can do than hoping it gets to her beloved. And she hopes he feels the same way. This feeling reflects one's tireless efforts to get someone whom they feel very distant from to notice them, even if their efforts are fruitless. This song is very relatable for adolescents and young adults in particular who have experienced a similar feeling of longing and jealousy, which can make them feel not seen or recognized.

The song *The Very First Night* seems like a sweet song about reminiscing about good times with your partner, but also reflects the dread and anxiety that comes with the passing of time. Many look at change as a negative thing, and Taylor represents that feeling as wanting everything to stay one way forever. The line that states how she wishes she could fly and swoop up her beloved and take him back in time is very beautiful as she hopes to write about their love into the sky and how she still misses her love as she did on their very first night apart. This reflects the feelings of nostalgia that make memories feel much brighter and happier, thus increasing the feeling of longing for the happier time.

Never Grow Up is one of Taylor's songs that resonates with many people, including those who don't typically like Taylor's music. It is a song that reflects on the happiness and joy of childhood, and the longing to grow up we often felt as kids, though now we all wish we could turn back time. Taylor gives this song a happy demeanor with the intent of resonating with her audiences of all ages. Taylor writes poignantly about how one needs to take mental pictures of what your room was like when you were a child and how you should take great pains to remember what it was like when your dad got home from work, even the sound of footsteps and what words were said and what children's songs your little brother sung because one day all of that will be gone and you will only have your memories. This is very impactful because it portrays the realization a lot of individuals have, as they begin to grow older, that they should cherish every moment they live because it will someday be gone.

The song *You Belong With Me* is a classic upbeat song about a girl wanting to get with a guy because she feels she is better for him than his girlfriend is. Though this is what it seems like on the surface, the song portrays the impact jealousy has on the mind, mainly negative and hateful thoughts. This is best relayed in the part of the song where the girl whom Taylor is jealous of doesn't understand the boy's sense of humor and can never understand him as well as she does and she always seems irritable. She then sings about his wonderful smile that was capable of lighting up an entire town and how going with this other girl made it disappear. Though the song is upbeat and happy, as well as portraying the main character as the hero, the one-sided thoughts about the boy's girlfriend show that her jealousy has brought her to become judgmental and hateful. This is someone many people can relate to, even if they won't admit it, because jealousy is a natural human reaction, which causes many people to view the person they are jealous of in a negative light.

Another song, *Teardrops on my Guitar*, is about a girl longing to be with a boy who is madly in love with another girl, so she writes sad songs about her distress. This song recognizes that everyone has unique coping mechanisms to deal with one's grief, whether it be large or small scale. In the song she is hopelessly in love with someone named Drew who occasionally talks to her and whom she finds so funny and how being around him prevents her from seeing anyone else in the room. But he only talks to her about how in love he is with another girl! He doesn't realize the affect he has on her and how she can't sleep at night because of him and how he is the reason for the teardrops on her guitar. She is left to making wishes on a wishing star and singing in her car this song she made up about him helplessly. This reflects the grief people feel from rejection, and how that can lead to self-doubt or jealousy, which many then deal with using unique and individual coping mechanisms.

Finally, the song "Slut!" is about a girl who doesn't mind being judged and is all right with being insulted if it meant staying with her boyfriend. This song relays the message that no matter what one does, he or she will always be judged, so the best thing to do is whatever makes them happy. In this sad song Taylor talks about how if people look at her all dressed up for this guy she's willing to pay the price of being called a slut because to her it is worth it to maintain this relationship. This song demonstrates that in order to be happy and confident, one needs to be open to judgment and criticism because it is ultimately inevitable.

Swift's use of Surrealism in her music videos, including *Fortnight* featuring Post Malone, represent the magical and supernatural feelings one often feels when they are blind-sided by a strong emotion, often love. It also showcases the distance many people feel when reflecting on old memories, often caused by a feeling of reminiscence and longing for the past. This is especially seen in Swift's music video and lyrics for *Fortnight*, as she reflects on a short relationship she had that only lasted the span of two weeks, but this relationship contained some of her fondest and most comforting memories. When she is seen typing the lyrics on a typewriter across from Malone, a brief moment of color is seen spreading across the top of the screen, strongly contrasting with the colorlessness of the rest of the video. This, alongside the fantastic nature of the scenery and situations of the video indicate that the memories she is reminiscing about are faint and unclear, perhaps due to the short length of the relationship or perhaps because it was fantasy rather than actual events, and yet it was still recalled as the most positive time in her recent life. This is supported by the lyrics of the song, including "and for a fortnight there, we were forever…now you're in my backyard, turned into good neighbors. Your wife waters flowers, I wanna kill her." These lyrics represent the narrator's grief over losing someone she once thought they would be with forever despite their relationship ultimately crumbling after only a fortnight. This is a situation often relatable to the feeling of adolescents and young adults, as many describe that in their first relationships they felt they had a type of love that could never be changed or replaced, despite the fact that they likely did not know what that type of love truly felt like yet. These lyrics also reflect the grudges and distaste often felt after breakups in one's early life, despite growing older and learning to accept and move on as time passes. Swift writes about hating her ex's new life and his wife, yet she is longing for his love the way she believes they once had it, and this also represents the way many recall a time when they would formulate a reality that was inaccurate in relation to their real life when they were young and they felt they were in love, so that they are feeling as if they'd lost something that had never even existed when the other person moved on. This song and music video are sentimental to me personally because I feel like the colorlessness and surreal nature very effectively represents the distance I feel from many of my memories, even my fondest ones. Knowing we will never be able to return to some of the best parts of our lives is a hard thing for anyone to accept, but seeing this feeling represented in Swift's music helps me as well as many others be more accepting of that and look to the present and future rather than solely the past.

Taylor Swift is a lyrical genius in the sense that she includes many hidden details and meanings in her songs that need to be analyzed in order to find and experience them, rather than just experienced by listening to her music. These meanings often attack topics that are brushed over due to embarrassment or sensitivity, but are very important for many individuals, including myself.

Each of these songs helped me realize something about myself I had never really thought about before, including the fact that I sometimes will create a negative persona of someone in my head if I am envious of them, or that I have a lot of different ways I cope with grief and rejection. I think Taylor Swift's music is beneficial for those of all ages and backgrounds because she writes about topics that can be related to by anyone, yet can still be lighthearted and enjoyable.

3

Taylor Swift's *Anti-Hero*: Her Personal Catharsis

By David Soren

(Note: Before reading this please go to the Internet if possible and view Taylor Swift's *Anti-Hero* video and have it ready to refer to and pause as needed).

It's never easy to try to read the mind of a poet who reveals herself in her work at the same time that she couches her revelations in so-called Easter Eggs of varying obscurity. An Easter Egg can be a subtle reference to Taylor's beloved cats, a harbinger of a song she will release six months from now such as writing the word "us" on a book in a video when you know she will soon release a song with that name, or it can be something deeply significant for the video you are watching but which has been cleverly hidden (Editors 2024). In Taylor Swift's recent videos, it is important to view them many times to observe every object or piece of writing that you see because nothing is in the video by accident.

Easter Eggs however are often a fun puzzle that young and old can delight in trying to solve. As I have been told by local teachers, it can even be used as a fun learning tool for elementary schoolers or teenagers who might discover something hidden in one of Taylor's videos such as a top hat or an old typewriter and it can lead the students and teachers into all sorts of searches and discussions to learn about what the past was like or how technology developed or it can even lead to a discussion of Sigmund Freud or the ancient Greeks and so on.

Sometimes reviewers are spot on at recognizing the Easter Eggs and their meaning. However, one often ends up learning more about the interests of the reviewer than one gains about the actual intent of the poet herself. Of course the fact that the poet doesn't dress as a poet but rather appears regularly in her shows in a form-fitting quasi-leotard makes her an easy target for those who don't believe she is a serious artist.

FIGURE 1: A teenage girl browses the magazine Taylor Swift: The Magic in Her Music from Key Publishing.

Numerous critics have taken a shot at interpreting the complex Taylor Swift song *Anti-Hero*, with one of the best efforts being done by Oliver Tearle, a lecturer on English literature at Loughborough University in the English midlands who compared the video to something he knows a good deal about: Shakespeare's play *Richard III,* at the end of which some of the main people Richard wronged come back to visit him in ghostly form (Tearle 2023).

Does this then tell us more about Taylor's literary interests or Dr. Tearle's interest in English literature? In any case, before we assess the abundant critical analysis and offer some suggestions of our own, let's take a deep dive into the video itself and try to figure out what is going on because Taylor describes it as one of the most personal and insightful songs and videos she's ever done and a "guided tour throughout all of the things she hates about herself" (Huff 2022).

The extremely catchy and ghost-filled song helped to make it possible on Halloween night of 2022 for Taylor to capture the first 10 song spots on the Billboard chart, the first time it had ever been done. Was that a coincidence to have a ghostly subject win a prime place at Halloween? Not too much in a Taylor Swift video is coincidence:

"Anti-Hero" is one of my favorite songs I've ever written. I really don't think I've delved this far into my insecurities in this detail before. I struggle with the idea that my life has become unmanageably sized and I, not to sound too dark, just struggle with the idea of not feeling like a person. This song is a real guided tour throughout all the things I tend to hate about myself, and it's all those aspects of the things we dislike and like about ourselves that we have to come to terms with if we are gonna be this person, so I like "*Anti-Hero*" a lot, because I think it is really honest."—Taylor Swift (Irvin 2022).

Before we start digging in I need to say a word about my own credentials for analysis of this video. I am not a professional psychoanalyst but over the last 53 years I have taught about 1000 univer-

FIGURE 2: David Garrick (1717-1779), renowned English actor, as Shakespeare's *Richard III*. Mezzotint by John Boydell, after painting by Nathaniel Dance, 1772.

sity students per year, some years fewer and some more, both in person and online at the Universities of Missouri and of Arizona. I have done a great deal of student counseling, directed student overseas programs and archaeological excavations in Italy, Cyprus and Portugal wherein all sorts of mental illness and anxiety-based complexes manifested themselves among the students, and where groups of people have to live together day in and day out for weeks and sometimes months in remote areas with little access to anything but one another and a radio.

I have even worked in Bedouin areas of central Tunisia and in the foothills of the Sahara desert with small teams. As such I have seen and had to deal with just about every neurosis and bizarre behavior manifestation there is, including even actual witchcraft exorcism and the believed possession of one person by another. Night terrors were a particular specialty on the long, isolated digs and we worked in areas where bombs were often deliberately placed so I had to learn from British intelligence forces how to check a car for explosives, deal with poisonous vipers and beware of on-site scorpions. I even did some Biosphere counseling for one of its inhabitants!

Besides all of that, I had the scariest job of all. I was a university department head for 12 years and almost nothing can prepare you for the neuroses that accompany the subtle care and handling of university professors! So I think I could do at least a shallow if not a completely deep dive into Taylor's personal nightmare here and see what we might discover.

We begin the video with Taylor speaking directly to us about getting older but not wiser and how she is having more midnights than afternoons, a time when she is restless and feeling particularly out of control of her life. Her entire album, *Midnights*, is, she says, about the things that keep her up at night and not in a good way: self-loathing, fantasizing about revenge, wondering what might have been, falling in love and falling apart (everlovelyjewel 2022).

FIGURE 3: iOctober 27, 2022: Kiosk display in a Target store in Minnetonka, Minnesota of Taylor Swift's new *Midnights* album.

The video begins in an ordinary kitchen. Taylor is eating bacon and eggs with broccoli. She is dressed very simply in a nice shirt and slacks, things she might have on when relaxing at home and being what all her friends and interviewers constantly call "normal" (Mohan 2024), and not doing anything fabulous such as entertaining 92,000 people at once and holding them spellbound for 3 ½ hours on the Eras Tour. But all is not normal here. Taylor finds that the meal forms a smiley face-- and when she cuts into one of the two sunny-side up egg eyes, it spews out a purple goo which some extraordinary Swifty Easter Egg hunters such as Alyssa Bailey (Bailey 2022) see as the ink from a Glitter Gel Pen which Taylor says she likes to use in her songwriting because of the joy it brings to the user :

"Glitter Gel Pen lyrics don't care if you don't take them seriously because they don't take themselves seriously. Glitter Gel Pen lyrics are the drunk girl at the party who tells you that you look like an angel in the bathroom. It's what we need every once in a while in these fraught times in which we live." –Taylor Swift (Swiftipedia 2022).

However, the breakfast she is eating seems to be occurring at midnight and the oozing eye suggests that her quest for the simple pleasure of a normal meal is not happening, since the eggs are bleeding out within this nightmare song. Like the rest of the video, this event is situated in a surrealistic universe wherein things are juxtaposed that normally wouldn't be or couldn't be: morning breakfast at night, food as a smiley face that has a bleeding eye, midnight that becomes her afternoon. And we've just started to enter the surreal landscape of Taylor's mind (see my other essays in this volume). Furthermore, we aren't sure if this video is a comedy as many interpret it to be (Rossignol 2022) or as something intended to be terrifying…or both at the same time.

FIGURE 4: Glitter gel pens in bright vivid colors.

As we continue she suddenly feels the presence of ghosts, reportedly played by her brother (2 of them) and her lawyer at the time (Taylor-Swift Nation 2022). One ghost is covered with a sheet so it resembles a traditional cartoon ghost such as Caspar the Friendly Ghost or more generally our traditional idea, since at least the 15th century, of what a ghost might look like (McDaniel 2019). This idea comes from a long tradition of burying people, especially poor people, wrapped in a linen shroud or a bedsheet so that if they were perceived as rising from the dead, they would be what were termed "bedsheet ghosts" or revenants wearing a sort of shroud. In order to frighten people a living person might dress as a dead revenant or the shrouded person would be interpreted as the living dead and brigands could frighten easily-swayed citizens by dressing up as a ghost.

FIGURE 5: Traditional Halloween ghost.

But this first ghost that Taylor encounters is wearing a cowboy hat and sunglasses and waves to her as if he/she/it knows her and expects her to recognize "him". It might represent her country music career from her early years in show business that she has now left behind to become a pop star. It doesn't menace her directly but its sudden and unexpected appearance terrifies her and she runs to hide beneath a kitchen cupboard only to be greeted there by a different ghost wearing fancy round sunglasses and featuring cat ears, perhaps a reference to her love of her cats and the cat world she loves spending so much time in, even to the extent of wanting to be a cat in the movie *Cats* and going to cat training school for four months for the role (Quinn 2019). So far the ghosts are unexpected but not directly menacing to her. Nonetheless Taylor is delicate and easily frightened, which has actually been true especially throughout her life. She dislikes someone confronting her unexpectedly and she loathes being in a funhouse and encountering a still figure that suddenly comes to life and she hated being scared to death by Ellen De Generes on the *Ellen Show* and actually falling in a bathroom and almost seriously injuring herself (Bailey 2015)! She was once punked by Justin Bieber who made her believe someone had been burned alive on a nearby boat and she went into a near total trauma (Cooper 2012).

Totally panicked in the *Anti-Hero* video (compare it to the Bieber episode!), she runs for the 1970s style wall phone with a rotary dial and a land-line, things that older, more traditional or not famously hip people might have still in their homes (I do!). The phone is placed beneath a regular round analog wall clock but she quickly discovers that the phone line has been cut so she cannot call for help and it makes her scream in terror. Meanwhile, the cat and country ghosts have moved to the kitchen breakfast nook and are having a light breakfast and coffee, another bizarre and comedic touch but once again not totally frightening as they are apparently the ghosts of her earlier and present life. But the cut phone line signals trouble ahead.

Taylor's drawing from her life and anxieties while engrossed in nightmares or just late-night malaise is an example of the Dali-esque Paranoiac-Critical Method that I have discussed often at the University of Arizona when I present painter and designer Salvador Dali's approach to his art and how he was governed by the logic of dreams and of course full-blown nightmares, a way of harnessing his fears and turning them into art, a device he had discovered by 1930 (Sarvé-Tarr 2023).

Now in our video Taylor runs again and this time a third ghost appears wearing heart-shaped sunglasses, a ghost that really likes Taylor and raises a glass filled with a dark liquid to her. Close inspection shows that this ghostly figure has a laurel crown—look carefully—it IS there. What can this be and what does it have to do with Taylor's life which was so secure and simple before this with country music, cats and …now we have this weird thing encountered after she has witnessed cut phone lines.

It is I believe a symbol of her growing might and power and fame, which she has difficulty handling well (at least in her own opinion). The laurel crown is associated with ancient Greek and Roman figures both divine and mortal and its presence on a ghost here calls to mind several possible meanings in our context.

The laurel crown is specially chosen for Olympic victors in ancient Greece and was worn by the Greek sun god Apollo who instituted the renowned Pythian Games featuring his symbol the giant python snake that winds around the *omphalos,* a symbolic marker for the very center of the ancient world as signified by the greatest Greek god Zeus (Fontenrose 1959).

Apollo was the god who came to Delphi, the center of the world and appropriated it as the center of mystical prophecy visited by all who sought to know wisdom and the truth. The sacred site was presided over by a priestess who breathed actual vapors emitted from a sacred spot deep within the earth. After ingesting these vapors, she foretold the future from inside the Temple of Apollo at Delphi, responding to questions asked of her through her

FIGURE 6: Portrait in profile of Greek god Apollo wearing laurel wreath on fifth century B.C. ancient coin of Leontini, Sicily.

FIGURE 7: Omphalos in the Delphi Museum, Greece.

priests. Scientific studies made in 2003 determined that there were actual fault lines running through the temple which gave access to a tiny spring deep in the heart of the building which produced a gas, ethylene, that made the priestesses fall into a trance and feel a heightened euphoria as if they were stoned. This may have been the inspiration for their cryptic predictions (Curchin no date).

Apollo slew the great python to take over control of this mystical area of Delphi in ancient Greece and how fitting it would be if the great priestess of this world, at the center of the universe where ancient prophecies were pronounced at the great Temple of Apollo, was the representative of the god who had vanquished the great snake Pytho and had taken it as one of Apollo's symbols.

Described as a vicious snake by Kim Kardashian and in much of the media frequently almost ten years ago (Holterman 2017), Taylor decided to embrace the snake image and move towards it instead of shrinking from it. She began using it as a symbol to face her detractors and even exact a measure of revenge. "*Look What You Made Me Do!*," she sings on her *Reputation* album and she begins to adopt snaky clothing in her more aggressive and less meek return to recording, touring and doing public appearances and her dress at the 2018 Billboard Awards is referred to as "very modern Grecian goddess" (Simmons 2018; Wasilak 2018).

Anton_Ivanov/Shutterstock.com

FIGURE 8: Ruins of the Temple of Apollo at Delphi, Greece.

If one cares to continue the parallels among Taylor, Apollo, snakes and prophecy that we encounter at Delphi, we can add that Taylor also has stated that she was set up by her detractors who used an edited version of her Kim/Kanye phone call to misrepresent her actions (Dailey 2023). Later, in *Tortured Poets*, she compared herself to the ancient Trojan priestess Cassandra who was condemned by the gods to always speak the truth and to never be believed even though she warned her people of impending attack and doom.

Kathy Hutchins/Shutterstock.com

FIGURE 9: Taylor Swift at the 2018 Billboard Music Awards at MGM Grand Garden Arena on May 20, 2018 in Las Vegas, Nevada. She is wearing a Versace gown, Jacquie Aiche snake ring, Fernando Jorge arrow ring, Casadei heels with snake-like detailing and Hueb earrings.

Cassandra was the Trojan royal priestess of Apollo! So we can see that despite being a celebrity in today's world, Taylor often draws on the ancient classical (Greek and Roman) world for her analogies and thinly masks her anguish while revealing her desire for retribution.

We are not permitted to quote her lyrics but she discusses in her song how Cassandra was killed right away at Troy because she was possessed by fears and tried to warn the town and she had her prison cell filled with snakes. She had told the truth that the Trojan horse should not be accepted as a gift to the Trojans from the Greeks and Cassandra asks if now that Troy is in ruins can she be believed now that she told the truth.

Also, the Pythian Games in honor of Apollo's victory over Pytho were special contests that offered prizes in many different areas, including music, poetry and dancing. Victors were offered laurel crowns as rewards for excellence in their competition and we get our terms Nobel laureate when referring to Nobel prize winners and, perhaps more importantly,

FIGURE 10: Neo-classical marble sculpture of the priestess Cassandra under the protection of a statue of the goddess Pallas Athena, made in 1877 by Aimé Millet (1819-1891), now in the Tuileries Park, Paris, France.

poet laureate from this classical reference. When THIS ghost raises a glass in her honor it may be hailing her as the poet laureate of her generation (Giltz 2024).

The laurel is also a symbol of power warn by Roman emperors and popularized by Rome's late Republican period dictator Julius Caesar who was captured by enemies early in his career but was later enormously successful in his military campaigns and was not averse to bragging about them ("*veni, vidi, vici*- I came, I saw, I conquered," he said; Brinks 2024) but he became filled with *hubris,* a Greek word for overarching arrogance, which led to senators revolting against him and conspiring to stab him to death in mid March (the famous Ides of March) (Suetonius, *Life of Julius Caesar* 37.2). Images of Caesar wearing the laurel were well known in Rome in his time and he was the first living dictator/leader to have his own head on a Roman coin.

By becoming a dictator and dishonoring his wife Calpurnia, who was much beloved in Rome, and consorting with Cleopatra and bringing her back to Rome with him he went too far in his arrogance and even his former friend Marcus Iunius Brutus turned against him and was one of the senators who attacked and killed him. Caesar's last words as he was being killed were alleged to be "et tu, Brute" meaning "even you,

FIGURE 11: Gaius Julius Caesar wearing a laurel wreath crown.

Brutus" but in fact this story and phrase comes from Shakespeare's play *Julius Caesar* and not from any specific ancient source even though most people believe it is from an ancient Roman author, such as Suetonius, who mentions the event.

Going too far and exhibiting too much *hubris* has always been a great concern to Taylor who is deeply worried about wanting to be normal in her relationship with the public and close friends and not obsess about herself or seem arrogant or needy (Haden 2023). If she goes into a football stadium she tries always to be respectful and "normal" to everyone whom she encounters and to never play the diva or be the elephant in the room despite her massive security needs and staggering fame. As a reminder to herself to keep humility, she kept and I believe still keeps in at least one of her homes a now commercially available couch pillow which displays the words IN LATIN (!) "et tu Brute" to remind her how to treat people and not to be arrogant so that friends turn against you (Fresh Pair 2018), and this may be a direct link to the possible laureate Julius Caesar ghost in *Anti-Hero*. It also appears on the front of the throne that she sits on in her video *Look What You Made Me Do*. It is only barely glimpsed in Latin but it is there! (VOGUE 2017; Thompson and Sblendario 2018)

FIGURE 12: *Assassination of Julius Caesar*, engraving from *Charles Rollin's Ancient History of the Egyptians, Carthaginians, Assyrians, Babylonians, Medes, Persians, Grecians, Macedonians* (1768). The assassination of Julius Caesar was a conspiracy involving several Roman senators; Suetonius, *Life of Julius Caesar* 82).

So, in sum, the laurel can have meanings of musical and poetic symbolic excellence, can be associated with the great sun god and ancient Greek and Roman patron of the arts Apollo, can be a symbol of enormous power but can also lead to hubris and at least, according to Shakespeare, friends turning into enemies. In other words if you don't get its radiant power and glory under control it can bring you to the heights of fame but also destroy you…and that is a major theme of this complex video. Are we right about this? Only Taylor knows for sure but the presence of the laurel has high significance in the video and seems to connect to Greco-Roman antiquity in an important way for subtle Easter Egg hunters.

Indeed we see that all of the increasing recognition, all of these highlights of her life, are becoming too much in our video and her life is literally getting too big, too complicated and as Taylor has said in her famous *Miss Americana* documentary "too loud" and it is all turning into a Freudian midnight nightmare. She cannot be left alone to "her own devices" because these ghosts all come with a price taken out of her and each of the three parts of her life revealed here has its own vices and problems. People attack her unjustly even though she's telling the truth, just like Cassandra. She's pulled in every direction at once. Everywhere she goes she is stalked and followed and pursued by the success that, ironically, she herself has so vigorously sought. She needs help desperately but who can provide it?

Up to now in the video we have met innocent and sweet young girl Taylor like the one at the end of her *Look What You Made Me Do* video who is trying to live simply, following her self-admitted credo revealed in the wonderful Netflix video *Miss Americana*: that she just always wanted to be very good and do what was right and stay really close to her mother and excel in school. This is what traditional Freudians would have called her Superego, the person here who dresses simply and modestly, uses her mother's land-line phone, uses basic analog clocks, has a simple breakfast and loves country music and cats and beautiful poetry and music. (Mannoni 2015).

FIGURE 13: Freud's psychoanalytic theory of unconsciousness in people's minds.

But this is now becoming a problem because she is being called to develop her talents to the next level and even beyond that by another version of herself who enters right in through her front door—this is her EGO talking which is dressed flamboyantly in a concert show outfit more blatantly exposing her body by showing off her sex appeal and especially her legs by means of a bodysuit/leotard, which has become an iconic symbol of her fame and more grown-up look partly in response to all the attacks on her that had taken away her aura of childhood innocence. She had first done it, partly for the shock value, on the *Reputation* tour in 2018 and it often involved a snaky look that came right in the face of her detractors. (Larrabee-Zayas 2018).

In her safer more traditional superego form, her body is covered up and she is easily frightened essentially by her life getting bigger and bigger across the country and the world, and she hardly recognizes herself in her constant scheming that she engages in to get ahead and survive in the tough music business like a Julius Caesar trying to negotiate the late Roman Republic and its senate. In fact she's so frightened that she fears that the friends or loves of her life (the Brutus types) will get tired of what she is becoming and leave or defame her. She is even sorry about burdening her mother with her problems and trauma which seem so minor when her mother (and father) have been so ill with cancer off and on from 2015 (Cinone 2024).

FIGURE 14: Taylor Swift performing on stage at the Aviva Stadium in Dublin, during the Eras Tour (Picture date: Friday, June 28, 2024). Photo by Liam McBurney.

Credit: Alamy Images.

We are not told how she is specifically scheming to get ahead but we know that she is being accused of all sorts of things by harsh media such as perhaps pushing too hard to get revenge for the cruel slights that were done to her by manipulation of her taped conversation made by her enemies or maybe by her releasing various versions of her songs to sell more material to her fans and keep her higher up on the Billboard charts. There is constant criticism of her private plane use (as if she could ever go anywhere by public transportation and survive all the personal threats to her and withstand the constant fan admiration and pressure)! It could be the staggering amount of money she is amassing for each recording and performance. Or it can be the fact that the family literally invested in her career and they could do this because they were wealthy. Nothing of all of this is illegal of course in any way and there are many many wealthy people who invested in their children's entertainment careers and the offspring never made it because they didn't have the ability (I personally know a number of these individuals), but all of this seems to weigh heavily on her conscience and provide seemingly endless uninvestigated and unsubstantiated grist for the mass media (Zambas and Stephanou 2023 lists a bunch of them for you).

She is desperate, however, in the video for some way to cope with the ravages of fame and the dark paths it can lead you down, including furious exercising to reshape her body into a perfect form and 00 dress size because she will be analyzed completely and mentally dissected by critics each time she appears in public or on a stage (Dador 2024). She is particularly sensitive about her buttocks and stomach areas and often has had to severely talk herself out of feeling acute body dysmorphia to avoid weeping and depression as was shown in the starkly revealing *Miss Americana* video (Tsintsiras 2023).

But now in our video we see at the front door a new and very different version of herself. And this second self announces "it's me" to which the Taylor superego self responds weakly with a simple "hi" and to which the ego Taylor responds "I'm the problem it's me. This now explains the curious, seemingly awkward positioning of the words in the lyric as it is actually revealed to be a CONVERSATION between superego and ego Taylor!

Her ego then shows her the way to greater success as they have a drink together to celebrate Taylor's glorious yet rather frightening future because as Taylor has said, after two drinks of mojitos she begins to think that she is a wizard (Brandel 2019). The very young Taylor once said she was not a party girl and never would drink significantly (Halter 2024) but now the two Taylors ARE drinking heavily and now are merging into one Taylor, a mix of the "normal" superego girl and the ego-driven superwoman performer.

There are several references in the video to *Tea Time* which became an enormously popular segment of the Ellen Degeneres tv show but which normally had two little girls Sophia Grace Brownlee and Rosie Grace McClelland back in 2011 who invited celebrities to tea and cookies and skones in the British fashion and then asked them questions which were partly scripted and partly just the little girls having fun on their own (Sims 2022). Their charming British accents and silly formal high tea served by infants became one of the most successful parts of the *Ellen* show. Many of the famous rock and pop celebrities of the time came on and Taylor's stint was one of the very best episodes.

But in the *Anti-Hero* video *Tea Time* has been subverted into a heavy booze drinking session, a dark parody of one of England's nearly sacred customs!! In England, traditionally (I lived there briefly) when you have problems it is considered customary to offer the upset person a "good cuppa" but it is not normally a boozing session. The drinking will continue again later in the video, causing more havoc.

After the binge drinking, ego Taylor calms superego Taylor's fears by showing her how to emerge from her cocoon and deal with life in the fast lane and superego Taylor takes notes furiously. While innocent Taylor demurely strums on her famous, trendy koi fish guitar, ca. 2011, from her *Speak Now Tour*, ego Taylor takes the guitar and gleefully smashes it to bits like rock musicians used to do in the psychedelic sixties.

FIGURE 15: Group of colorful Koi fish swimming and making ripples on the surface of a pond.

Guitar smashing became a symbol of drug-induced, alcoholic haze rock and roll and was pioneered by Pete Townshend of *The Who*, *Rage Against the Machine*, Jimi Hendrix and Kurt Cobain (and don't forget the famous scene with Jeff Beck and The Yardbirds in Michelangelo Antonioni's 1966 classic movie *Blow-Up*)—in short, it was an act which is a rite of passage from passivity and youthful innocence to a wakeup call to survival in life through action/aggression (Metzger 2016). Townshend, the pioneer, is known for doing it as an act of rage against the music industry and its corruption, something Taylor has learned a bit about (Bonner, Garcia and Olson 2024). The act of guitar smashing has in fact become a symbol of rebellion against the status quo as indeed it symbolizes in this video (Trapp 2023).

Swifties know that the koi fish is all over the *Midnights* album and traditionally they are symbols in Japan of good luck, prosperity, endurance and the ability to persevere and transform yourself in the face of adversity which certainly applies to Taylor's survival as an artist (Swimming in Beauty 2023). But it is her second self here, her ego, which emerges and throws caution to the wind by smashing this traditional symbol of success.

The biggest revelation of the ego Taylor to the superego Taylor is that EVERYONE WILL BETRAY YOU, done all in capital letters. Don't trust anybody, not even as it would turn out Scott Borchetta who has been like family to you, even making your recording ambitions and dreams possible, but even he will sell you out to one of your worst enemies for $300,000,000. Taylor had wanted to buy the rights to her earlier work but Borchetta sold them to Scooter Braun, whom Taylor had, according to her, always detested, accusing him of being a perpetual bully. Upon seeing this key revelation in the video from her ego, emphasized by pounding with a pointer onto a portable blackboard, superego Taylor, eager to learn survival techniques, takes furious notes just like a school student.

You are living in the fast lane now, baby, the ego seems to tell her, where everybody appears to be a sexy baby and you just haven't fit in. This term, many Swifties have noted, apparently comes from the tv show *30 Rock* where Tina Fey's character Liz Lemon hires a female comic name Abby (Cristin Milioti) as a writer to combat accusations of misogyny against Liz but Liz and Abby don't get along and Liz tells her to "drop the sexy baby act" to which Abby says that the "sexy baby thing isn't an act…I'm a very sexy baby." (Mercado 2022; Huff 2022b).

Superego Taylor is the sweet innocent country music-loving high school girl we've known back in 2006 and, at least up to the *Red* album when she began to swing more towards pure pop, loving to sing to anyone who will listen. At this time she was beautiful but about six feet tall, awfully thin and gawky in her dance movements, being described then by British talk-show host Graham Norton as "a gangly giraffe teenager country girl" (Duran 2024). Members of her high school class would hardly recognize 2018 Taylor from the *Reputation* tour after ego Taylor transformed her. The Kardashian /Kanye incidents (which we will discuss more in detail later) may have been the final catalyst to her coming to terms with her new life wherein she confronts her dysmorphia and builds up her body with an Olympic athlete style training program and healthier diet (Durkan-Simonds 2024).

Superego Taylor complains that she is not feeling like a sexy baby herself in the way that ego Taylor is; in fact she feels more like a monster on a hill, and here we meet Taylor number 3 who appears to be the id, a Taylor of gigantic size who may generally mean well but cannot be bottled up and soon goes out of control doing what she should not do. This giant creature is unable to relate to humanity, a misunderstood monster who arrives at an African-American family dinner party uninvited thinking she can join them if she brings the wine but she turns out to be like a giant bull in a tiny china shop, causing the entire group to panic and seek weaponry to save themselves, with one individual shooting her supposedly through the heart with an arrow but actually only wounding her in the shoulder, which gushes out more purple goo. She is described as a monster on a hill slowly lurching towards "your favorite city". This Taylor, once unleashed, can be shot through the heart but even then not ever killed.

This appears to be an image derived from American and Japanese horror movies of the 1950s, and ultimately, originally from RKO pictures' famous 1933 classic *King Kong* but manifested in numerous low budget fifties atomic radiation generated monster movies such as the Japanese classic schlock film *Godzill*a, as well as American productions such *as The Amazing Colossal Man, Tarantula, War of the Colossal Beast*, and most especially in the schlock horror classic *Attack of the Fifty Foot Woman* (1957) with a giant Allison Hayes storming a town.

Producer/director Bert I. Gordon was a 1950s specialist in this kind of low budget horror which relied on cheap special effects that were laughable even by standards of that day. Often the monster headed towards your favorite city (usually Tokyo in the Japanese films or a small town in the cheap American efforts) and it had to be stopped somehow before it destroys humanity or at least a few stores in the town.

Shutterstock AI Generator

FIGURE 16: *Attack of the Fifty Foot Woman* illustration has her picking up a 1950s car.

FIGURE 17: Godzilla attacking Japanese city of Tokyo with Mount Fuji in the background).

In both the 1957 and 1993 versions of The *Attack of the Fifty Foot Woman* (Allison Hayes and Daryl Hannah respectively), the "monster" runs amuck provoked by an unfaithful husband—i.e. male trouble.

When Taylor as the Id Monster crawls into the dining room bringing a bottle of wine to dinner she doesn't seem to realize that she is too big to fit in the room, a symbol now of how Taylor's life has become unmanageably large and she will pay a price for her behavior, especially the drinking session. Is she now no better than a disingenuous congressman who says *Vote For Me For Everything* and wears a campaign button. How can she not tell people her feelings about whom to vote for or why a particular candidate is corrupt and evil? Her sins are "covert narcissism I disguise as altruism". Yet in real life when headlines suddenly attacked her because homeless people were being driven off so her Eras tour could come blissfully into Edinburgh, Scotland, she immediately gave a large contribution to the Food Bank there to help feed the homeless, not something that many billionaires would worry about doing but as she said in the documentary Miss Americana she is tremendously concerned about being "on the right side of history" (Daley-Harris 2024). An actual id monster by the way was found in the science fiction classic movie *Forbidden Planet* (1956) starring Walter Pidgeon, Anne Francis, Leslie Nielsen and Earl Holliman.

In our video, id Taylor has already been shot with a bow and arrow but cannot bleed true blood, rather only the purple goo discussed before. She is drunk and forages the table for booze finding only a tiny bottle which does not offer enough liquid to quench her powerful and apparently uncontrollable thirst for alcohol.

The quintessential 1950s id horror movie to match up with this video is *Fiend Without a Face* (1958) in which a meek and batty scientist at an atomic power research and NORAD military base in Canada (payed by Kynaston Reeves) is doing research on the power of thought transmission when he learns that he has developed the power to combine his own mental prowess with atomic power at which point his ego comes forward and takes over control of him. By the film's end he has lost control of his life and thoughts

FIGURE 18: Robby The Robot, one of the popular creations from the 1956 sci-fi movie *Forbidden Planet*. Presented by the Alex Film Society, Alex Theater, Glendale, California, July 7, 2007.

and has begun to produce thought monsters which look like gooey crawling brain stems with legs and these creatures when shot emit a sort of putrid goo which, although this is a black and white film, starkly resembles the goo emerging from the giant Taylor when she is shot. *Fiend Without a Face* is a cautionary tale about the dangers of leaving scientists (for this inference read in J. Robert Oppenheimer at Los Alamos developing the atomic bomb from 1943 to 1945) who are doing dangerous unregulated experiments (and see the recent movie *Oppenheimer*).

At this point in our video as the superego and ego Taylors bounce on the bed, ego Taylor triumphs by pushing her simpler, weaker self backwards off of the bed. At this point ego Taylor and id Taylor, both drunk, have led superego Taylor's life to lose all meaning as her beloved is abandoning her. At another *Tea Time*, with still more alcohol drinking, the diminished superego Taylor throws up in the lap of ego Taylor who is shocked and disgusted mostly because superego Taylor is such a wimp.

The next lesson in our video has superego Taylor on a bathroom scale which only reads that Taylor is too fat, a reference to her struggles with *anorexia nervosa* in which she tried to not eat while still exercising and was constantly finding herself quite weak when doing her shows and struggling to maintain a 00 dress size instead of the 6 she now settles for. On the wall in the background of the bathroom is just barely visible a photo portrait of Taylor's opera singer, tv show host and recording artist grandmother Marjorie Moehlenkamp, later Finlay, who looks amazingly like Taylor (Gibson 2023). Marjorie was the inspiration for Taylor taking up music and she looks out over her granddaughter here from the wall, perhaps trying to exert a counter influence to ego Taylor who is fat-shaming superego Taylor.

FIGURE 19: The father of the atomic bomb, Julius Robert Oppenheimer.

In the original video the closeup of the scale that Taylor stands on just says fat and gave no numbers. Taylor has often spoken of her body dysmorphia which has caused her to cry (again in the *Miss Americana* video) (West 2020), and to feel that her stomach was too large or her posterior too small, as we have already seen. Matters were not improved by fans who criticized this video for exhibiting fatphobia, leading Taylor to remove that part of the video, which was followed by fans protesting the removal since those suffering from the affliction were identifying strongly and positively with this part of the video (Georgi 2022). At this point superego Taylor in our video doesn't know what to do. Her grandmother is watching and the ego is dominating and the lyrics say that it must be exhausting rooting for the anti-hero… and so it seems.

The scene now leaves the music and shifts to a funeral service with her offspring gathered but they don't appear to be there to honor the dead Taylor Swift who seems now to be invisible to them and who can hide within her own coffin. Everyone is hanging around due to the lure of inheritance money. At the service one sees an image of Taylor in older age, surrounded by cats, but the painting looks astonishingly like Taylor's mother, perhaps indicative of the superego influence she has had on Taylor.

Often influenced from films she has seen, Taylor may be referencing the 2019 film *Knives Out* in the bridge of the song (Townsend 2022). In our video Mary Elizabeth Ellis portrays Taylor's daughter in law Kimber (reference likely intended here to Kim Kardashian as a murderess!) who has likely killed Taylor for the money she believes she will inherit, but Kimber receives a copy of a will that says that Taylor is only leaving 13 cents (13 is of course Taylor's life-long lucky number she often has written on her arm often by her own mother when performing) and Kimber is shocked into disbelief, claiming she and Taylor were so close which is of course a lie (here one could footnote *Thank You Amy* and *Cassandra* on the *Tortured Poets Department* as thinly veiled Kim references).

Taylor's "sons" in the video are portrayed as equally horrible, being raised with too much money and no ethics, apparently like their self-torturing mother. Mike Berbiglia is son Preston who uses his mother's name and fame to get into a prestigious country club while John Early, who appeared in the tv show *30 Rock* mentioned above is son Chad, who whines that he has had to fly all the way in from Ibiza for the funeral, a place noted as a getaway for the idle rich and famous or at least for their feckless offspring, an island known for young clubbers and wild open-air party-goers (Whyte 2009).

The will indicates that all of the money has been left to Taylor's beloved cats Meredith Grey, Olivia Benson and Benjamin Button and Preston notes that Taylor is laughing up at them from hell. Her fabulous beach house (at Westerly, Rhode Island and sung about in her *Last Great American Dynasty* song) is also left to the cats to be made into a cat sanctuary. Kimber shouts that cats don't even like the beach. (Andriotis 2020)

Insults and accusations are hurled back and forth and it is finally stated by Chad that he believes that Kimber pushed Taylor off of a balcony from which she fell to her death below.

Unable to accept that they've been cut out of the will, the trio decide that it's all a joke and that Taylor has left some other clue as to what they really are getting, a secret encoded message that means something else because that's what she was known for doing (i.e. an Easter Egg). But Taylor has added a codicil to the will stating that there was no secret message!

The insults continue as Chad is accused of trading on Taylor's name with his book *Growing Up Swift* and his podcast *Life Comes At You Swiftly*. And Kimber has taken Taylor's clothes from the 2009 *Fearless Tour* to wear (Denman 2024). The funeral degenerates into screaming and brawling as horrified superego Taylor watches and yet is somehow still invisible to them.

FIGURE 20: The Taylor Swift seaside residence High Watch formerly Holiday House, with its sweeping lawn down to the sea, on iconic Watch Hill, in Westerly, Rhode Island.

At the end, ego Taylor reappears and greets superego Taylor again and they both sit on the roof of the house and share a bottle of wine. In the distance, the gigantic id Taylor approaches as superego Taylor beckons her to the two other Taylors. The joke here is that in the 1950s movies it was never quite possible to show the giant creature and the normal people interacting and it always had to be done not with animation or superimposition but with separately made phony-looking giant mechanical hands reaching out to menace normal-sized people. But now it is possible to use modern technology to fully make all of the Taylors appear to truly interact, and the giant id Taylor is able to take the wine bottle directly from their hands and drink from it, a scene you will never see and could never see in a 1950s low budget giantism horror movie. In the end all of the Freudian Taylors have seemingly realized that they are all part of one Taylor and they have to learn to live with it.

The entire video was usually viewed as a comedy—Berbiglia IS a well-known stand-up comic—by the general public and various blog writers and talk-show hosts, among them Taylor's friend Jimmy Fallon (Rossignol 2022), but once one digs into it as we have been doing we see that *Anti-Hero* plays both as a comedy and an imagined tragedy in the landscape of Taylor's mind and this duality appears in many of her works, including *I Can Do It With a Broken Heart*. After all, her legacy in *Anti-Hero* is a spoiled, even murderous family with a huge sense of entitlement amid dissipated lives.

In this video as in many with Taylor there is also a timeless quality and we aren't sure what age Taylor is. Her cats are apparently still alive but the children are grown and entering middle age and she looks like her own mother in a photo even though she is young in her casket. All 3 Freudian Taylors are still young here, especially as she is looking on everything as if she is the young superego Taylor. But her portrait shows an older Taylor so it can only fit together in the logic of nightmares.

In this video, Taylor seems to be coming to terms with the various aspects of her personality. She is still able to be frightened and disappointed with herself but she seems to be better at exorcising her demons and managing her emotions. Although terrified to the point where things get oversized and, as she puts it in *Miss Americana*, "loud" in her life, she can take a step back as director and see the humor in it all: the multi-cat portrait, the ridiculously behaving "children", the plot contrivance of how wretchedly each one of the kids has grown up, and of course the silly ghosts. It is 2022 and she has more maturity and, especially, perspective and more ability to confront who she now is at this point in time after having taken so many cruel hits.

This was not so when she composed what must stand as an earlier companion song to this one, written at a time when she was depressed and increasingly isolated by the initial action of Kanye (now known as Ye) which she feared had collapsed a large section of her fan base. Later on, these fears would prove justified when Kanye again entered her life with his phone call and subsequent video and claims, supported by Kim, that she had given her okay to the degrading imagery and bitch language that he chose for her in his lyrics and video. At the time she was widely accused of being a liar.

There was also resentment at her having the audacity to have personal anguish when in fact she was already a multi-millionaire and it was even periodically claimed, falsely, that she didn't even write her own music (Nolan 2022). She was described repeatedly as annoying, polarizing and even deserving of being slapped around and having all of her fans turn against her (Hawthorne 2024). It hit her so hard that she had to remove herself from public view for a year (again, according to the *Miss Americana* documentary).

In 2010 her brilliant fifth album *Speak Now* came out and on it was supposed to be a wonderful song called *Castles Crumbling*. This was to be a strong expression of her conflicted feelings of the time, hopeful at some times as exemplified by the song *Long Live*, from the same album. But *Castles Crumbling*, which forms a firm antecedent to *Anti-Hero*, feels like the end of youth and a sad, cruel welcome to the dangers of adult life and the fragility of a career in the minefield of popular music where Taylor asserts recently in her *Fortnight* song that "you wouldn't last an hour in the asylum where they raised me."

Thinking when she first started that she had a charmed life with many wonderful fans, and winning all sorts of awards, she ran into the buzz-saw that was Kanye West and then wife Kim Kardashian when Kanye interrupted her acceptance of her MTV VMA award in September of 2009. Not fully understanding what was happening, the 19 year old thought that she was being booed by the audience for receiving the award, as reported in the *Miss Americana* documentary.

Much later on, in 2016, when she had been phoned by Kanye, she thought she was being alerted to and asked to approve a vulgar request

FIGURE 21: December 8, 2024 - A crowd of Taylor Swift fans outside BC Place Stadium in Vancouver, Canada, where Taylor Swift is performing the last concert of her Eras Tour,

which she felt initially didn't seem so bad that he was making to feature her in one of his songs. However, what seems to have been a big mistake on her part in retrospect was taking a phone call from Kanye after what he had done to her in the first place at the awards show. Hindsight suggests that she should have known she was playing with fire. There should have been a lawyer present or at least a more legally sophisticated adult. When she tried to protest what Kanye had done in full without her knowledge and put on his recording, strongly implying sexual relations and calling her a bitch, the media rather universally took his side when Kim publicly played part (and only part) of the phone conversation.

FIGURE 22: A still teenage Taylor Swift in 2009, wearing a Milly dress, in the press room for the 44th Annual Academy of Country Music ACM Awards on April 5th, MGM Grand, Las Vegas, Nevada.

Taylor was viciously attacked in the media for allegedly playing the victim perennially in her music and her life and just being generally annoying about the situation. Later evidence apparently emerged that the West call had been strategically edited. Taylor thought that Kim had manipulated the situation to deliberately cause the end of her career and has never forgiven her. Taylor said that she was sent into a mental hibernation and felt that her career which she had so carefully built up was over or as Taylor put it "cancelled" (Mier, Spanos and Harris 2024).

In the song *Castles Crumbling* (originally written in 2010 after the first Kanye episode) she talks about how she had built a dynasty with a fabulous castle but which was all now crashing down. As someone who performed on tv as a kiddie "star" in the early 1950s, I can tell you that you get used to everyone telling you that you are wonderful and when that suddenly stops and turns to disinterest and even harsh criticism it hurts deeply because your career is what you have built your life upon even though you are young—hard work, being nice to everyone and trying your best in your performance. When you are basically cancelled, to use the old vaudeville term which referred to the exercising of a clause in your performance contract, or "handed your walking papers" as we used to say when I was performing, it is a complete shock to the system. The fans don't hang out at the stage door anymore, the money stops and you find you cannot get hired after the media blackballs you.

You begin to self-examine and self-destroy and in her case she held a grudge against Kanye and especially Kim for what she considered to be major backstabbing and lying about what she agreed to allow, trying once again to be nice and give in as much as she felt she could but without realizing that with some people you cannot give them an inch because they might take your career away with deft manipulation. In the media the jury is still out on this and several other cases regarding Taylor Swift's life and actions but I can feel the frustration that comes through in her music, especially in the song *Cassandra* about her treatment by the media and the two principals involved (Huff 2023).

In the song *Castles Crumbling*, Taylor says that those who tried to help her stayed loyal but she drove them away although she gives no details. People were talking openly about hating her and how she was finished. I can tell you from first-hand experience that when you are in the bright lights of show business and you fail and important sources don't believe your story and complain about your complaining and your alleging victimization and they make you out to be the liar, you just don't know what to do and you begin to punish yourself if you are so inclined by your nature. We know that Taylor suffers from a number of disorders which she chronicles in her musical diaries. Being outmaneuvered and outsmarted by Kanye and hung out to dry afterward must have seemed in Taylor's darker moments evidence that she was losing her entire fan base and her entire career that she had worked so hard for and in fact she was losing much of her reason for living.

She compares herself in the song to a king in a castle losing control and driving off friends just as Shakespeare's King Lear did to his own daughter, as has been stated earlier (Hutchinson 2023; Tearle 2024). Taylor talks about dynasties and how she was like a queen with people hanging on her every word. The song reaches its climax, to my mind, when she says her people who once loved her are screaming that they hate her and she replies that she "never wanted you to hate me" in a tiny, little girl voice that is deeply effective as it cracks pathetically, reminding us of her power as an emotive singer (Discover Music 2019). It is ironic that the person she thought would be best to invite to sing it with her was Haylie Williams of the group Paramour, the group that contained her very first friends she met in the country music business, and the first ones to be really nice to her when she was starting out (Krol 2023).

This song may have only been a minor memory, if even that, to those who follow Taylor's career but it and *Anti-Hero* particularly reveal the "delicate" nature of Taylor's mental landscape. When you are a composer whose lyrics are based on chronicling the true details of your life in poetic form it is absolutely devastating to have someone else gain control of your life's narrative and use it against you, especially if you are already beset by a wide variety of neuroses and fears. "Cancellation" not only blocks your ability to communicate in the way you need to in order to survive as a musical artist but it also tears you apart inside and leaves you feeling powerless.

FIGURE 23: Dark and sinister old King Lear with his castle crumbling.

Anti-Hero and *Castles Crumbling* reflect a career crisis that she has managed to pass but she cannot forget nor forgive the people involved who worsened her already existing fears and insecurities. All of this anguish plus romantic turbulence no doubt ultimately led to the creation of *The Tortured Poets Department* which she says has been "cathartic" (see my chapter one of this book where I discuss Taylor on catharsis) and above all necessary to do for her mental health (Longman 2024). We can only buy a ticket (and they are expensive!) on the roller coaster of her life and be grateful that we get to experience something of the feeling and the remarkable glow of the ride.

NOTES

Andriotis, Mary Elizabeth, "A New Taylor Swift Song Tells the Story of the Former Owners of Her Rhode Island Home," *House Beautiful* 7-24-2020 https://www.housebeautiful.com/design-inspiration/a33417436/taylor-swift-holiday-house-folklore-last-great-american-dynasty/

Aniftos, Rania, "Damon Albarn Apologizes 'Unreservedly & Unconditionally' to Taylor Swift for Songwriting Comments," *Billboard* 1-24-22 https://www.billboard.com/music/pop/damon-albarn-apologizes-taylor-swift-1235022420/

Bailey, Alyssa, "#FBF: That Time Taylor Swift Fell on Ellen DeGeneres' Bathroom Floor", *Elle* 11-20-2015 https://www.elle.com/culture/celebrities/news/a32030/ellen-degeneres-greatest-celeb-scares/

Bailey, Alyssa "All of Taylor Swift's 'Anti-Hero' Music Video Easter Eggs So Far," *Elle* 10-21-22 (https://www.elle.com/culture/music/a41734324/taylor-swift-anti-hero-music-video-easter-eggs/)

Bailey, Alyssa and Lauren Puckett-Pope, "Taylor Swift's 'Anti-Hero' Lyrics Are An Earnest Portrait of Her 'Self-Loathing,'" *Elle* 10-21-2022 https://www.elle.com/culture/music/a41727143/taylor-swift-anti-hero-lyrics-meaning-joe-alwyn/

Bate, Jonathan, "Why Taylor Swift is a Literary Giant—by a Shakespeare Professor," *The Sydney Herald* 6-4-2023 https://www.smh.com.au/culture/music/why-taylor-swift-is-a-literary-giant-by-a-shakespeare-professor-20230518-p5d9cn.html

Bonner, Mehera, Gretty Garcia and Samantha Olson, "Taylor Swift and Scooter Braun's Drama, Explained," *Cosmopolitan*, Published: Jun 17, 2024 (https://www.cosmopolitan.com/entertainment/celebs/a29807801/taylor-swift-scooter-braun-scott-borchetta-tyrannical-control-amas-netflix-doc/

Brandel, Lars, "Taylor Swift Tells Jimmy Fallon She Turns Into a 'Wizard In Two Drinks,'" *Billboard* 10-4-2019 (https://www.billboard.com/music/music-news/taylor-swift-mojitos-snl-lover-fallon-watch-8532149/)

Brinks, Melissa, "What Does "Veni Vidi Vici" Mean? Why Do People Say It?," Prep Scholar 2024 https://blog.prepscholar.com/veni-vidi-vici-meaning

Cinone, Danielle, "Both of Taylor Swift's Parents Had Cancer— The 'Shake It Off' Singer-Songwriter Says It Taught Her To Focus On 'Real Problems,' Not Small Anxieties," *Survivor Net* 8-22-2024

Cooper, Brittany Jo, "Taylor Swift Brought to Tears After Ruining a Wedding on Punk'd," A Taste of Country 3-30-2012 https://tasteofcountry.com/taylor-swift-justin-bieber-punkd/

Cord-Cruz, Nicole, "The Real Reason 13 is Taylor Swift's Lucky Number," *Nicki* 9-5-2022 https://www.nickiswift.com/993921/the-real-reason-13-is-taylor-swifts-lucky-number/

Curchin, L. A., "Breaking the Vapour Barrier: What Made the Delphic Oracle Work?." No date given. https://uwlabyrinth.uwaterloo.ca/labyrinth_archives/breaking_the_vapour_barrier/

Dador, Denise, "Researchers study Taylor Swift lyrics' impact on disordered eating, body image," *ABC Eyewitness News Los Angeles* 8-16-2024 https://abc7.com/post/taylor-swift-lyrics-videos-help-fans-cope-body-image-issues-disordered-eating-researchers-say/15179667/

Dailey, Hannah, "Taylor Swift Says Kim Kardashian & Kanye West's 'Frame Job' Phone Call 'Took Me Down Psychologically'," *Billboard* 12-6-2023 https://www.billboard.com/music/music-news/taylor-swift-kim-kardashian-kanye-west-phone-call-frame-job-1235540478/

Dailey-Harris, Sam, "Taylor Swift: 'I need to be on the right side of history'," *Fulcrum* 5-30-2024 https://thefulcrum.us/pop-culture/taylor-swift-miss-americana

Denman, Phoebe, "Taylor Swift Eras Tour outfits: What to wear for the Fearless era," *Heat World* 5-20-2024 https://heatworld.com/shopping/fashion/taylor-swift-fearless-eras-tour-outfits/

Discover Music, "Is Taylor Swift actually a good singer?," *Classic fm* 4-26-2019 https://www.classicfm.com/discover-music/music-theory/taylor-swift-good-singer/

Duran, Anagricel, "Graham Norton praises Taylor Swift for being "so close to normal" despite fame: "It's remarkable"," *NME* 10-8-2024 https://www.nme.com/news/tv/graham-norton-praises-taylor-swift-for-being-so-close-to-normal-despite-fame-its-remarkable-3800818

Durkan-Simonds, Deirdre, "Taylor Swift's personal trainer says the pop star's workouts would make other people throw up: 'She is the most resilient person I've met'," Dailymail.com 4-20-2024 (https://www.dailymail.co.uk/tvshowbiz/article-13332185/Taylor-Swift-workout-personal-trainer-intense.html)

Editors 2024, "40+ of Taylor Swift's Most Brilliant Easter Eggs, Decoded," *Cosmopolitan* 2-26-2024 https://www.cosmopolitan.com/entertainment/celebs/g45551106/taylor-swift-easter-eggs/

Eley, Amy, "Taylor Swift reveals how she got in shape for 'Eras' and why she quit drinking on tour," *Today* 2024 https://www.msn.com/en-us/health/other/taylor-swift-reveals-how-she-got-in-shape-for-eras-and-why-she-quit-drinking-on-tour/ar-AA1l656K

Everlovelyjewel on X: Taylor Swift (speaking) .   https://www.youtube.com/watch?v=foitkQyUnyg 2022

Fontenrose, Joseph Eddy, *Python; a study of Delphic myth and its origins* (Berkeley: University of California Press,1959) https://uwlabyrinth.uwaterloo.ca/labyrinth archives/breaking_the_vapour_barrier/

Fresh Pair, "Where To Buy The Et Tu Brute Pillow From The Taylor Swift Direct TV Commercial," *Fresh Pair of IIS* 10-28-2018 https://freshpairofiis.com/2018/10/28/where-to-buy-the-et-tu-brute-pillow-from-the-taylor-swift-direct-tv-commercial/

Georgi, Maya, "Taylor Swift let fans down by removing 'fatphobic' scene from 'Anti-Hero' video," Think 10-29-2022 https://www.nbcnews.com/think/opinion/taylor-swift-should-not-remove-fatphobic-scene-anti-hero-video-rcna54617

Gibson, Kelsie, "All About Taylor Swift's Grandparents," *People* 7-7-2023 https://people.com/all-about-taylor-swift-grandparents-7558166

Giltz, Michael, "Taylor Swift (For)Evermore: 113 Poets Pay Tribute #1," *Parade* 11-12-2024 https://www.msn.com/en-us/entertainment/news/taylor-swift-for-evermore-113-poets-pay-tribute-1/ar-AA1tY30d

Haden, Jeff, "Taylor Swift Says Living a Happy, Successful, and Meaningful Life Comes Down to 5 Simple Things," *Inc.* 11-10-2023 https://www.inc.com/jeff-haden/taylor-swift-says-living-a-happy-successful-meaningful-life-comes-down-to-5-simple-things.htm

Halter, Marjorie, "Proof That Taylor Swift Drinks Way More Alcohol Than You Think," *Showbiz Cheat Sheet* 1-23-2024 https://www.cheatsheet.com/entertainment/proof-that-taylor-swift-drinks-way-more-alcohol-than-you-think.html/

Haupt, Angela, "Why Taylor Swift's Music Makes Us So Emotional," *Time* 4-19-2024 https://time.com/6968864/why-music-makes-us-emotional-taylor-swift/

Hawthorne, Nathaniel, "Taylor Swift: More Vicious? A Look Back at Two Decades of Evolution," *Buzz Viral* 11-18-2024 https://top1.us/2024/11/taylor-swift-more-vicious-a-look-back-at-two-decades-of-evolution/

Holterman, Alexandra, "The History of Taylor Swift & the Snake," *Billboard* 8-21-2017 https://www.billboard.com/music/pop/taylor-swift-the-snake-history-kim-kanye-instagram-7934297/

Huff, Lauren "Taylor Swift says new *Midnights* track 'Anti-Hero' is 'a guided tour' of her insecurities," *Entertainment*, 10-3-2022 https://ew.com/music/taylor-swift-midnights-anti-hero-meaning/

Huff, Lauren, "*30 Rock* fans think Taylor Swift's new song 'Anti-Hero' features a funny reference to the show," Entertainment Weekly 10-21-2022 b) https://ew.com/music/taylor-swift-midnights-sexy-baby-30-rock-reference/

Huff, Lauren, "Taylor Swift says leaked Kanye West video proves 'I was telling the truth the whole time,'" *Entertainment* 3-23-2023 https://ew.com/music/taylor-swift-leaked-kanye-west-video-focus-what-really-matters/

Hutchinson, Emily, "What's The Real Meaning Of Castles Crumbling By Taylor Swift? Here's What We Think," *Nicki Swift* 7-7-2023 https://www.nickiswift.com/1333336/real-meaning-castles-crumbling-taylor-swift-lyrics/

Irvin, Jack, "Taylor Swift Says 'Midnights' Track 'Anti-Hero' Is an 'Honest' Exploration of Her 'Insecurities'", *People* 10-3-22 https://people.com/music/taylor-swift-says-midnights-track-anti-hero-explores-her-insecurities/

Jones, Nate, "When Did the Media Turn Against Taylor Swift?," *Vulture* 7-21-2016 https://www.vulture.com/2016/07/when-did-the-media-turn-against-taylor-swift.html

Krol, Jacklyn, "The Story Behind 'Castles Crumbling' By Taylor Swift and Hayley Williams," Stage Right Secrets 7-6-2PS023 https://www.stagerightsecrets.com/the-story-behind-castles-crumbling-by-taylor-swift-and-hayley-williams/

Larrabee-Zayas, Dora, "Taylor Swift Shows Off Long Legs In Sequin Mini Dresses For 'Reputation' — See Tour Outfits," *Hollywood Life* 5-19-2018 https://hollywoodlife.com/2018/05/09/taylor-swift-outfits-reputation-tour-stage-dresses-looks/

Legaspi, Althea, "Taylor Swift Performs 'Castles Crumbling' With Hayley Williams at London Show," *Rolling Stone* 6-22-2024 https://www.rollingstone.com/music/music-news/taylor-swift-hayley-williams-castles-crumbling-performance-london-1235045157/

Longman, Molly, "The Tortured Poets Department" Is Cathartic as Hell — Experts Explain Why," *Pop Sugar* 4-19-2024 https://www.popsugar.com/fitness/taylor-swift-cathartic-music-49355355

McDaniel, Spencer, "Why Are Ghosts Depicted Wearing Bedsheets?," *Tales of Times Forgotten* 10-27-2019 https://talesoftimesforgotten.com/2019/10/27/why-are-ghosts-depicted-wearing-bedsheets/

Mannoni, Octave, *Freud: The Theory of the Unconscious (Radical Thinkers)* (Verso Books: London, 2015) https://www.amazon.com/Freud-Theory-Unconscious-Radical-Thinkers/dp/178168894X

Mercado, Mia, "I Can't Shut Up About Sexy Babies," *The Cut* 10-28-2022 (https://www.thecut.com/2022/10/what-does-taylor-swift-mean-with-that-sexy-baby-lyric.html

Mena, Nayana, Tiffany Wertheimer, "Taylor Swift edits Anti-Hero video after 'fat-phobic' backlash," *BBC* 7-27-2022 https://www.bbc.com/news/entertainment-arts-63414044

Mendez, Michelle, "Taylor Swift's 'Anti-Hero' is All About Being An Outsider," *Elite Daily* 10-21-2022 https://www.elitedaily.com/entertainment/taylor-swift-midnights-anti-hero-lyrics-meaning

Mercado, Mia, "I Can't Shut Up About Sexy Babies," *The Cut* 10-28-2022 https://www.thecut.com/2022/10/what-does-taylor-swift-mean-with-that-sexy-baby-lyric.html

Merinuk, Madeleine, "How Taylor Swift turned fandom into a scavenger hunt of clues," *Today* 10-21-2022 https://www.today.com/popculture/music/taylor-swift-easter-eggs-hidden-messages-rcna51887

Metzger, Richard, "The Yardbirds: The legendary supergroup that boasted of Eric Clapton, Jimmy Page & Jeff Beck, *Dangerous Minds* 8-26-2016 https://dangerousminds.net/comments/the_yardbirds_the_legendary_supergroup_that_boasted_of_eric_clapton_jimmy_p

Mier, Tomas, Brittany Spanos and Keith Harris, "From VMAs Drama to 'thanK you aIMee': A Timeline of Taylor Swift's Feud With Kim Kardashian, Kanye West," *Rolling Stone* 4-23-2024 https://www.rollingstone.com/music/music-features/taylor-swift-feud-kim-kardashian-kanye-west-timeline-1235008539/

Mohan, Isabel, "Taylor Swift Is 'So Close to Normal,' Says Talk Show Host Graham Norton as He Dishes on Star Guests," *US* 10-8-2024 https://www.usmagazine.com/entertainment/news/taylor-swift-is-so-close-to-normal-says-talk-show-host-graham-norton/

Nolan, Emma, "Does Taylor Swift Write Her Own Songs? Full List of Her Songwriting Credits," *Newsweek* 1-25-2022 https://www.newsweek.com/does-taylor-swift-write-own-songs-full-list-songwriting-credits-damon-albarn-1672546

Parkins, Njera, Kirsty Hatcher, "Taylor Swift Thrills Edinburgh Food Bank with Generous Donation. Will 'Leave a Lasting Impact,'" *People* 6-12-2024 https://people.com/taylor-swift-thrills-edinburgh-food-bank-with-generous-donation-8662274

Perez, Lexy, "Taylor Swift Details Meaning Behind 'The Tortured Poets Department' Songs," *The Hollywood Reporter* 4-22-2024 https://www.hollywoodreporter.com/news/music-news/taylor-swift-explains-tortured-poets-department-songs-1235878743/

]Quinn, Dave, "Taylor Swift Spills Secrets of Filming 'Cats' Movie: 'I Had More Fun Than Anyone Else,'" *People* 5-24-2019 https://people.com/music/taylor-swift-cats-movie-school/

Ross, Gemma, "The history of the White Isle: How did Ibiza become a party island?,"Mixmag 8-21-2024 https://mixmag.net/feature/history-of-ibiza-how-did-white-isle-become-party-island

Rossignol, Derrick, "Taylor Swift Put A Surprise Comedy Sketch Featuring Mike Birbiglia And Others In Her Wild New 'Anti-Hero' Video," *Uproxx* 10-21-2022 (https://uproxx.com/pop/taylor-swift-anti-hero-video-mike-birbiglia-sketch-mary-elizabeth-ellis/

Sarvé-Tarr, Marin, "Doubling and Duplicity in Dalí's Inventions of the Monsters," *Art Institute Chicago* 3-7-2023 https://www.artic.edu/articles/1036/dali-s-blended-selves-and-truest-monsters

Schocket, Ryan, "Taylor Gave Her First Sit-Down Interview In A While, And Here's 13 Things We Learned", *BuzzFeed* 8-25-2019 https://www.buzzfeed.com/ryanschocket2/taylor-swift-cbs-this-morning-interview

Simmons, Shea, "Taylor Swift's Billboard Music Awards Dress Was TOTALLY Unexpected," *Bustle* 5-20-2018 https://www.bustle.com/p/taylor-swifts-2018-billboard-music-awards-dress-was-unexpected-for-more-than-one-reason-9150125

Sims, Brittany, "ALL GROWN UP! Where Ellen DeGeneres Show guests Sophia Grace & Rosie are now- from Super Bass viral video stars to budding pop singers," *U.S. Sun* 5-12-2022 https://www.the-sun.com/entertainment/5324711/where-ellen-degeneres-show-sophia-grace-rosie-are-now/

Somers, Caitlyn, "Taylor Swift and Paramore's Hayley Williams' Complete Friendship Timeline," *US Weekly* 6-26-2024 https://www.usmagazine.com/celebrity-news/news/taylor-swift-and-hayley-williams-complete-friendship-timeline/

Suetonius, *Life of Julius Caesar* 37.2. This was a simple phrase to celebrate his triumph of 46 B.C. in the Pontic area, and it could be put on a placard carried in a military parade as he displayed behind it booty pillaged from the region and brought back to Rome. On the Ides of March 44 B.C. when Caesar was assassinated see H. H. Scullard, *Festivals and Ceremonies of the Roman Republic* (Cornell University Press: Ithaca, New York, 1981) pp. 42-43

Suetonius, *Life of Julius Caesar*, 82; see also Plutarch *Caesar* 66

Swiftipedia 2022, "Glitter Gel Pen Songs," Taylor Swift Fandom 2022 https://taylorswift.fandom.com/wiki/Glitter_Gel_Pen_songs

"Swimming in Beauty: The Fascinating World of Japanese Koi Fish," *Creature Companion* 11-16-2023 (https://creature-companions.in/japanese-koi-fish/)

Taylor-Swift Nation, "Fun Fact: Taylor Swift's Brother and Lawyer as Ghosts in 'Anti-Hero' Music Video," *Taylor-Swift Nation* 2022 https://www.youtube.com/watch?v=cmp968-JccY

Tearle, Oliver "The Real Meaning of Taylor Swift's 'Anti-Hero'," *Interesting Literature* 2024 https://interestingliterature.com/2023/10/taylor-swift-anti-hero-meaning/

Thompson, Laura and Peter Sblendario, "Every reference you missed in Taylor Swift's 'Look What You Made Me Do' music video," *Daily News* 4-7-2018 https://www.nydailynews.com/2017/08/28/every-reference-you-missed-in-taylor-swifts-look-what-you-made-me-do-music-video/

Townsend, Chance, "Taylor Swift's 'Anti-Hero' Lyrics: A Detailed Analysis by the Internet," *Mashable* 10-22-2022 https://mashable.com/article/taylor-swift-anti-hero-break-down

Trapp, Philip, "The History of Guitar Smashing in Rock 'N' Roll," *Loudwire* 5-1-2023 (https://loudwire.com/guitar-smashing-history-rock-destroyed-smash-instuments/)

Truong, Kimberly, "Taylor Swift Opened Up About Being Publicly Canceled After the Kim Kardashian Drama," *InStyle* 8-8-2019 https://www.instyle.com/news/taylor-swift-cancel-culture-kim-kardashian-vogue

Tsintsiras, Aya, "Taylor Swift's Body Dysmorphia Caused Significant Issues In Her Life, Here's How She Battled It," *TheThings* 10-1-2023 https://www.thethings.com/taylor-swifts-body-dysmorphia-mental-health-issues/

VOGUE.COM.AU, "Taylor Swift drops new video, is a takedown of anyone who has wronged her," *Vogue Australia Edition 8-29-2017* Clue 6 https://www.vogue.com.au/culture/features/taylor-swift-drops-new-video-is-a-takedown-of-anyone-who-has-wronged-her/image-gallery/a0f1b89a3cf50b42da487da44a106e9a

Wasilak, Sarah, "We Don't Know What's Higher, Taylor Swift's Platform Heels or That Slit on Her Dress," *PS* 5-30-2018 https://www.popsugar.com/fashion/taylor-swift-versace-dress-billboard-music-awards-2018-44865309

West, Kelly, "Miss Americana: 13 Things We Learned From Taylor Swift's Netflix Documentary," *Cinema Blend* 2-1-2020 https://www.cinemablend.com/news/2489468/miss-americana-13-things-we- learned-from-taylor-swifts-netflix-documentary

Whyte, Barry, "7 Crazy Nights in Ibiza's Summer of Lust," *Matador Network* 7-23-2009 https://matadornetwork.com/nights/seven-crazy-night-in-ibiza-2009/

Willett-Wei, Megan and Eve Crosbie, "Inside Taylor Swift's $17 million Rhode Island mansion where she hosts parties for her A-list friends," *Y! Entertainment* 8-26-2024 https://www.yahoo.com/entertainment/inside-taylor-swifts-17-million-160659386.html?guccounter=1&guce_referrer=aHR0cHM6Ly9kdWNrZHVja2dvLmNvbS8&guce_referrer_sig=AQAAANlS6tmpoIOxAFF0cjP4qLHjY2TMWwcL9GN8yVMQ2oNMLb6hh-C3TTRi1AfoF4THi33Y4ZFmDcbF6ikUXbL3BFx7MLPGN7B2ltm5iWK_6NR0xsaz1EgooHt62JPd4EIDa91J_9HuzIoftiWERzgZJ2HVzFR-wvH0OeXj6UVwv-Ay

Willman, Chris, "Taylor Swift Opens Up About Overcoming Struggle With Eating Disorder," *Variety* 1-23-2020 https://variety.com/2020/music/news/taylor-swift-eating-disorder-netflix-documentary-miss-americana-1203478047/

Zambas, Joanna and Angela Stephanou, "Taylor Swift – 16 Scandals & Controversies," *Tell Tales* 5-17-2023 https://www.telltalesonline.com/51218/taylor-swift-controversies/

The Swifties Weigh In: Taylor Swift: A Roadmap for Growing Up

By Arielle Sare

(Arielle Sare is currently a Junior at the University of Arizona majoring in Operations and Supply Chain Management. Some of her hobbies include yoga, trying new restaurants, and listening to live music. She is hoping to become an Operations Manager at a well-known company some day).

Taylor Alison Swift is more than just another pop star- she's revolutionary. With an insanely large fan base and an undeniable influence on music, culture, and even politics, she has been able to reshape the industry and inspire artists all around the world. However, for me, and for many young adults like me, Taylor's impact is larger than chart-topping hits.

I'm a 19-year-old girl navigating a world where expressing yourself can feel like walking a tightrope. Living in a society where young girls are often told to not be too much, too loud, too outspoken, too confident, Taylor's music gives me that safe space I crave where I feel validated and heard, a space no other artist has ever been able to imitate. It feels as though she's writing about my own struggles, victories, and experiences. Her lyrics resonate so deeply to me, and others similar to me, by expressing emotions and experiences with an immense authenticity that speaks directly to her audience.

In her song "Mad Woman", she challenges gender stereotypes by giving a voice to women who are afraid to be angry and show it. Taylor is able to reclaim a societal expectation by asserting that it is okay to be loud and outspoken, once again proving the need to tear down these voices in our heads to simply sit and look pretty.

Beyond her writing and songs, Taylor Swift embodies fearlessness. Even while navigating the spotlight, she's unapologetically herself, a role model for girls everywhere. In an industry that tries to box women in and creates restrictive standards for women, Taylor breaks free. She is able to challenge these norms through her art but also through her public image. Her song *The Man* isn't just a song; it's a statement against the double standards women face every day. It advocates for equality and breaks down these barriers with each word.

Taylor Swift's song *The Man* completely flips the script on gender norms by taking on a male persona to critique the double standards in society. By doing this, she is able to highlight the imbalance in ways men and women are perceived and treated, more specifically in professional environments or personal choices. Since this song is written through a male perspective, Swift is able to prompt listeners to reconsider the expectations and biases on gender roles. It is as if she is saying "why should we allow our gender to determine how much respect we are given? Why are we creating these societal norms and sticking to them? Let's break them down and celebrate the successes of everyone despite what they look like." Taylor's approach on this theme and this song encourages a reflection on inequalities and how we can disassemble them.

Taylor's music isn't just catchy tunes; it's a journey through life's ups and downs. From love and heartbreak to finding your voice and standing tall, she covers it all. Her lyrics are like a roadmap for growing up and staying true to who you are. With each album she writes, her songs serve as anthems for strength and power, resonating with her fans on a deeply personal level. And that is what I admire most about Taylor- how she has evolved with each album. She has never been afraid to speak her mind or share her vulnerabilities. Her music isn't just art and entertainment; it's empowerment. She shows us it's okay to be ourselves, imperfections and all.

One of my all-time favorite songs by Taylor Swift is *Clean*, from her fifth studio album, *1989*, released in 2014. This song delves into themes of healing, self-discovery, and moving on from a past situation that caused pain. The lyrics convey a sense of freedom and renewal following emotional turmoil. Taylor reflects on the process of letting go and finding clarity, whether it's about a breakup, family trauma, or other personal experiences. She emphasizes the importance of self-growth and acceptance, acknowledging that it's okay to miss a period in your life while still healing and evolving. This song is particularly special to me because I first heard it when I was about 10, but it wasn't until I was older that I truly understood its meaning. After going through my first heartbreak, among countless songs by Taylor Swift, *Clean* became a source of comfort and strength. It taught me that even when it feels as though I am drowning, I will eventually breathe again and be free of the pain.

She wrote in the lyrics that she was ten months sober but that that didn't mean she didn't miss "it" even though she had gotten clean and that she was ten months older but wouldn't go back to her former ways.

This is my favorite part of the song because it resonates deeply with me. Here, "sober" symbolizes leaving past experiences behind, representing true growth and self-acceptance. It acknowledges that moving on can be challenging and that you might miss what you've left behind, but ultimately, you learn and grow from it. Overall, *Clean* captures Swift's approach to songwriting and her ability to express personal experiences with vulnerability, allowing listeners to relate and find comfort in her words.

As Taylor Swift continues to redefine pop culture, her influence remains extreme. She's more than a singer and an artist; she's a voice for our generation, challenging and allowing us to break down conventional social "rules" and embrace our true selves. Her legacy is more than what is in her songs; it is in those whom she touches and in whose lives she influences.

Who's Afraid of Little Old Me?

By David Soren

(In order to more fully appreciate this essay the viewer is asked to view the Internet postings from the Eras Tour regarding this song. You may need to view several different ones in order to more fully see the backgrounds projected onto the large screen and onto the stage floor). A particularly useful backscreen video was projected during the performance at https://www.youtube.com/watch?v=sNwe_e7BL14 *in Cardiff, Wales and* https://www.youtube.com/watch?v=RMsvwWoSdL8 *in Milan.*

This is a dark, frightening number from Taylor Swift's *Tortured Poets Department* which suggests what might happen if all of Taylor's rage were to be unleashed at all of the individuals who attacked, slighted and bullied her and tried to ruin her life. It is pure uncontrolled, unregulated id with a pretty frightening demonic/vampiric finale on the Eras tour which caused viewers to gasp when first seen. About it Taylor has stated:

"What do we do to our writers, and our artists, and our creatives? We put them through hell. We watch what they create, then we judge it. We love to watch artists in pain, often to the point where I think sometimes as a society we provoke that pain and we just watch what happens (Evans 2024)."

We begin our look at this strange song on the Eras Tour with a look at a creepy ca. 1900 period house which is visible on the giant screen and evokes old fashioned ghost stories. This place with its Queen Anne Style corner tower and gables and its pair of Gothic rose windows on the ground floor to the left and its 3 lancet windows projecting from the 2nd floor is a mishmash of styles typical of its eclectic era and it sets the tone for the rest of the video, especially when we see Taylor silhouetted eerily in a window on the top floor.

FIGURE 1: Detail of rose window at Trento Cathedral of San Vigilio; Trentino-Alto Adige, Italy.

FIGURE 2: Lancet cathedral windows.

In many of Taylor's videos the landscape of her mind is dominated by impossible combinations of things which inhabit her dreams and nightmares. This fondness for Surrealism we have already mentioned as the Paranoiac-Critical Method employed by Salvador Dali. But in her ultra-dark vision of this video for the Eras Tour she uses at its core a trip along a strange corridor which at its exit is particularly angular and out of symmetry entirely, leading to a strange back room where Taylor sits on the ground as if shackled to her spot. Where does this frightening, dark, black and white world come from?

To understand this we must go back to near the end of the 19th century and first visit with a Dutch wannabe artist named Vincent Van Gogh who was, to say the least, extremely unsuccessful at what he did throughout his entire life, so much so that after his death his own mother burned up the paintings she had from him. His brother Theo owned an art gallery in Paris and worried about his younger brother who was not able to join the clergy due to his erratic social behavior and poor Latin skills. As an artist he was an even bigger failure. His paintings were charged, however, with a kind of forceful energy and he painted passionately and boldly in a manner not done before but not considered very skilled either. In 1888 he wrote:

"Instead of trying to reproduce exactly what I have before my eyes, I use color to suggest any emotion of an ardent temperament." (National Gallery 2024).

FIGURE 3: Self-portrait by Vincent Van Gogh on stamp from Burundi.

Through his art he was trying to forge a link between himself and the exterior universe. If he felt a certain way, the entire world around him would swirl and vibrate and be filled with appropriate coloring to reflect his mood. In paintings such as *The Night Café* (1888), he underscored the feeling of a pathetic world of losers by using intensely ugly color pairings involving orange, green and an intense piss yellow with the result that we see a portrait not only of the lowest levels of human society but we also feel it in the overall atmosphere of the painting.

FIGURE 4: Vincent van Gogh, The Night Café (Café de l'Alcazar, Place Lamartine in Arles), September 1888. Oil on canvas, 70 × 89 cm. New Haven, Yale University Art Gallery.

Credit: Alamy Images.

While Van Gogh was failing and flailing in the French art world, there were other artists known as Impressionists, such as Claude Monet in France, who recorded their responses to the sunlight playing over such things as water lilies or cathedral surfaces and causing different light effects at different times of day. These could be painted as short impressions of color which when viewed from a distance were able to form coloristic versions of the original subject matter.

Almost without emotion and certainly without the boldness of a Van Gogh, Claude Monet could sit detachedly as the sun played over a surface and record his visual sensations. These took the form of strong blobs of color which when fused with other colors and viewed from a respectable distance took shape and formed a realistic painting with real depth (Wullschläger 2024). His use of complimentary colors such as red and green, blue and yellow, done with choppy brush strokes made his works appear highly individualized but also calm, restful and evocative of time spent in quiet contemplation, much resembling a modern-day yoga break from the intensity of modern life.

Georges Seurat, another French artist following in the Impressionist tradition, was even able to make little points of color which could appear to fuse when seen from a short distance into fascinating views that weren't photographically real and weren't totally abstract. Other artists began experimenting with opening up paintings until they were starting to lose images of reality entirely and turn reality into intensely stylized areas of color. Such an artist was Edouard Manet. Other artists too, especially in Paris, were experimenting with filling the canvas with splashes and broad areas of color, in part as a response to the development and perfection of photography which could replace realistic painting in a fraction of the time.

Credit: Alamy Images.

FIGURE 5: Claude Monet 1840–1926, *Rouen Cathedral* 1893, Oil on canvas, 91 × 63 cm. (Photo Erich Lessing). Paris, Musée d'Orsay.

The Norwegian Edvard Munch was another artist who explored his inner fears and anxieties with emotional Expressionistic types of paintings such as *The Scream* where one was treated to a series of zombie-like passersby and dreary apartment dwellings each complete with a garish Van Gogh influenced piss yellow window.

FIGURE 6: Tourists observe the famous Edvard Munch composition *The Scream* at the National Gallery in Oslo, Norway.

Munch had lost a number of family members while still young and like many others he lived in fear that he would contract tuberculosis for which there was then no cure and he would die a slow, horrible death.

FIGURE 7: Edvard Munch. Portrait on Norway 1000 Kroner 2001 Banknotes

In Berlin, the bizarre art that Munch created found a niche in the flamboyant experimental theatre of impresario Max Reinhardt in the early 20th century. In plays by August Strindberg, popular at the turn of the last century, characters brooded and repressed strong emotions while the garish or distorted physical environment of the sets expressed their malaise and fears. Like Van Gogh, Munch was not only a creator of this kind of anguished art but in a strong sense a victim of it, as his intense creative expression, his fear of women and his general compulsive shyness, thanatophobia (fear of dying) and anxieties regarding day to day living culminated in a massive nervous breakdown from which he never fully recovered (Bischoff 2016).

Most intense of Munch's paintings however was *The Scream*, an expression of total rage and frustration at the horrors one encounters in life when one's nightmares become a reality. That painting, several times stolen and now destroyed, has embodied human rage and fear for whole generations. It used the highly effective disorienting diagonal, the tilt or distortion of reality which makes one feel slightly out of kilter, as evidenced in the bridge in the painting. The color scheme also adds to the garish, intense effect while there is also the sense of paranoia as mysterious figures follow behind. We are in an apparent seaside area but as in a Van Gogh painting the water seems to swirl up menacingly and add to the overall sense of dread. The human figure is nothing more than a little frightened doll at the mercy of a hostile universe.

Into this pre-Expressionist world came another movement which looked at reality as shattered apart, as if through a broken mirror, full of fracture lines, sharp angles and approximately geometric forms. This movement which achieved its greatest prominence in France was spearheaded by Georges Braque and Pablo Picasso, a Spaniard active in Paris. Although not originally charged with deep emotion, this Cubist movement was soon combined with Expressionism around 1910 and developed into a movement which became known as Expressionist-Cubism which is very important for our Taylor Swift Eras Tour video of her song (Artlex 2024).

FIGURE 8: Crowd of people near the Pablo Picasso painting *Les Demoiselles D'Avignon* in the Museum of Modern Art in New York City.

The new movement combined the shattered, hard-edged look of Cubism with the blacks and dark broad brush strokes of Expressionism and was pioneered in the early part of the 20th century by artists in Germany (Meyer 2024), a land of traditionally emotional artistic and literary expression. Even their fairy-tales are charged with horror (Laskow 2017). Lyonel Feininger (1871-1956), an American who worked mainly in Germany, was one of the pioneers, fascinated by shattered mirrors and jarring reflections seen in store windows as he walked the streets and also by the use of bold black colors and the piss yellows and bubble gummy colors of the early Expressionists (Luckhardt 2019). As early as 1911 he had created his *Carnival in Arcueil*, a suburb just south of Paris. It had people made up of garish colors and considerable angularity, piss yellow house walls, a menacing black aqueduct which hovered above the apartment houses and a sky charged with atmospheric blackish highlights. Carnival settings, places of intense emotion and exuberance, were always of primary interest to Expressionist artists (Robbins 2011). Feininger also did woodcuts which brought forth a forceful shattered angular look in intense black and white as in his *Villa am Strand* or *Villa on the Shore* from 1920 clearly shows.

FIGURE 9: *Karneval in Arcueil* by Lyonel Feininger, 1871–1956. 1911. Chicago Art Institute.

FIGURE 10: Lyonel Feininger, *Villa am Strand* 1920. New York Metropolitan Museum. On Exhibition in Altenberg, Germany. Woodcut. DPA Picture Alliance/Alamy Stock Photo. This print style by the artist inspired such films as *The Cabinet of Dr. Caligari.*

Karl Schmidt-Rottluff (1884-1976) was another German artist working in the Expressionist-Cubist style who drew jagged strange scenes that seemed to fuse Munch and Picasso together and he shared Picasso's fascination with African masks because of their stark simplicity and, often, bold angularity. In his religious woodcut print *Walking to Emmaus* he featured two disciples encountering Jesus after his death and resurrection, according to Luke 24: 13-35 in the Bible, but they did not know who he was at first despite speaking with him.

Credit: Alamy Images.

FIGURE 11: **Karl Schmidt-Rottluff,** *Der Gang nach Emmaus – Walking to Emmaus/The Way to Emmaus* 1918, Pushkin Museum of Fine Arts, Moscow.

The image shows Jesus giving a blessing with his head crowned with a radiate *nimbus* as he confronts the viewer frontally and boldly and the disciples slump to the side. There are sharp cubist angles and the path appears jagged and terrifying, reflecting the intensity of the moment.

What does all of this have to do with Taylor Swift? A little patience will reveal all!

In the early 1900s Germany became involved in a program of super-nationalist aggression designed to increase its power across Europe under Kaiser Wilhelm II (1859-1941) who had been emperor of powerful Prussia within the confederation of German states.

The Germans had won the Franco-Prussian war in 1870 and what had been a loose grouping of individual states now became a unified industrial and military force. The assassination of the Archduke of Austria-Hungary in 1914 in Sarajevo, Bosnia was followed by various European nations and Russia choosing up sides in what was to lead quickly to World War I as the Germans feared the might of Russia united with Serbia while the French were still eager to avenge their loss in 1870 and Germany decimated Belgium while heading for France.

FIGURE 12: Kaiser Wilhelm II (1859–1941), last German Emperor, early 1920s.

This led to terrible carnage in World War I which included the use of poison gas and the killing of 20 million people plus another 20 million people getting crippled and maimed, although these numbers can only be estimates. Reconstructive surgery and the development of artificial limbs became serious professions due to all the horrifying casualties!

FIGURE 13: Soldiers wearing WW1 gas masks. L-R: American, British. French, German. 1917-1918.

Within Germany the young people had been led by their government to believe that they were going to win the war when in fact the youth of the country was used for cannon fodder with tremendously high death and wounded tolls (Soren 2018). The defeat and reparations following World War I led to a new republic called Weimar which hoped to achieve democracy there but which was riddled by corruption. One movie sought to expose the misdeeds of the government and was created by Hans Janowitz and Karl Mayer, both young victims severely traumatized by the horror and government lies in Germany during World War I.

They sought to make a film that would reflect their anguish but there was little money to do so. They decided to employ two young artists Walter Reimann and Hermann Warm who were affiliated with an Expressionist group known as *Der Sturm* (The Storm). There was no chance to do the film in color which would have no doubt had the look of a Munch or Feininger painting. Instead it was all done with mostly painted and partly built sets done in the Expressionist-Cubist style with bold swashes of black and angular sets which strongly resembled the woodcuts of Karl Schmidt-Rottluff. It was called *The Cabinet of Dr. Caligari (Das Kabinett des Dr. Caligari)* and despite its low cost it caused a sensation. Anything that was bizarre and profoundly disturbing came to be known at the time as Caligaresque (Kaes 2006).

The film deals with murders in the German town of Holstenwall and the fact that no one can discover the culprit. However, a traveling mountebank or carnival magician named Dr. Caligari was discovered to be using a young perpetually hypnotized young man named Cesare to commit the murders while functioning in a zom-

FIGURE 14: *Das Kabinett des Doktor Caligari (The Cabinet of Dr. Caligari),* Germany 1919; Director: Robert Wiene; Screenplay: Hans Janowitz, Carl Mayer). University of Arizona School of Anthropology Collection.

bie-like trance. The idea was that the established members of the society (judges, politicians, police, military leaders, bankers), controlling everything, were using the young people as dupes, plying them with hopes of great conquest and super-nationalism. The police in the film were no help as they arrested a petty thief for the murders and threw him in prison with a ball and chain fastened to him so he couldn't escape.

The film was made in 1919 at the beginning of the great German depression and it was shot entirely in black and white. *The Cabinet of Dr. Caligari* has remained a classic for more than a century now and is regularly studied in art and film schools (Eisner 2008). It was intended to reflect an insane world and the film itself, made as a protest film against the government, was in fact taken over by the government film organization known as Ufa and had a false ending put on it where the young man who had discovered the insane killer Caligari turned out to be himself the madman and Caligari was nothing but a respectable leader of a psychiatric clinic! The young man telling the truth was thus completely undermined and the original intention of the film was contradicted.

All of this, believe it or not, brings us back to Taylor Swift and her Eras Tour wherein she wished to stage the song *Who's Afraid of Little Old Me*? As the song progresses toward its middle we have been told in the lyrics how she has managed to go from her simple joyful beginnings as a high schooler coming to prominence in show business with only the desire to be a good girl and good to her fans but she reports that she was tame and gentle until "the circus life made me mean". This is a reference to how artists are treated by media, by horrible rivals and even by fickle fans who crave the destruction of their one-time idols.

She is compared sarcastically to a lion in a circus which has to have all of its teeth removed before she can be released again to perform in a cage. But in the lyrics she is serving notice that she's been made into a kind of demon with extraordinary powers of retaliation. Witch does not quite cover it, for in the Eras Tour's theatrical imagery she is portrayed as a demon with the power of levitation and the ability to go down your street where you live. Such a frightening creature reminded me of Meroe, the terrifyingly powerful female demon in Apuleius' mid second century A.D. Roman period proto-novel *The Golden Ass* and indeed one should be afraid of such a creature (Crumbie).

At a certain point she tells her audience that she wants to snarl and show you just how disturbed what has been done to her has made her…and so she does just that. Suddenly on screen we find ourselves going down a horizontal tunnel that looks like a mine shaft. Its walls are all tiny black dots or bold slashes of black color in the Expressionist painting style and as we come to the end of it we see that the tunnel is misshapen and has not a simple lintel block at its exit, like a mining tunnel would have, but rather a strange, distorted angular lintel area to it, tilted out of whack, and through it we can glimpse a large room which contains massive disorienting diagonal slashes which are hard-edged and all in black and white, resembling a woodcut by Karl Schmidt-Rottluff about whom we have written above and the room bears a striking resemblance to the Expressionist-Cubist scene from *The Cabinet of Dr. Caligari* wherein a prisoner, falsely arrested, detained and confined to a large room

is hailed as the Holstenwall murderer when in fact he was only guilty of petty crimes and it is the society around him that has become corrupt and arrested the wrong man just as Taylor has told us she has been wrongly accused and persecuted.

But now in the dead center of the room in our Eras Tour scene sits not a falsely accused male prisoner but a WOMAN in the prisoner's position with her hands hiding her face in agony. It is Taylor herself and at this time the lyrics tell the audience that you yourself if placed in this "asylum" wouldn't last an hour. In fact it is a symbolic jail that Taylor has been placed in BUT in the German silent movie Dr. Caligari was *actually* the director of a mental asylum which subverted and hypnotized the innocent young anti-hero Cesare and forced him to do his bidding, including serial murders.

FIGURE 15: Image of the falsely accused prisoner from *The Cabinet of Dr. Caligari* 1919 German film. University of Arizona School of Anthropology Collection

And in case you didn't get the message the background screen dissolves immediately and directly from the closeup of the woman in the Expressionist-Cubist room to an image of Taylor Swift herself actually singing the song on the stage and the backscreen rotates her around 360 degrees in a completely bizarre video somersault to show her manipulated state of mind. It is a stunningly powerful moment which the audience only half understands because most do not know the inspiration for the image.

Nonetheless, it is still dramatically effective if you are physically there to see it. You get enough of it to make it work. And by the way, as to the disorienting diagonals for psychological effect, Taylor herself has been recorded during the actual filming of the video for *Fortnight* with Post Malone saying for her crew to be sure and include the angled cocking of Post's face because "nothing says crazy like a tilt to the head" !!! (see the chapter included in this book on *Fortnight*). As the Eras Tour continued the background video for this song was changed periodically and the version I am describing was used in a number of sites early in the tour, including Cardiff, Wales where a number of our Swifties viewed it and reported in.

The rest of this video compares Taylor to a caged wild beast who is subjected to all sorts of cruelty such as has been done to Taylor by hostile media (which by the way affected her mother deeply and moved her to tears frequently during times when she needed to be recovering from cancer treatments) (Hardington 2024). Taylor describes herself as being lured, hurt and taunted, caged and called crazy, all of which in the song she considers her training and when she lashes out now, with this hardened soul, don't be surprised because now she knows how to do it and she isn't about to take any more crap from anybody about anything. It's a declaration of attitude and a warning, one conditioned by the blatant abuse whereby it was even publicly stated that she needed to be slapped around and that she had become an annoying liar—it's all well documented and was well orchestrated at the time she was having her career systematically attacked (Carlson 2016).

The use of the *Cabinet of Dr. Caligari* as an expression of madness in a popular music context is not however unique to Taylor Swift. Robert Bartleh Cummings (1965-), better known as Rob Zombie, founder of the heavy metal band *White Zombie,* made a video of his song *Living Dead Girl* (1999) (Davis 2023), which incorporated some shot by shot reconstructions of scenes from *The Cabinet of Dr. Caligari* and fused it with

FIGURE 16: Robert Bartleh Cummings performs under his stage name Rob Zombie at Shoreline Amphitheatre in Mountain View, California in 2016.

Sterling Munksgard/Shutterstock.com

influences from the Caligari-derived American talking picture *Svengali* (1931) and also *White Zombie* (1932) from which his group's name was derived. At the Eras tour performance I witnessed, the audience was astonished to see this image and there were audible gasps and then oohs and ahhs that revealed yet again her amazing ability to surprise and entertain an audience, even for 3 ½ hours and have them wanting to go again and again to see her and even experiencing withdrawal symptoms when the concert and the overall tour was over (La Grassa 2024).

One question I would really love to ask Taylor about the Eras Tour is where do the specific concepts come from that are used on the backscreen projections and on the floor. We know that she creates the music and uses technicians to help create the sounds she basically hears within her head, but is she that brilliant that she can draw on earlier masterworks of artistic expression and repurpose them in the imaginative way that she does in this video or is it something she works out with suggestions and consultations from artistic advisers. We know that she worked on the Eras Tour with many technicians and consultants to achieve her visions and we know that from as early as her Fearless Tour preparations in 2008 she has been visually documented advising her backup group on what she wants in her accompanying music and her designers on how she sees her set design and overall tour concept (Behind the Scenes 2010; Shania M 2009), but for the Eras Tour how much is total Taylor and how much is consultation with experts at set design?

We know that one of her quiet gurus for the tour was a man named Ethan Tubman whose task it appears to have been to carry out her cerebral fantasies (Burke 2024) and who was responsible for developing the production design of Taylor's 10 minute video of *All Too Well* plus eight other major Swift videos, including the amazing *Fortnight*. Is the concept of making each song into a mini-story partly his or totally hers? Taylor is known for arriving at her collaborative sessions with a complete idea which she has already either composed or seen in her head (The Week 2023). Whatever happens in these meetings of incredibly creative people it is truly amazing to see the result as the Eras Tour crowd sits or stands enthralled singing along, periodically surprised at the visual effects and above all, at least for me, learning the deeper meanings that Taylor experienced and quoted within the songs as she conceived them (Greive 2024).

NOTES

Artlex, "Cubism vs Expressionism: Similarities and Differences," *Artlex Art Dictionary* (2024) https://www.artlex.com/art-movements/cubism/cubism-vs-expressionism/

Behind the Scenes 2010 - *Behind the Scenes of the Fearless Tour* 9-24-2010 posting https://www.youtube.com/watch?v=MNRhiJ0Uh4g

Bischoff, Ulrich, *Edvard Munch: Images of Life and Death* (Los Angeles: Taschen America, 2016)

Burke, Sammi, "Taylor Swift's Creative Director Reveals the Most Difficult Part of Working on the Eras Tour," *MSN* 11-22-2024 https://www.msn.com/en-us/music/news/taylor-swifts-creative-director-reveals-the-most-difficult-part-of-working-on-the-eras-tour/ar-AA1uAaGJ

Carlson, Nicholas, "Something else is going on with Taylor Swift — and it's ugly," *Business Insider* 7-18-2016 https://www.businessinsider.com/something-else-is-going-on-with-taylor-swift-and-its-ugly-2016-7?op=1

Crumbie, Lawrence, "The Typicality of Apuleius' Witches," *Scribd*, no date given https://www.scribd.com/document/332558228/The-Typicality-of-Apuleius-Witches

Davis, Hector, "The Meaning Behind The Song: Living Dead Girl by Rob Zombie," *Beat-Crave* 12-30-2023 https://beatcrave.com/the-meaning-behind-the-song-living-dead-girl-by-rob-zombie-2/

Eisner, Lotte H., Haunted Screen: Expressionism in the German Cinema and the Influence of Max Reinhardt (University of California Press: Berkeley 2008)

Evans, Olivia, "Taylor Swift Reveals the Real Meaning Behind *The Tortured Poets Department* Songs," *ENews* 4-22-2024 https://www.eonline.com/news/1399924/taylor-swift-reveals-the-real-meaning-behind-the-tortured-poets-department-songs

Greive, Duncan, "Don't understand the appeal of Taylor Swift? Let a critic explain it," *The Spinoff* 2-24-2024 https://thespinoff.co.nz/pop-culture/24-02-2024/dont-understand-the-appeal-of-taylor-swift-let-a-critic-explain-it

Hardington, Brooke, "What We Know About Taylor Swift's Mom Andrea's Cancer Diagnosis," *Nicki Swift* 2-17-2024 https://www.nickiswift.com/1509911/taylor-swift-mom-andrea-cancer-diagnosis-what-we-know/

Kaes, Anton, 'The Cabinet of Dr Caligari: Expressionism and Cinema' in Ted Perry (ed.), *Masterpieces of Modernist Cinema* (Bloomington, IN, Indiana University Press, 2006), pp. 41–59.

La Grassa, Jennifer, "Here's why you might be 'down bad' after Taylor Swift's Eras Tour," *MSN* 11-23-2024 https://www.msn.com/en-ca/news/canada/heres-why-you-might-be-down-bad-after-taylor-swifts-eras-tour/ar-AA1uyz2m

Laskow, Sarah, "The 19th-Century Book of Horrors That Scared German Kids Into Behaving," *Atlas Obscura* 6-14-2017 https://www.atlasobscura.com/articles/original-struwwelpeter-illustrations-childrens-moral-lesson-book

Luckhardt, Ulrich, *Lyonel Feininger* (Hirmer Publishers: Munich, 2019)

Meyer, Isabella, "German Expressionism- One of the Greatest German Art Movements," *Art in Context* 2-10-2024

National Gallery (Washington, D.C.), "In the Mind of Van Gogh," *National Gallery* 2024 https://www.nga.gov/learn/teachers/lessons-activities/sense-of-place-france/van-gogh.html

Robbins, Eleanor, "The carnivalesque expressionism of Lyonel Feininger," Cassone 9-2011 http://www.cassone-art.com/magazine/article/2011/09/the-carnivalesque-expressionism-of-lyonel-feininger/

Shania M 2009- Fearless Tour 2009 First Show Behind the Scenes https://www.youtube.com/watch?v=NBYUB6tFU8Q

Soren, David, Art History, *Popular Culture and the Cinema* (Dubuque: Kendall Hunt 2018)

The Week, "The Taylor Swift phenomenon," *The Week* 11-12-2023 https://www.youtube.com/watch?v=NBYUB6tFU8Q https://theweek.com/culture-life/music/the-taylor-swift-phenomenon

Wullschläger, Jackie, *Monet: The Restless Vision* (Knopf: New York, 2024)

Taylor Swift: Behind the Magic

By Gerardo Quintana Bernal

(Gerardo Quintana Bernal is a 20-year-old Student at the California Institute of the Arts in Santa Clarita, California. He is studying Theatrical Design and Production with a focus in Lighting Design at the School of Theater. He plans to work in the theater world and the film industry. His inspirations include Science Fiction, Fantasy, Mythology, and History. Apart from Lighting, he enjoys set building and sound design, as well as animation and illustration.)

For this article there are frequent notes which refer to relevant articles and images on the Internet that should be viewed in order to better visualize what is being discussed).

Spearheaded by Ethan Tobman, Creative Director and Production Designer of the show, the lighting and video technology and its execution in *Taylor Swift's Eras Tour* is truly something spectacular.

Along with the standard, but still very impressive, lighting and rigging, this production was elevated to its legendary status thanks to two unique elements. The first is the gorgeous showcase of the LED wristbands that included the audience in the show and turned the crowd into an artist's canvas (Talreja 2023). The second is the main showpiece, the LED Panels that animate the stage and bring the show to life and it is fascinating to view the

Pixmob Wristbands and Solotech Panels at work washing the venue in rainbow (https://medium.com/@ieeemuj/glowing-in-harmony-wristband-wonders-that-illuminate-the-concerts-9d7f4f21c0cf).

So how does everything work?

To start with, everything comes from the programming software. In this case, a program called TAIT is used through one of their programming boards. The program is fed all the data by the designer for what, when and how all the lights will do something. This includes all the standard fixtures along with the wristband lights. This data is sent through a DMX, or Data Multiplex, to the individual lights, sometimes directly or sometimes through a black box that serves as an external processor to help send more data over long distances. The data being sent through includes all sorts of things, from how bright the lights are to the color and temperature of the lights, and if the fixture allows it, panning and tilting of the light.

Pixmob (https://pixmob.com/products/led-wristbands) is a leading supplier of LED wristbands. Their technology had been used at the closing ceremony of the 2024 Paris Olympics. In 2022, they teamed up with the rock group Coldplay for their World Tour to create compostable wristbands, which reduced carbon emissions by 400% while still creating a great result.

For the Eras Tour, Pixmob provided the X3 Wristband and, in the U.S., a Custom VIP ID Badge show. The X3 wristband was one of their brightest options at the time, designed to give audiences the best possible experience (Pixmob Wristband https://pixmob.com/products/led-wristbands). It is fully bendable and comfortable to wear. Its Ultrabright RGB LEDs and data technology allow stunning animations integrating the crowd into the performance with different colors and other special effects (https://pixmob.com/projects/taylor-swift-eras-tour). The VIP ID Badges are also available for ticket holders looking for a memorable experience (wristbands and VIP ID badges are worn by our own Swifties in Chapter 8 Figure 2 of this book). While they are not as bright as the wristbands, they offer more branding options and serve as a beautiful keepsake (https://nz.pinterest.com/pin/919086236457537975).

They have three fixtures that send data directly to the wristbands. Instead of controlling each wristband individually, two infrared lights handle the control and data. When the lights shine on a wristband, sensors inside convert the light signals into instructions for the LEDs.

The first fixture is called Wash. It sends data to large parts, if not all, of the audience, creating unified visuals and animations.

Pixmob then uses Moving Head and MVT fixtures for more detailed animations in specific sections. These smaller lights can be remotely adjusted to pan, tilt, and rotate, providing smooth projections across the audience. The difference between them is that the Moving Head projects static images, while the MVT (Moving Video Transmitter) is capable of projecting Video content for dynamic animations. However both are similar in appearance.

LED PANELS

The stage also features beautiful LED panels provided by Solotech and designed by Roe Visuals. Solotech also provided many of the other fixtures and stage equipment for the show, but this discussion will only focus on the LED panels. These panels cover almost every part of the stage, from the floor to the large back wall. Each panel is connected and assigned a specific position in both the real world and the TAIT software program. In lighting design software, it's important to input the exact position of the lights. This is because the software controls patterns that the lights create, which often involve them moving in relation to one another. Therefore, the actual arrangement of lights must match the setup in the program for everything to work correctly on stage.

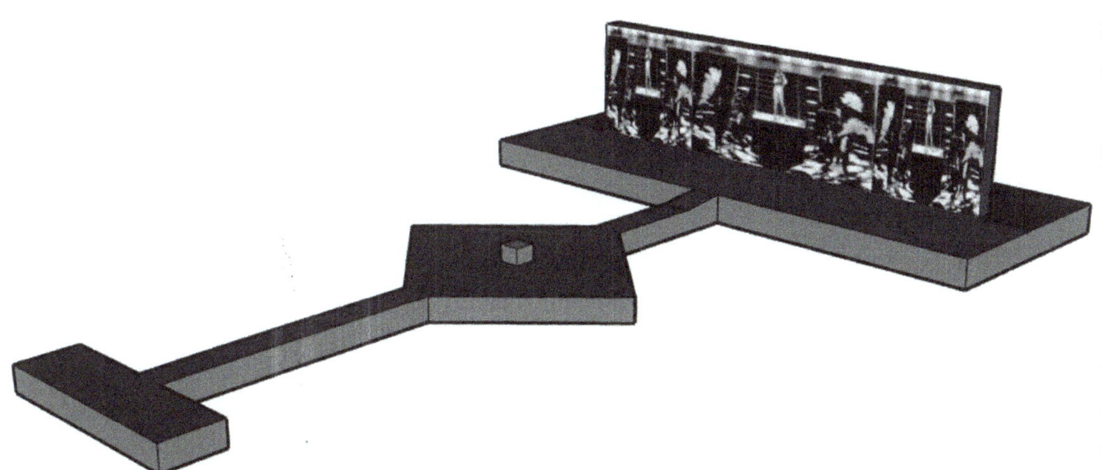

The same principle applies to video walls, like those used in this tour. Each panel acts as an individual fixture in the software. Each one can display its content, or they can be synced together to show one video across all panels, based on their arrangement in the software. For example, in the original video for the song *Blank Space*, you see a real car being hit with golf clubs (watch the official video!) and on the Eras Tour you see a raised LED panel showing an image of the car being "hit" with golf clubs (Torchinsky 2023).

Or there is her deep stage dive, where Swift dives into a gap in the panels that opens up quickly and then she is seen "swimming" upstage. Later she reappears "miraculously" in a new outfit (Stopera 2023); these are pre-programmed sequences that sync with the choreography. Usually, a person operates the computer to time these sequences, but in musical performances, the system often runs automatically on a timer while the performers adjust their timing to sync up with it.

While not anything new, the execution of these technologies was truly something phenomenally unique, and groundbreaking. And the lighting world seemed to agree, with Solotech receiving the Parnelli "Lighting Company of the Year" award in 2023 for their work on this show, and it was well-deserved.

From the most standard of lighting fixtures to cutting edge Infrared Projectors and wristbands, Taylor Swift's *Eras Tour* is a beautiful showcase of the power of illumination, and the current level of performance technology available now on the market, ready for the next brilliant designer to pick up and make the next groundbreaking show.

Since I have to do or assist doing this kind of work periodically, I find that there are a few basic questions that people often ask that are worth going over here:

With this technology at one's fingertips, how long do the performers and tech experts have to rehearse a song to make it work smoothly?

Based on my experience, it is likely that each song is practiced hundreds of times before it is pronounced perfectly synced up. One of the benefits of it being a musical performance is that each song has an established time limit so that the singers, the band playing the music and the dancers are expected to pull off the same song the exact same way every time they play. The musical performers can even have a literal metronome in their ear to keep time with each other, but sometimes it's not even needed with skilled professionals.

When it comes to the visuals it's the same thing so that everyone including the stage manager and technicians work together. Having a drummer like Matt Billingslea who keeps an even beat can also be very important and the drummer's consistency is absolutely as important as his skill at creating enhancing power flourishes for a song. The performers and the technical designer can animate the required synchronizations for the song using a demo track which is what you would hear if you listened to the song on Spotify. This need for everyone to be working together is one reason why Taylor's songs live sound virtually identical to her recordings even down to her breathing and tiny verbal exclamations within the song.

Does all of the choreography also have to match with every other aspect of the performance?

Yes, and the dancers can come up with unique sequences such as the hitting of the car in the *Blank Space* song on the Eras Tour. To make this fit together perfectly, the dancers must practice on what beat they hit the car and where they hit it and keep doing the same thing until the technicians create the sound and the reaction appropriately timed to the action. The person running the visuals can always change his or her timing to match that of the performers. If they want the timing to be perfect, they just need to practice on what beat they hit and where they hit and just repeat that until it all matches.

But that's just the sequencing if it is running on a timer.

How does all of this work without a timer but with manual cues?

Something I actually have been in charge of is running manual cues for a concert program. Take for example Taylor Swift diving into the stage. Since something like that can vary based on how and when she decides to dive, that's instead left to a board operator and a stage manager.

A stage manager would have a full list and/or script with notes of what happens when. These notes or "cues" will usually be tied not to a time or timer but instead to a specific verbal phrase or an action such as a walk to the area where the stage panels slide open so that no matter how a performer does something it's always synchronized or tipped off to the board operator through a signal from the stage manager. But for things like this a board operator needs to manually press a "go" button that runs that cue, so it can be a bit tense to get it exactly right, but when it works it works amazingly.

Each rectangle making up the stage can be programmed individually, in groups or collectively. If the little rectangles in the ground receive messages and so does the screen how do the performers time their performances to be in sync with the overall operating board. " Must they use a metronome to get it all programmed right?

Each panel is its own screen that can show images. It's not too different from connecting your computer to a monitor so that you can either have the monitor show its own display, or it can be an extension of the same display, by adding just a few more steps. A metronomic device could be used but certainly after frequent rehearsals may not be necessary once everything is in sync. A world class drummer can be enough to make a show run smoothly with his consistency and innate sense of timing for a song.

SOURCES

Pixmob on the Eras tour; https://pixmob.com/projects/taylor-swift-eras-tour
Pixmob on IR Fixtures: https://pixmob.com/our-effects
Analysis of the tech: https://youtu.be/5qmqXbggxFY?si=hvHQBdMq51Fn_Lvq
Solotech on Eras Tour: https://solotech.com/en-uk/tag/eras-tour-en-uk/
Roe Visuals; https://www.roevisual.com/us-en/

NOTES

Stopera, Matt, "People Are Laughing At Taylor Swift After Discovering What She Does After Her Viral Stage Dive," *BuzzFeed* 8-11-2023 https://www.buzzfeed.com/mjs538/taylor-swift-stage-dive-crawling-video

Talreja, Suhani, "Glowing in Harmony: Wristband Wonders That Illuminate the Concerts," *Medium* 6-29-2023 https://medium.com/@ieeemuj/glowing-in-harmony-wristband-wonders-that-illuminate-the-concerts-9d7f4f21c0cf

Torchinsky, Jason, "Taylor Swift Is Dancing On A Strange Car On Her New Tour, What The Hell Is It?," *Autopian* 4-4-2023 https://www.theautopian.com/taylor-swift-is-dancing-on-a-strange-car-on-her-new-tour-what-the-hell-is-it/

Doing It with a Broken Heart and Lots of Pre-Planning

By David Soren

(Before viewing this it is helpful to view the Eras Tour video for the song and production which can be seen on YouTube at https://www.youtube.com/watch?v=uJI9S8LmzPk *in Miami and* https://www.youtube.com/watch?v=tBmgagml6Sw *Gelsenkirchen, Germany, and* https://www.youtube.com/watch?v=GE7JDu0VOkw, https://www.youtube.com/watch?v=k02y0o-EdPG4 *London, and especially* https://www.youtube.com/watch?v=3DxJr6vlo7I *Paris)*

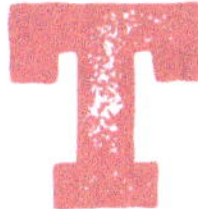aylor Swift is the most underappreciated celebrity on the planet.

That may seem like an absurd statement considering that for the past few years she has been the number one female celebrity in the entire world and is a billionaire several times over.

Catrina Haze/Shutterstock.com

FIGURE 1: Taylor Swift promotional poster for the Eras Tour Australia, from Sydney, March 5th, 2024. Pictured at the ticket booth stand.

Featureflash Photo Agency/Shutterstock.com

FIGURE 2: Taylor Swift arriving for the Brit Awards 2013 at the O2 Arena, Greenwich, London. 20/02/2013 Picture by: Henry Harris.

In fact, so much has been written about Taylor Swift that it would appear that there could be nothing left to say or to learn about her. She has been studied by scholars at Harvard (Inampudi, Parker and Reimann 2023) and at many other universities, institutes and museums, given an honorary Ph.D. by New York University (Miller 2022), assessed by online psychotherapists (McGuire 2024), stalked everywhere she goes by super-aggressive *paparazzi* (Thompson 2023), and documented in her every waking moment and movement by gossip columnists often making up vicious, untrue and/or deliberately hateful and misleading stories to meet deadlines and garner money.

But it is doubtful that she has been studied by a 79 year old professional archaeologist before and that is a shame because an archaeological approach to Miss Americana seems to be just what's needed now or at least doesn't seem to have been done. Generally, much of the documentation on Taylor so far has been either so intellectual and discipline-restricted or so low level (whom she's dating, what's she wearing, who likes or hates her, who's in her pack, what are the latest Easter Egss, etc.) that it seems not enough has been written for people who appreciate Taylor but who want to dig a little deeper into what she has achieved. I came to this conclusion after I noticed several articles had been written about how she has to go to the bathroom in a public environment (Flavius 2025). It struck me that there isn't enough appreciation of what she actually does and too much trivia about the megastar diva she's become, triggering both an adoring public and an enraged public without quite enough appreciation for or awareness of what she actually is doing.

What we have in Taylor is a pioneering songwriter, production stager, video director, game designer and thrilling show-stopping entertainer who is developing new venues for artistic expression all the time and in so doing has created some of the most striking examples of Performance Art ever made (Woltmann 2023) and has been reinvigorating popular music dynamically in many ways while improving the business side of it for the artists doing it. Taylor doesn't just write popular music. She sees it in her mind, creating a total concept parallel universe that involves everything from music and lyrics to the final presentation on a stage or in a video or short film complete with attention to every detail she can imagine of the production design, stage movement and sound, including above all how it will be perceived by her precious fans. She works with fabulous hand-picked collaborators but the end result is always something that reflects her vision.

Her vision is, initially, usually spoken into and saved on her phone and then composed in its entirety out of the pieces, often first as a song or song fragments and then lyrics, emphasizing a key turn of phrase that will be memorable and she deliberately writes in different styles as the mood hits her, including a more poetic Emily Dickinson sort of style called her Quill Style, a more contemporary or "Fountain Pen Style" which features modern problems and a poetic twist within it, and there is her bouncy frivolous Glitter Gel Pen style which never takes itself seriously, and every Swiftie should read her comments at the Nashville Songwriter of the Decade Award Show in 2022 on how she does it (Rahman 2022).

Once a song is formed and polished it is still not through, for at this point, if it is deemed worthy, it is storyboarded and constantly refined through her artistic skills into whatever look she wishes to follow until the final resulting tour or video presentation meets with her approval. When she can no longer think of things to further embellish the work, it is then considered done and ready to share (Raza-Sheikh 2022). And she's been producing the overall look of her concert tours with increasing degrees of interaction, direction and total audience involvement since she was still a teenager, supervising the creative input into her enormously successful *Fearless Tour* as early as 2009 at the age of 19 and making it look unique. There is footage of her overseeing her dancers, musicians and technicians as a young high school equivalency-educated kid (Whitaker 2024). It shows every one of her touring team listening intently because she is so precise and knowledgeable about everything that is needed to make a successful tour and she talked about it with *Access Hollywood*:

FIGURE 3: Taylor Swift at age 19 on stage for Taylor Swift *Fearless* Tour Concert at Madison Square Garden, New York City, August 27, 2009.

""I love living that way, where you have control over everything that happens creatively and artistically, like putting a tour together and knowing that you had a hand in every decision that was made."(*Access Hollywood* 7-7-2023)

She considers herself, above all, to be a storyteller which she began doing through her writing as a child of 11 (and even becoming a novelist, writing *A Girl Named Girl* at the age of 14!) (Bhattacharya 2021), Today, she is still learning and is currently on her way to becoming a feature film writer, producer and director with likely also a Broadway show or two thrown in which would explain the title she recently copyrighted: *Female Rage: The Musical* (Irvin 2024). In fact, diving deeper, we should note that she is the foremost exponent today in popular culture of what used to be called the Paranoiac-Critical Method of artistic expression in which one takes one's own phobias, life concerns and nightmares and records them, often at night, without the need to limit them to the realities of this world but instead with the option to use Surrealism, an alternate reality where all things are possible (and color sensitive).

This was the technique pioneered by Salvador Dali in his timeless, sizeless and airless paintings which presented his personal obsessions and phobias, leading to such works as *Persistence of Memory* where we can view familiar things in his life including the background cliffs of his boyhood home, a distorted portrait of himself, frightening grasshoppers, and a watch crawling with ants (part of his obsession with time and fear of insects). Dali kept an easel by his bed to record his night-time or nightmare sensations while Swift, also a frequent midnight devotee, uses her phone and also sketches things as she feels them and sees them in her mind, storyboarding them with the help of professional artists such as Vincent Lucido (Mamo 2020).

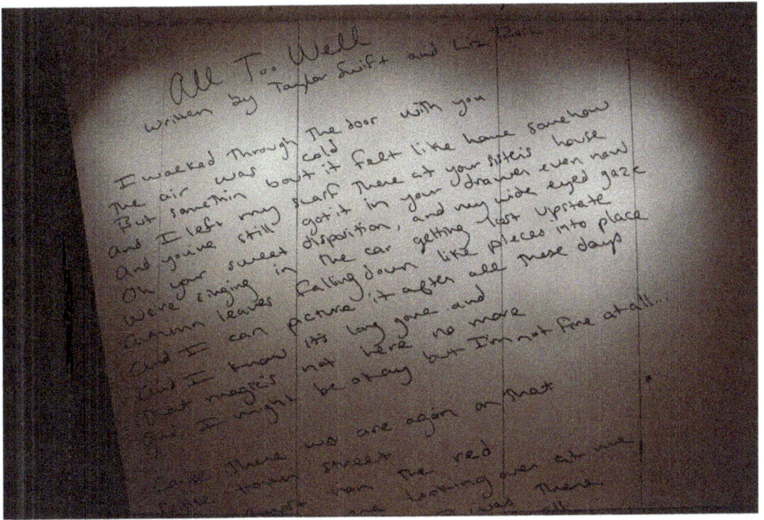

FIGURE 4: Taylor Swift—Original writing for the words of her song *All Too Well*, written with Liz Rose, from the Red Album. Storyteller exhibit at Museum of Arts and Design in New York City, as seen on October 14, 2023.

FIGURE 5: A photograph of famous painter Salvador Dali looking through the window of an art gallery exhibiting some of his works on Via Rodeo, near famous Rodeo Drive in Beverly Hills.

Dali was also a pioneer of interactive exhibition before the invention of the computer. In Figueroa, Spain, for example, he created a walk-through exhibit where one experienced what seemed like stylized everyday objects such as photographic images, a sofa and curtains but when one completed the exhibit and looked at it from a higher vantage point all at once it formed a facial image of vaudeville, theater and film star Mae West, one of the most iconic women in the entertainment field.

FIGURE 6: Famous Mae West room in Dali's Theatre—Museum building, Figueroa, Spain, opened on September 28, 1974, housing the largest collection of works by Salvador Dali.

The idea of interactivity with the audience and being able to be a mastermind and read their mind would also become a part of experiencing Taylor's shows along with her music and explains in part the repeated audience comments that she seemed to be singing to each person individually, that she was describing the life of her listener, and that the time of the show flew by despite being 3 ½ hours in length.

In her Eras Tour, Taylor has expanded Dali's Paranoiac-Critical Approach to involve her enormous audiences in dramatic and surprisingly new interactive ways. To attempt to illustrate this I would like to do a deep dive into one of her most amazing creations, the song and Eras Tour production number entitled *I Can Do It With a Broken Heart*.

The song began by her listing it as number 13 on the *Tortured Poets Department* album song list

FIGURE 7: The Mae West room from further away.

which tells you that it has been given a place of prominence in Taylor's mind,13 being her lucky number (Jeffrey 2024). When the song was released, however, I wondered how it could ever possibly be performed in her tour program because it tells the audience that her performance is fake and not truly sincere because she is doing it night after night with a broken heart due to all the horrible things that have been done to her both romantically and professionally. Wouldn't her fans, who believe in the honesty of her affection and sincerity for them, reject her performance as a phony effort/masquerade if she dared to present it as such?

What I hadn't understood was that she was not only going to present the song but to feature it as the lynchpin of her Eras Tour homage to old movies and the glory days of 1930s Hollywood. When the song was conceived apparently Taylor thought of it as a complete vision and not just as a song. It would not only be a vehicle for confessing her own rage at her treatment at the hands of some others in the entertainment profession but also her profound and repeated disappointment in the men she had chosen and believed in, a subject which is displayed prominently throughout The *Tortured Poets Department.*

She has noted that when she begins with a song she often finds it comes to her with a mental visual display of what the song is about, enhanced more easily if it is based on her actual life but which could be also a made-up or even a fairy story as was the case especially in the earlier albums produced during co-vid confinement: *Folklore* and *Evermore* (Penn and Trust 2024). So how does *I Can Do It With a Broken Heart* fit into her stage show and the rest of the album?

FIGURE 9: Taylor Swift's *Folklore* Songbook cover, arranged for easy piano with lyrics. 17 songs from Swift's 2020 surprise release of tunes she recorded during the COVID-19 pandemic.

To stage the song she used a technique which those of us who grew up in the entertainment business and in my case vaudeville used to call "routining". This means that she has a pre-designed stage that is custom-made for her usual striding out and dancing around to offer the possibility of more intimacy with her audience and flexibility for her dance troupe and backup singers (Little 2024).

FIGURE 10: Taylor Swift performs in concert at Wembley Stadium on June 23, 2018 in London.

But for many of her songs on the Eras Tour and even her earlier tours too, a simply "routined" stage is far from sufficient to contain her energy and desire for total artistic expression of her song. In this case the stage itself is full of what used to be called "vampire traps" or openings under the stage to allow state of the art machinery of all sorts to be employed and which could do LED projection of imagery onto the artificially created stage floor itself (see the previous article in this volume). These images on stage and screen would then be visible from the audience. Unlike a standard "vampire trap" which was just an opening in the stage which dropped down to allow someone to seem to vanish instantly, these openings could be made to rise up to elevate her on the stage. There could also be camouflaged carts which could be employed to cause her to travel or slide around the stage (as she does for *Who's Afraid of Little Old Me*) and seem to be flying in the air when this is combined with imagery projected onto the large screen behind her.

Summing up then, her "routining" necessitates a total concept approach. Through the manipulation of the stage itself and its lighting and the integration with it of giant back-screen projection, it allows her free expression to explore the landscape of her mind in producing the presentation she desires, encompassing the stage area itself, the back-screen, and the beneath-the-stage openings as well as imagery projected on the stage itself. In another part of routining or gaining control of your presentation, dance numbers must be learned and timed with rising and falling areas of the stage itself, so that she and her 15 dancers must hit precise places on the stage (there don't seem to be actual marks) at precise times in the song so as not to collide and so as to take advantage of the movable stage parts and the LED projection. She is therefore required to sing, dance in tandem, and hit precise places on the stage simultaneously for 3 ½ hours, quite a chore for someone not really trained in her early life as a dancer. I used to have to do it all working in television but for perhaps as much as 15 minutes at a time, never 3 ½ hours for 175 shows!

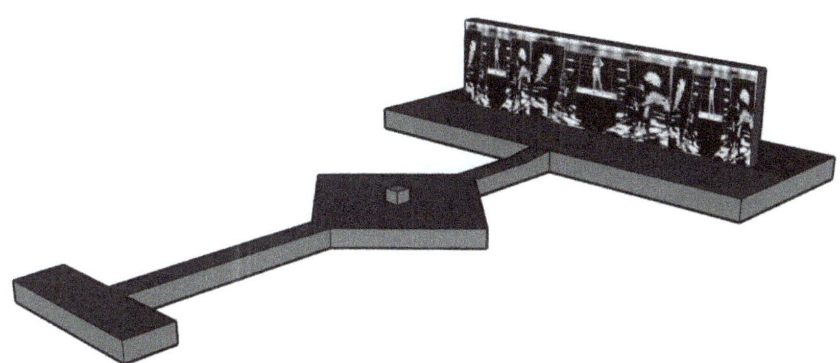

FIGURE 11: General reconstruction of the Eras Tour stage arrangement, featuring backscreen, central performing area and front rectangle. Drawing by Barbara Bernal.

But the inventive stagecraft is far from the complete vision of this song in Taylor's mind. In keeping with the depressed feelings of *Tortured Poets*, the entire video portrayal of that album of songs is cast dramatically and daringly in black and white, suggesting the absence or draining of all color from her life. But black and white also allows her to blend well with her song, *I Can Do It With a Broken Heart*, which was inspired by the plot of old-time Hollywood black and white musical movies. The staging hasn't been talked about very much by the critics but seen in person it was a wow for lovers of 1930s musical cinema!

Taylor has expressed her love of old-time show business many times and comedian and former late night talk show host David Letterman has said how her performances are "reminiscent of real show business, everything you want in a performance—glamour, lovely music, beautiful woman" (Late Show 2014). She has stated on the same program that she loves the whole idea of building up to the big show and giving the patrons something special as a reward for spending their hard-earned money on a night out with her.

And so, with this background, let's now look at how *I Can Do It With a Broken Heart* is actually presented as best we can without having the video precisely before us. At this point the reader is encouraged to watch one of the fan videos taken of this song on the Eras Tour before we start if you are able.

Taking a page from 1930s movies, we can quote that old vaudeville, circus and theatre mantra that "the show must go on" no matter what, and Taylor in this section of her Eras Show is shown as wounded and lying practically dead on the stage from acting out her previous heartbreak song (*The Saddest Man Who Ever Lived*). In the link to the next song, she is subsequently scooped up and carried off by two apparent showmen who revive her and tell her that she can perform again, while the music plays a raucous jazzed-up ragtime comedic version of the title song that seems especially out of place with all of the rest of her musical numbers in the Eras Tour show and there seems to be a feeling that is comedic but also at the same time tragic about this scene, the sort of dualism that Taylor sometimes effects in her videos, such as *Anti-Hero*.

The attendants are elegantly dressed in top hat and tails and yet one of them, Kameron Saunders (Sen Gupta 2024), brazenly strips her clothes off as the real-life audience collectively gasps and oohs loudly at the bold shock of this, while the other man raises her limp arm as if trying to get her to express some sort of victory and helps her to put on her dancing shoes. They quickly redress and revive her and push her off amid her protests that she is not ready and she is staggered by her own confusion, but suddenly the pounding music starts and the sound of it miraculously revives her and she heads out again to take her place on the stage as the audience cheers this playlet within the big show.

The entire plot of this is achieved with no script and owes a great deal to Warner Brothers musicals of 1933 and 1934 which featured the often-used story of bringing the show to a successful conclusion despite every sort of heartbreaking personal problem exacerbated by the Great Depression and of course often a heartbreaking love affair or an unknown chorus girl seeking stardom and getting her chance when the lead woman suffers misfortune of her own making.

Having grown up in live vaudeville and entertained on early (mid 1950s) television, I know personally about performing no matter how you feel (*Say Etcetera* 2014). On tv and in live vaudeville performances we often closed our show by singing Irving Berlin's 1946 song *There's No Business Like Show Business*" which contains the lyric "You Smile When You Are Low" and "Still You Wouldn't Change It for a Sack of Gold. Let's Go On With The Show". Taylor literally believes this as one can see from her performances in heavy downpours and bitter cold so bad it froze her guitar picking hand in Edinburgh (Frost 2024).

As the two men revive Taylor from her exhausted state on stage, they, for some reason, end up holding and actually waving ostrich feather fans, which are a callback to old-time vaudeville shows as presented in the *Ziegfeld Follies,* going all the way back to 1906 and continuing on stage into the early 1930s. The Follies were resplendent in plumes and walking lovelies who were the toast of New York and known as Ziegfeld Girls (Brideson 2015; Pagkalinawan 2024).

FIGURE 12: **Close up of ostrich feathers.**

FIGURE 13: **Showgirls with white feather fans.**

The pounding music then transforms the song into a strong visual which is further developed by integrating the surrounding giant screen, stage props and even the floor itself into devices for enhancing the comparison to 1930s Hollywood. The audience is able to witness LED projections done onto the central floor of the stage where arranged rectangular panels of the stage are layed radially to surround the central rising and lowering rectangular stage opening area. These rectangular LED panels show us a large number of scantily clad female dancers arranged in a circle around the stage floor opening, reminding us, I think deliberately, of the Busby Berkeley overhead film shots in the early 1930s Warner Brothers musical extravaganzas, done in the original films in black and white of course.

Credit: Alamy Images.

FIGURE 14: On the set of the Film, *Roman Scandals*, United Artists, 1933 with choreographed sequences by Busby Berkeley. This is the type of circular surrounding imagery represented by the showgirls in the Eras Tour song while the central area, fixed in one place here, can rise up from within the stage on the Eras Tour.

FIGURE 15: Design of the Eras Tour stage showing the central performing area where 1930s dancers have been projected in black and white onto the stage floor via LED surrounding the central square area while the square area rises and falls with Taylor on it.

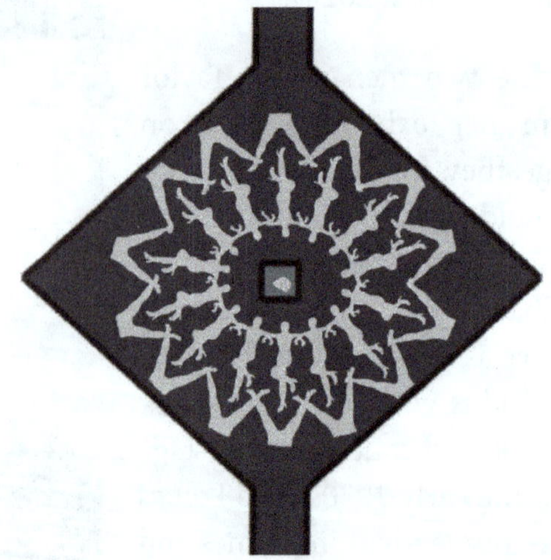

FIGURE 16: Detail of previous image. All stage drawings are by Barbara Bernal based on film evidence that we could gather from fan projections of Eras Tour photo images.

There is also a chorus line of Taylor's dancers in typical 1930s style top hats and costumes showing off their legs while they do routines featuring canes. In the film they even do a "fadeaway" as we used to call it where each dancer, following the one preceding, does the same movement and fades away from the camera, similar to a wave in a stadium. Such a fadeaway was a staple of the Busby Berkeley musical as were the leggy showgirls and the blatant taken-for-granted sexism of the era.

In the movie *Dames*, from Warner Brothers in 1934, Dick Powell sings the title song which states: "Their knees in action. That's the attraction." In Taylor's sequence, the 1930s showgirls projected onto the floor are each shown lying down but are leaning up against some sort of circular border that surrounds the raised central rectangular area upon which Swift dances (we have not been able to see it clearly in any of the fan projections). In the Eras tour stage design there is such a circular area placed near the cen-

Credit: Alamy Images.

FIGURE 17: Jack Oakie with *Rows of Chorus Girls* wearing top hats, on the set of the Film, *Let's Go Native*, Paramount Pictures, 1930

Everett Collection/Shutterstock.com

FIGURE 18: Shutterstock A beach official checks the amount of thigh exposed by a young lady's bathing suit to make sure it complies with public regulations. Hemlines on all women's clothing reached new heights in the 1920s.

tral area of the massive stage (see our drawings). In the Berkeley films the central area is completely round and layered like a colossal wedding cake with showgirls on it and all around it. Taylor changes this to a squarish central area but with a circular surround against which a series of moving images of dancing girls is projected onto the stage through the individual stage pieces.

The overall effect is similar to what Busby Berkeley created but with the added possibility of raising and lowering the central square. It appears that Taylor's technicians did this (as we have seen in the previous article) by projecting filmed LED images onto the stage which in this area has been specially arranged in a circular custom-fit pattern so that the images of black and white beautiful girls are placed around the central stage area where Taylor is singing and dancing. In order for this to work effectively Taylor has to "hit my mark" which is that central square (and she even tells you in the lyrics she is doing just

FIGURE 19: Busby Beauties 1933: A scene from the musical *Footlight Parade*, choreographed by Busby Berkeley, showing chorus girls draped over a typical Berkeley "wedding cake", suitable for overhead kaleidoscopic shots.

that!) so that the geometry and timing of the sequence syncs and she performs exactly on top of the raised square while the projected 1930s chorus girls dance in time to the song below her and her actual dancers perform around her and above the projected girls. It is something surprising and extra to astonish the perceptive viewer at the Eras Tour and even if you were there you might easily miss the subtleties of creating this amazingly timed sequence. It is not only hard to do but very difficult to even explain what they did! And numerous people went to the Eras Tour more than once in order to take in all the things you didn't realize were going on the first time they went!

In one video sequence we saw from a Stockholm Eras Tour visit Taylor was not quite in the center of the rectangular raised area in center stage and the geometry was just slightly off when seen from an upper balcony view. The key to making all this seem effortless is to have perfect timing in raising and lowering the square central area and all of the live dancers must be precisely hitting their "marks" as well so that the integrated 1930s dancers fall in line with them. Projected imagery must occur at the exact rate of the live action to coordinate with it and this synchronicity would have to be done each time either with a metronome device or an incredible amount of rehearsal to monitor the beat of the song while the live action people are hitting precise spots to integrate with the filmed people and back-screen images.

We have examined this Eras Tour footage with technicians from the University of Arizona over and over again and nobody can come up with any other way this complicated technique could be done. It requires perfect coordination among musicians, dancers, and technicians, and it is a seemingly miraculous live showcase when executed perfectly night after night—a blend of high engineering, set design and LED coordination with live performance and perfectly coordinated timing. There hasn't been that much written by Taylor herself about exactly how this was all achieved nor is there a great deal in the popular media, perhaps because people doing it prefer to keep their trade secrets under wraps or because Taylor doesn't want the general public to know how she creates the magic that she does so that it just seems to flow seamlessly.

Such an effort requires enormous technical setup and coordination and that is likely why the technicians moving one version of the Eras Tour into place are complimented by a second unit doing the same thing well enough ahead of the next concert date. So the tour has to be planned in two places at once to provide time for the technicians to put the mechanics of the Eras Tour into place. The entire effect is achieved with state of the art engineering (Peltz 2023).

The projection onto the giant backscreen and even onto and through the individual floor panels is an idea that had been started in movie picture palaces and theaters in the later 1920s continuing into the 1930s where a device known as a Brenkert Brenograph or Brenograph Junior hidden in the floor of the theater would actually project clouds and cupids onto the sky and other wondrous scenes to dazzle picture goers (Embassy Theatre 2024). Picture palace builder John Eberson was particularly fond of using this technique in the 1910s and 1920s, leaving the ceilings of the auditoria of his theaters blank so that moviegoers could be waiting for the show to start and in the meantime be treated to heavenly projected scenes on the ceiling. Taylor's sequence is clearly the super-modern descendant.

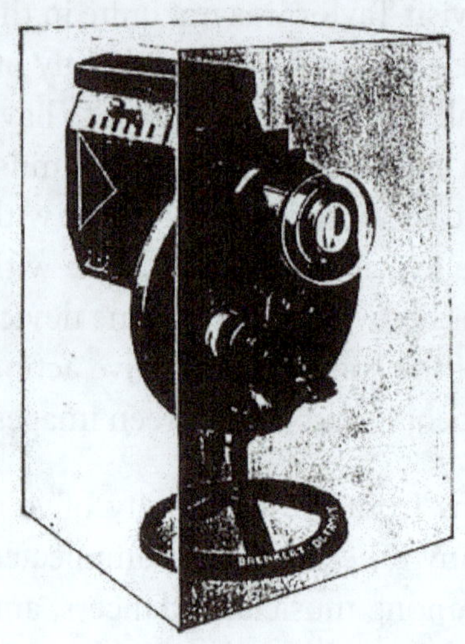

The space requirements of **Brenograph Junior** as shown above for concealed work are as follows: 24″ wide, 30″ high and 30″ deep.

FIGURE 20: The Brenkert Brenograph projector of the 1920s projected everything else in a movie theatre but the movie. University of Arizona Vaudeville Collection.

FIGURE 21: Atmospheric Theatre with blue evening sky projected on the ceiling. Auckland Civic Theatre, New Zealand, 1929.

But that's not all of the fertile ideas pouring from Taylor's mind regarding the presentation of this number. On the back screen we get images which remarkably integrate Taylor and her dancers with what is supposed to resemble an old-time movie premiere apparently in Hollywood because the old Hollywoodland sign (dedicated in 1923) is prominently featured on the big screen at the beginning of the song (Smith 2023). Huge searchlights of 1930s style fill the sky at an old-time Hollywood movie premiere as we see a group of three buildings in front of which are a group of cars which seem all identical and which seem to be primarily of vintage 1939. Searchlights were in use in warfare to blind enemies or illuminate targets since the 1870s even before the development of electricity but they became synonymous with Hollywood movie premieres of the later 1920s and 1930s (and into the 1940s) to give glamour and visibility to the events (Kittler and Winthrop-Young 2015).

The buildings shown in the background behind the cars on Taylor's giant screen include what might be a later 1920s Art Deco high end restaurant on the left which is called *Cassandra's*. But there again that reference is part of the landscape of Taylor's mind because

Cassandra is the name of one of the other songs on the *Tortured Poets* album which may be intended to show how Taylor was smeared by falsehoods about the awful things that had been done to her reputation even though few would believe her and it caused her enormous pain and suffering to the point where she had to withdraw for a long time from public life (Stivale 2024).

But Cassandra is also a classical reference to Homer's *Iliad*, an oral epic poem believed to date from the 8th century B.C. but finally written down in the 6th century B.C. in Athens, Greece. It dealt with the tragedy of the Trojan War between the invading Greeks under King Agamemnon and the defending Trojans led by King Priam (Hiltz 2023). Cassandra was the Trojan priestess who constantly spoke the truth but could find nobody to believe her, telling the Trojans to beware of Greeks bearing gifts and leading to the bringing in of the Trojan Horse as the fatal gift in question (Padman 2023).

FIGURE 22: Hollywood hills and Hollywood sign, colorful billboards, palm trees, and traffic.

FIGURE 23: Old huge military searchlight for detecting enemy targets in the sky during World War II.

Once the horse was allowed within the city gates of Troy, under cover of darkness, Greek soldiers hidden inside emerged and opened the gates leading to the secretly returning Greek army entering the city and causing the fall of Troy, or so the story goes. Cassandra had been cursed to prophesy but to never be believed supposedly because of her rejection of the advances of the Greek god Apollo (we've met Apollo with Taylor before, in my *Anti-Hero* essay). Cassandra's unhappy demise came after the result of the Fall of Troy as she was brought back to the mainland of Greece as a captive and was subsequently murdered.

FIGURE 24: Modern rebuilding of the Trojan horse, Canakkale, Turkey on the site of ancient Troy.

The created/projected building in our Eras show is then both a salute to old Hollywood and at the same time a reference to the Kanye West and Kim Kardashian affair when Taylor was so emotionally damaged over her heinous treatment in a video and rap lyrics and gossip in the media disparaging her that, as she has said, she could not forgive or forget what had been done to her (Benitez-Eves 2024).

In the mythological story Cassandra is taken by the king of Mycenae, the leader of the Greek forces, as a concubine to be used for sex (!) but may have been murdered by his wife Clytemnestra (!!). Readers of this may explore the possible parallels between Cassandra, Agamemnon, Clytemnestra, Kanye and Kim at their leisure but it is beyond the scope of this book to deal with it in detail here (Mier 2024).

Another building just to the right of Cassandra's and created for the big backscreen of this Eras Tour song appears to be intended as an actual theatre but its sketchy features do not allow it to be interpreted meaningfully as a structure that could actually be built while its topmost cresting seems to be an exaggerated Art Deco rhomboid keystone, an art movement and design pattern very popular around 1930). This decoration was also featured in the movie *Just Imagine* which depicted a crystalline and rhomboid Martian planet surface (Butler 1930).

On the right on the backscreen behind Taylor on stage is a third building which appears to be a Spanish mission such as one might find in the American west or southwest, which features two towers in the front, strongly resembling the San Xavier Mission Church in Tucson, Arizona near my home, an historic Spanish Catholic mission founded originally in 1692.

Evgeniya Litovchenko/Shutterstock.com

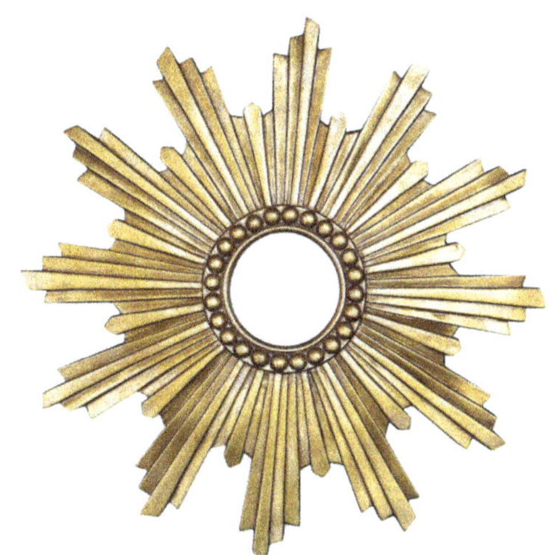

FIGURE 25: The uppermost part of this image was similar to that used as an exaggerated rhomboid fantasy building keystone in Taylor's video.

Nick Fox/Shutterstock.com

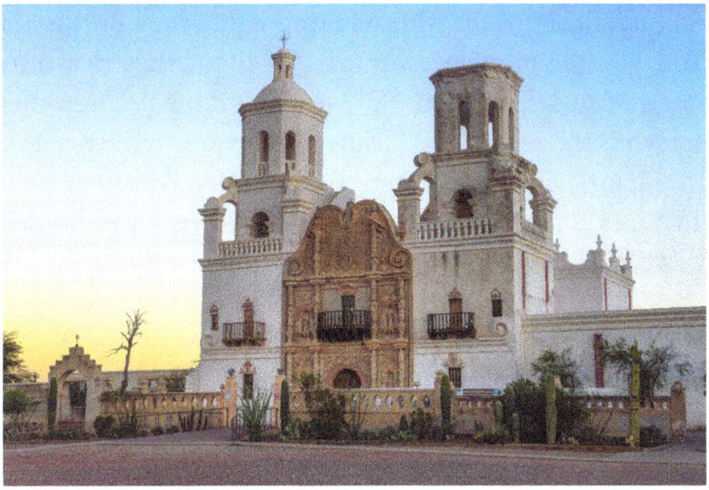

FIGURE 26: Sunrise at the San Xavier Mission Church in Tucson, Arizona This historic Spanish Catholic mission was founded in 1692 and is located on the Tohono O'odham Nation Indian reservation.

Vintage cars are shown in what looks like stop-motion animation (!) passing by the buildings along the street in front of them and the setting with searchlights playing about seems to have been inspired by the 1939 movie premiere of *Gone With the Wind* (Cavendish 2014). The comparison is made between Taylor's Eras Tour and an old-fashioned Hollywood fancy show business premiere with the searchlights and elegant cars at a huge theater with a packed audience—she's turning the clock back and bringing back old time show business on a grand scale as David Letterman had noted and time can run backwards as it literally does on the backscreen timer that Taylor uses in this sequence.

Yet another building featured on the backscreen is an apparent theater which is called Peter's which appears to be a reference to another song on the *Tortured Poets* collection entitled *Peter* which tells the sad tale of Peter Pan and Wendy whereby Wendy, a mortal girl, waits for years for Peter to grow up and come back for her as he promised to do but never did, yet another reference to Taylor waiting patiently for the arrival of true love that is thus far never to be (Kettler 2020). An even more poignant reference to Peter and Wendy came in the song *Cardigan*, the lead single from the album *Folklore* (Thompson 2024).

And there are more theatre buildings that appear on the backscreen. On the next theater one can read vertically that the theatre name is *Applause* and on the marquee below is added twice the words "Hearts for Sale". This is a reference to Taylor's strong desire for fame, symbolized by the tremendous satisfaction she derives on the tour from the thunderous almost non-stop applause with which her devoted fans greet her at certain times during virtually every show. It is the time and place where she feels most intensely alive, supported and sustained, and incredibly happy (as she stated in Los Angeles during the 2009 *Fearless* tour) while at the same time what's playing at the theater is Hearts for Sale which indicates indeed that her personal life remains unfulfilled, that she is doing this with a broken heart and that life away from the stage has not been as completely fulfilling as her life in front of and among her fans.

Still another theatre with blinking lights next on the right is playing "Taylor Swift's Eras Tour" as if to provide a summary of all the theatrical attractions one could find in *The Tortured Poets Department*. But we aren't done yet. Another building displayed on the backscreen is the *Black Dog Theatre*, an obvious reference to a British pub allegedly frequented by Taylor Swift and former boyfriend Joe Alwyn and mentioned in *Tortured Poets* where Taylor says that she watches her beloved walk into some bar called *The Black Dog* and how this causes her heart to be pierced with new holes.

Once a quiet local pub in London, it is quiet no more in recent months due to an invasion of Swifties wanting to be where Taylor and/or Joe had allegedly once hung out at times. The Swifties seem almost like religious pilgrims to Jerusalem following various versions of the Way of the Cross depending on their faith (Chapman 2024). *The Black Dog* is also an example of the constant dualism in Taylor's work. As she puts it, her time in London was a "fleeting and fatalistic moment in time - one that was both sensational and sorrowful in equal measure" (LeGardye 2024). So much of her work is joy mixed with sadness, extreme happiness and extreme disappointment, and this combination of vulnerability and joy tempered with the attitude that "the show must go on" no matter what happens in her life pervades her career right up to the present day. She is a superstar who listens to and cares about her fans but who can also manipulate them in an auditorium because just as they think they know her, she believes she knows them too and knows how to move them emotionally. But to them she also seems real and caring and vulnerable, like a mother goddess who feels their pain and shares their dreams. The Swifties I know all respect and worry about her vulnerability to outside attack either physical or via mass media and they long for her happiness just as they find comfort and solace in her lyrics. On the original *Fearless* tour as early as 2009 she would sing an emotional song and then kneel down and tuck her head downward towards the floor while extending her arms out beyond the edge of the stage. There as if to console her fans would literally grab onto her hands and do so even though the song was a performance and there was no real need to console her…but they consistently did so anyway! This is performance art instinctive genius—she apparently just began doing this to link with her fans.

But we are not yet through with our theatrical tour of Taylor's Eras Tour projections. Among the other "throw-ins" that evoke 1930s Hollywood in this remarkable song and video presentation is a commonly used editing device from the silent movie and early talkie period to go from one scene to another called an "iris shot" whereby the motion picture camera aperture closes down or opens up again to change the scene.

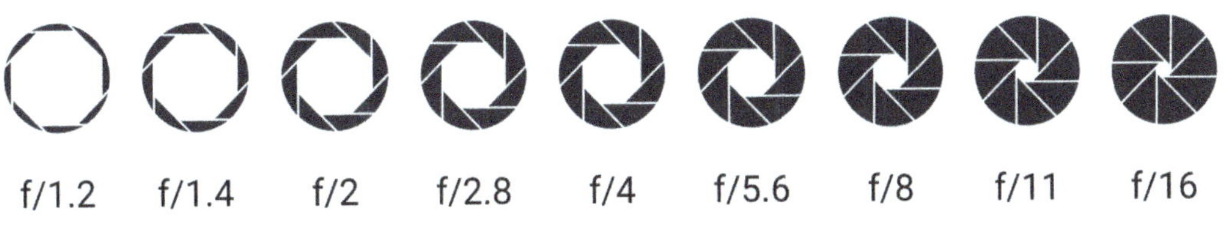

FIGURE 27: Camera iris shot.

Another 1930s reference is the beat of the middle part of our video which becomes a conga rhythm, a popular Cuban dance of the later 1930s and early 1940s in Hollywood movies such as *Too Many Girls* (1940) where it was popularized by Desi Arnaz, the young Cuban bandleader and later producer and co-star of the Lucille Ball television sitcom success of the 1950s called *I Love Lucy*.

In the conga a line of dancers follow one leader around the stage in a "conga line" while executing a few rhythmic steps back and forth or side to side and wiggling the body as may be done while holding on to the person in front of you. The dance is perfectly displayed by Taylor and her dancers in this video. The conga was later revived in the Miami Sound Machine hit song *Conga* and video with Gloria Estefan in 1985. The movement itself was big in

New York city from 1929 through the 1930s and into the 1940s and it originally had been introduced in Cuba before that by West Indian slaves. Arnaz would always sing his Cuban music while wearing and beating on a conga drum, his big hit Afro-Cuban hit song from 1939 entitled *Babalu*.

FIGURE 28: Postage stamp printed in USA in 1999 commemorating the tv sitcom comedy I Love Lucy (1951-1957), starring Lucille Ball and Desi Arnaz.

FIGURE 29: Black vector silhouette of a dancing conga line.

Still another 1930s convention is played with in this song, that of the counting of the numbers 1 through 4, which is done in a different language depending on what country Taylor is in and it is always done by her African-American dancer from St. Louis Kam Saunders who had to learn to count to four in many different languages during the tour. On the backscreen while he counts, the image displays the numbers 1 through 4 but does it as if it is showing the flashing countdown numbers from an old-time film leader or piece of film placed in front of the actual movie to protect it and to cue in when the projectionist needed to switch reels of film in a movie theater projection booth. In the days of silent and early talking pictures, the projectionist had to change reels of film sometimes several times in a single showing. This meant

FIGURE 30: **Man playing conga drum.**

that each film came with a countdown leader that flashed numbers on the screen from 10 down to 1 so that at 1 the projectionist could stop the film at that point and transfer to the new cued-up next reel to start at just the point where the previous film reel had been entirely shown. The "countdown leader" as we used to call it in the old days when I was a university projectionist would also provide a lead-in to the film that would protect the film itself from being harmed in case the leader got entangled in the projector and the projectionist always carried spare leaders in case one got damaged. In this sequence however the film leader is counted forward and not backward.

FIGURE 31: **Illustration of an old film movie timer countdown frame. Universal leader.**

Apart from the 1930s background atmosphere and the references to other parts of *The Tortured Poets Department* and the daring and risky unifying album concept of doing all of the background visuals in black and white imagery and basing them on old Hollywood, there is once again the remarkable creation of an on-stage audience interaction. This achievement is much more than a display of album cohesiveness and an expression of the fantasy landscape of Taylor's mind. The audience interaction is a high water mark in the history of theatrical performance art and shows Taylor to be a show business producer and stage director who is really a mastermind, so let us examine that part of the presentation now.

Most critical to remember here is that the audience has a major role to play in the presentation of this song. They are the fans who, according to Taylor, have created and sustained her long career but she has now told them that her performance is in a sense not genuine for she has a broken heart that has almost killed her and has been displayed in the previous number in the show about a real-life recent breakup, *The Smallest Man Who Ever Lived*, which has left her seemingly all but dead on the stage (Wehniainen 2024).

And it is this current Eras Tour audience who is part of the desire to push her quite brazenly in spite of all this to give them MORE as her lyric video of the song has the live audience literally shout out to agree with the recording. When she is almost stripped naked, revived, redressed and pushed forward in this sequence it is the audience that seems complicit in her exhausted near-death exposure, for the live audience leers, howls, oohs and ahhs as her dress is removed quickly on stage and she stands in what appears to be underwear facing the crowd, shattered, half-naked and partly oblivious to her manufactured plight.

Are the two males involved in this rescue of her generously helping her to revive or just pushing her forward for their own mercenary ends so they can exploit her talent? We can't be sure here how to think of them…and what WE as her audience have become in our desire to see and hear Taylor perform this number. All we know is that "the show must go on" for whatever reason and the audience likes her and is demanding "more" and the "more" is emphasized by the audience shouting it at the top of their lungs. So it seems that the audience is a great ugly beast just egging her on and only caring about such things as seeing her stripped and demanding more of what she does, regardless of her health or heartbreak just as she is describing her plight with her lyrics!

But wait a minute! In real life the audience already knows that she is saying how difficult this is for her and we see that that same audience is apparently now complicit in and indifferent to her real suffering, demanding loudly that she perform anyway. So she has in this performance both included the audience in her real-life agony and also used them interactively to provoke the reason for having to perform no matter how painful or how difficult it is because of her need to stay on top ("Try and come for my job" and "applause" and "I'm good"). The manipulation of the audience in this song is something I have never seen before on a stage and it is managed in a live performance with 70 or 80 thousand people participating in the grand deception without fully realizing it—it is almost unimaginable but it happened and continued to happen in every country at every performance and she told the audience straight out that "I can read your mind" and she does! The audience is a pawn, both sympathetic supporters and manipulated provocateurs and the fans don't seem to realize the interactive role they have been seduced into playing. How does she do it? About this time in the video Taylor informs us how good she is and reveals in her lyrics that "It's an art". We've been had and we don't even realize it! And what is more her current flame and possible marriage partner Travis Kelce is brought in as one of the two enabling men used to revive her (he wears a top hat and tux as well) in one of her London performances, which of course complicates the seduction of her audience even further (Richards 2024)!

It was a tradition in film and in Las Vegas for the female star to be lifted up by dancers and tossed around as Janet Leigh was in the movie *Bye Bye Birdie* (1963) for example, but in this video Taylor also is picked up and carried about horizontally by the dancers in this typical Hollywood/Vegas lift and everyone is thrilled to watch it as she boasts that you know you're good when you can do it with a broken heart and she states proudly that she IS good.

But the audience can barely hear her exclaim as she is lifted and moved around in the air " 'cause I'm miserable and nobody even knows!" And yet even though she is miserable she calls out the challenge to others to dethrone her ("Try and get my job").

FIGURE 32: Theatre dressing room makeup table.

Another easily missed aspect of the backscreen projection is the shooting of much of this number as if it were filmed through a mirror surrounded by small lights, the kind of mirror one would find in an old-time dressing room for a superstar. This is supplemented by stock films of showgirls rehearsing, adjusting their stockings (and occasionally their girdles) and preparing their makeup. This is all in there but it is very easy to miss!

This is the largest and greatest piece of interactive audience manipulation, as well as a reflection of the landscape of an artist's mind, that I have ever witnessed in a popular art form. You'd have to compare it to the force of Hitler at Munich as seen in the Leni Riefenstahl movie *Triumph of the Will* (1935) to appreciate mass audience control such as this. Whether or not you are a Swiftie, when you observe the power of a great artist to literally engage and manipulate a gigantic group to this level, causing them to cry out, gasp, involving them in the imagined and real-life drama as both sympathizers and villains and mixing up reality and theater, humor and drama—this is Performance Art at the highest level. It is literally a deeper dive into the possibilities of mass entertainment, even involving deep diving!! In fact it is at such a high level that we don't realize the total manipulation other than the fact that we are drawn in as participants and entranced (Abreu 2023).

It should be noted here that the stage itself is the main place where Taylor appears to have almost superhuman power and control and her stage productions, always centering completely around her, have grown in size and complexity beyond anything ever seen in a pop-star tour before, hence no one is surprised that it's been honored as the Tour of the Century by IHeart Radio (West 2025). Performance is also the place where her ego is able to be completely fulfilled and you can see it as the crowd goes wild with adoration of her at every stop in every country, often when she sings *Champagne Problems* (Dailey 2023) but generally with everything she sings and that has been going on in earnest since the *Fearless* tour began all the way back in April of 2009.

Fans lucky enough to meet her backstage on the last tour in Japan appeared to be about to go into cardiac arrest from the shock of seeing her live and one can witness her complete sense of inner fulfillment to be standing on a stage looking out at 80,000 people and seeing them singing the words back to her of her songs written over the past 20+ years. It has even become traditional now to do wedding proposals during her performances or in the special backstage meetings (Vargas 2023).

The stage is the one place in her life where she can be totally herself and completely in control and that includes everything the stage generates from executive business meetings to tour preparation design to every aspect of her empire. She has also learned to control her body through proper eating and phenomenal exercise. She can display her famous legs (National Enquirer claimed they were insured for $40,000,000 now) in a body suit (Willis 2015), having built them up through an exercise program so intense it is like training accomplished by a major athlete (Hibbard 2024). On stage you can note a few of her familiar looks—

The Supermodel Look- She has learned how to walk like a model and has hung out with models (including a gig with Frederick's of Hollywood) and learned from them and she no longer flails wildly around in a gawky manner as one can still see in her performances of her first albums (Santino 2024)

The Power Gaze- She will sometimes stop and just look over her shoulder and stare diva-like at the audience during or at the end of a number, suggesting she is taking in the joy and power of the moment.

Total Control of the Crowd- She has the rare ability to make 3 ½ hours fly by, even when you really have to go to the bathroom! In some of her earlier shows she used to even control the level of the crowd by raising her hands

FIGURE 33: Taylor Swift (left) performs as model Karlie Kloss walks the runway during the 2014 Victoria's Secret Fashion Show on December 2, 2014 in London, England.

FIGURE 34: Power Gaze. Waxwork statue of Taylor Swift in a Power Gaze, displayed at Madame Tussaud's waxwork museum in London.

up and down to increase or decrease the roar but as it can appear hubristic she seems to have stopped directly regulating the crowd and allows the adoration moments now to just come naturally—*All Too Well*, the 10 minute version, usually brings the house down with only Taylor and her piano playing.

FIGURE 35: Taylor Swift takes a moment to enjoy the love of her fans at the 2019 Z100 Jingle Ball at Madison Square Garden in New York.

Dance- Taylor is not a professional dancer but she is naturally graceful and is able to re-member a tremendous amount of precision simple choreography and to gracefully and fully use a stage with her characteristic stride followed by her dancers. Typical examples are her side to side movements in many of her songs and her little head slides as in the word "boy" of *London Boy*. Her ability to do a beautiful full split is also remarkable (as in the video *Delicate*). Had she undertaken more dance training when younger she could have de-veloped into an outstanding jazz/modern dancer—I say this as a former professional dancer who performed regularly on television. She does dancing of limited complexity on the Eras Tour but what she does is done with good solid definition which is a hallmark of dancing coach and choreography stager the great Mandy Moore. Her self-mocking of her dancing ability in the official video for *Shake It Off* isn't really justified and she is also an extremely quick study at choreography.

The Power Stride- Taylor's confident stride using all of the stage back and forth and side to side are also earmarks of her owning the stage and reaching out to all of her fans scattered throughout the arena and is a hallmark of all of her concerts.

And Swifties appreciate the honesty of the show and music. Everything is based on elements from Taylor's real life or inspired visions. One has the feeling that *Tortured Poets* was truly written and staged as a cathartic experience just as she says. All through her life she has gone out of her way to confront her enemies directly through music. In fact she has ONLY been able to do it through her music so as she has said, with all of the heartbreak and lies about her, she had to write that album. Swiftie listeners understand that *Tortured Poets* is Taylor's catharsis—it had to come out to be cast off.

Taylor could have written more catchy pop tunes such as she had for 1989 but listeners appreciate that this album was a sincere call-out of those who worked against her to undermine her and destroy her career. She had reached an emotional level after her last breakup and before she started to feel "so high school" again she told her fans she had to put out this album in order to preserve her sanity (Lawson 2024). The fact that it became a smash hit all over the world is a testimony to Taylor's international draw. With a star of this magnitude, there is a much stronger chance that people would give it that extra listen and begin to identify even with the many downbeat slow songs.

Even if there was no obvious hit single within the album, she had to write it all from the heart, go with her instincts and take a chance that her new work would touch others. As throughout her career, her albums took risks, changed genres and created new ones. News outlets however were not so forgiving. They leaped to write reviews of it after less than half a day of the album's release and criticized it basically because it was too much not like her 1989 album and too slow paced but as Swifties gave it time and began to listen to the lyrics more deeply, they became aware of the beautifully expressed poetry and numerous classic songs including the evocative *Peter, Who's Afraid of Little Old Me* and *The Smallest Man in the World*. Some of these songs such as the latter two really required to be seen on the Eras Tour to be comprehended fully and completed in meaning for Swift devotees.

I Can Do It With a Broken Heart has become an Eras Tour fan favorite because it is a song full of dualisms that pull and tug. It vicariously involves the fans in her life by evoking their reactions as direct participants in her world. And the more one examines this remarkable lady the more one can see how although she is the number one superstar on the planet, it is not generally realized how hard she works just about every day at her craft and how she produces not only extraordinary poetry and popular music but how she designs her art as a total concept experience.

NOTES

Abreu, Rafael, "What Is Performance Art?", *Studio Binder* 2-26-2023 https://www. studiobinder.com/blog/what-is-performance-art-definition/

Access Hollywood 2023, "Taylor Swift Reflects On Having Control Of Her Creativity In 2010 'Speak Now' Intv," *Access Hollywood* 7-7-2023 https://www.accessonline.com/ videos/taylor-swift-reflects-on-having-control-of-her-artistry-in-resurfaced-2010- speak-now-interview

Benitez-Eves, Tina, "The Meaning Behind Taylor Swift's "thanK you alMee" and "Cassandra" and Why Fans Believe Both Are Aimed at Kim Kardashian," *American Songwriter* 4-19-2024 https://americansongwriter.com/the-meaning-behind-taylor- swifts-thank-you-almee-and-cassandra-and-why-fans-believe-both-are-aimed-at- kim-kardashian/

Bhattacharya, Srimoyee, "Did you know Taylor Swift penned a novel when she was a teenager?," *Republic* 6-19-2021 https://www.republicworld.com/entertainment/ hollywood/did-you-know-taylor-swift-penned-a-novel-when-she-was-a-teenager

Brideson, Cynthia and Sara Brideson, *Ziegfeld and His Follies: A Biography of Broadway's Greatest Producer (Screen Classics)* (University Press of Kentucky, 2015)

Butler, David (director) 1930- *Just Imagine, Internet Movie Archive* (you can watch this entire Art Deco movie for free here, including the fascinating rhomboid Mars sequence at 1:13:40) https://archive.org/details/JustImagine_97

Cavendish, Richard, "Premiere of Gone With the Wind," *History Today* 12-2014 https:// www.historytoday.com/archive/premiere-gone-wind

Chapman, Rachel, "Is The Black Dog a real place? The Bar in Taylor Swift's Song Revealed," *Elite Daily* 4-22-2024 https://www.elitedaily.com/lifestyle/taylor-swift- black-dog-bar-real-place

Dailey, Hannah, "Taylor Swift Left Wonderstruck Over 8-Minute Standing Ovation at L.A. Eras Tour Show," *Billboard* 8-19-2023 https://www.billboard.com/music/music-news/taylor-swift-standing-ovation-eras-tour-show-reaction-1235388168/

Embassy Theatre 2024- "Historic Brenograph," *Embassy* 2024 http://fwembassytheatre.org/about-us/historic-brenograph/

Flavius, Lou, "Social Media Is In Shambles Over Bathroom Photos Of Taylor Swift From Super Bowl 59," *TPS Total Pro Sports* 2-16-2025 https://www.totalprosports.com/nfl/social-media-is-in-shambles-over-bathroom-photos-of-taylor-swift-from-super-bowl-59/

Frost, Caroline, "Taylor Swift Shakes Off Frozen Hand Mid-Show For "Scotland's Biggest Ever Stadium Concert"" *Deadline* 6-7-2024 https://deadline.com/2024/06/taylor-swift-frozen-hand-mid-show-edinburgh-eras-stadium-concert-1235962908/

Hibbard, Thomas, "How Much Are Taylor Swift's Legs Worth? The Weird World of Insuring Celebrity Body Parts," *The Hollywood Reporter* 6-21-2024 https://www.hollywoodreporter.com/lifestyle/lifestyle-news/celebrity-body-parts-insurance-taylor-swift-j-lo-1235926124/

Hiltz, Madeleine, "Did the Trojan War Actually Happen?," *War History Online* 6-28-2021 https://www.warhistoryonline.com/war-articles/trojan-war-myth-or-reality.html

Inampudi, Annika , Adelaide E. Parker, and Thor N. Reimann, "Taylor Swift: Harvard's Version," *Harvard Crimson* 11-9-2023 https://www.thecrimson.com/article/2023/11/9/taylor-swift-harvards-version/

Irvin, Jack, "Taylor Swift Files Trademark for 'Female Rage: The Musical' — Here's What This Could Mean," *People* 5-14-2024 https://people.com/taylor-swift-files-trademark-for-female-rage-the-musical-8648318

Jeffrey, Joyann and MC Suhocki and Ariana Brockington, "The full history of Taylor Swift and her 'lucky number' 13," *Today / Y Entertainment* 4-17-2024 https://www.yahoo.com/entertainment/why-taylor-swift-loves-number-235859466.html

Kettler, Sarah, "7 Facts About 'Peter Pan' Author J.M. Barrie, *Biography* 10-2-2020 https://www.biography.com/authors-writers/peter-pan-jm-barrie-facts-biography

Kittler, Friedrich and Geoffrey Winthrop-Young, "A Short History of the Searchlight," *Cultural Politics* 11- 1- 2015 pp. 383-390 https://read.dukeupress.edu/cultural-politics/article-abstract/11/3/384/25842/A-Short-History-of-the-Searchlight

Late Show – "Taylor Swift Loves New York, Not Lousy Boyfriends," *Letterman* 10-28-2914 https://www.youtube.com/watch?v=ozrrUio3AB0

Lawson, Ayla Cruze, "From Pain to Poetry: 'The Tortured Poets Department' in Review," *The Cornell Daily Sun* 4-22-2024 https://cornellsun.com/2024/04/22/from-pain-to-poetry-the-tortured-poets-department-in-review/

LeGardye, Quinci, "Taylor Swift Says 'The Tortured Poets Department' Is the End of Her "Fleeting and Fatalistic" Era," *Marie Claire* 4-19-2024 https://www.marieclaire.com/celebrity/taylor-swift-tortured-poets-department-fleeting-fatalistic-era/

Little, Sarah, Lynn Sharpe & Amanda Bruce, "Eras Tour Performer Guide: Every Taylor Swift Backup Dancer & Vocalist In The Concert Movie," *Screen Rant* 7-17-2024 https://screenrant.com/taylor-swift-eras-tour-backup-dancers-vocalists-in-concert-movie/

Top of FormBottom of FormMcGuire, Panicha, "A Therapist's Take on "The Tortured Poets Department," *Psychology Today* 4-30-2024 https://www.psychologytoday.com/intl/blog/embracing-neurodiversity/202404/a-therapists-take-on-the-tortured-poets-department

Mamo, Heran, "Taylor Swift Shares the Story Behind 'Willow' Video With These Before & After Shots," *Billboard* 12-15-2020 https://www.billboard.com/music/music-news/taylor-swift-willow-music-video-storyboard-9499892/

Mier, Tomás, Brittany Spanos, Keith Harris, "From VMAs Drama to 'thanK you aIMee': A Timeline of Taylor Swift's Feud With Kim Kardashian, Kanye West," *Rolling Stone* 4-23-2024 https://www.rollingstone.com/music/music-features/taylor-swift-feud-kim-kardashian-kanye-west-timeline-1235008539/

Miller, Korin, "Did Taylor Swift Go To College? Everything To Know About The Pop Star's New Honorary Doctorate Degree From NYU," *Women's Health* 5-19-2022 https://www.womenshealthmag.com/life/a40037299/taylor-swift-college-nyu-honorary-doctorate-degree/

Padman, Rhianna, "Cassandra: Princess of Troy, Cursed Prophetess, Tragic Prisoner," *The Collector* 9-13-2023 https://www.thecollector.com/cassandra-troy-princess-prophetess/

Pagkalinawan, Brandon, "WATCH: Travis Kelce joins Taylor Swift on stage for surprise Eras tour appearance at London's Wembley Stadium," *CBS Sports* 6-23-2024 https://www.cbssports.com/nfl/news/watch-travis-kelce-joins-taylor-swift-on-stage-for-surprise-eras-tour-appearance-at-londons-wembley-stadium/

Peltz, Brandon, " Taylor Swift's Eras Tour: A Deep Dive into the Tech Behind the Show," *Live Production Mastery* 6-2-2023 https://www.youtube.com/watch?v=5qmqXbggxFY

Penn, David and Gary Trust, "Taylor Swift's Songwriting and Production Analyzed: 13 Secrets to Her Chart Success," *Billboard* 4-30-2024 https://www.billboard.com/lists/taylor-swift-songwriting-production-analyzed/differences-between-swifts-earlier-and-recent-eras/

Rahman, Abid, "Taylor Swift Reveals Her Writing Process In Nashville Songwriter Awards Speech," *The Hollywood Reporter* 9-21-2022 https://www.hollywoodreporter.com/news/music-news/taylor-swift-songwriting-process-nashville-speech-1235224700/

Raza-Sheikh, Zoya, "How Taylor Swift mastered the singer-songwriter blueprint," *Independent* 10-19-2022 https://www.independent.co.uk/arts-entertainment/music/features/taylor-swift-eras-tour-songwriting-midnights-b2275506.html

Richards, Bailey, "Taylor Swift Shocks Fans by Bringing Travis Kelce Onstage at 3rd Wembley Show: Watch Him Carry Her!," *People* 6-23-2024 https://people.com/taylor-swift-joins-travis-kelce-onstage-london-show-eras-tour-8667894

Santino, Catherine, "Taylor Swift's Best Fashion Moments of All Time," *People* 1-6-2024 https://people.com/style/taylor-swift-best-fashion-moments-of-all-time/

Say Etcetera 2014, "The Horn and Hardart Children's Hour," *K12* 2014 https://www.k12academics.com/educational-television/childrens-television-programming/horn-hardart-childrens-hour

Sen Gupta, Manas, "All about Kameron Saunders, who is winning hearts on *The Eras Tour* with Taylor Swift," *Lifestyle Asia* 3-8-2024 "https://www.lifestyleasia.com/sg/entertainment/celebrities/who-is-kameron-saunders-taylor-swift-eras-tour-dancer/

Smith, Nathan, "The Hidden History of the Hollywood Sign, *Smithsonian Magazine* 7-13-2023 https://www.smithsonianmag.com/history/the-hidden-history-of-the-hollywood-sign-180982518/

Stivale, Shelby, "Who Is Taylor Swift's 'Cassandra' About? Lyrics Might Hide Message About Kanye West or Scooter Braun?," *Us Magazine* 4-19-2024 https://www.usmagazine.com/entertainment/news/who-is-taylor-swifts-ttpd-song-cassandra-about-lyrics-explained/

Thompson, Eliza, "A Complete Guide to Taylor Swift's Literary References: From Debut to 'Tortured Poets Department,'" *Us Celebrity News* 4-19-2024 https://www.usmagazine.com/entertainment/news/taylor-swifts-literary-references-before-tortured-poets-department/

Thompson, Mychal, "People Are Talking About How Taylor Swift Handled Paparazzi Swarming Her After The VMAs," *BuzzFeed* 9-16-2023 https://www.buzzfeed.com/mychalthompson/taylor-swift-paparazzi-reactions

Vargas, Chanel, "A Surprising Amount of Fans Are Getting Engaged on Taylor Swift's Eras Tour," *Pop Sugar* 6-2-2023 https://www.popsugar.com/love/taylor-swift-eras-tour-marriage-proposals-49191292

Wehniainen, Grace, "Taylor Swift's "The Smallest Man Who Ever Lived" Is A Venomous Breakup Song," *Bustle* 4-18-2024 https://www.bustle.com/entertainment/taylor-swift-the-smallest-man-who-ever-lived-lyrics-meaning

West, Bryan, "Taylor Swift's Eras tour named 'Tour of the Century' at upcoming iHeart Radio Music Awards," USA Today 1-22-2025 https://www.usatoday.com/story/

entertainment/music/2025/01/22/taylor-swift-tour-of-the-century-iheart-radio-music-awards/77880158007/

Whitaker, Sterling, "Remember When Taylor Swift Launched Her First Headlining Tour?", *Taste of Country* 4-23-2024 https://tasteofcountry.com/taylor-swift-first-headlining-tour-fearless-tour/

Willis, Charlotte, "This is why Taylor Swift's legs are worth $40 million," *news.com.au* 3-10-2015 https://www.news.com.au/entertainment/celebrity-life/this-is-why-taylor-swifts-legs-are-worth-40million/news-story/8f0387751250090166708a31b1811b0b

Woltmann, Suzy, "What Is a Performance Artist?," *Backstage* 4-18-2023 https://www.backstage.com/magazine/article/what-is-a-performance-artist-75760/

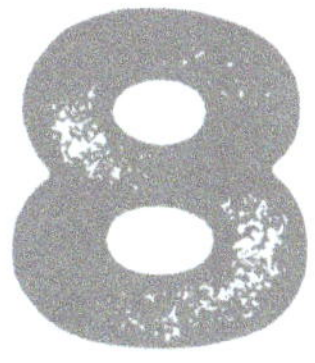

Why I love Taylor Swift So Much

By Liz Rossi

(Liz Rossi is currently a senior at the University of Arizona and will be graduating Spring 2025. She is majoring in Political Science with a concentration in International Relations and is hoping to work in intelligence and counterterrorism. Aside from being a full-time Swiftie, some of her hobbies include writing and reading, astronomy, volunteering, historical research, collecting antiques, and exploring. She says that there is nothing she loves more than spending time with her sisters, family, two dogs and one precious cat.)

She is my friend when I'm all alone

She is always there for me

My sister always said, "For anything you go through there's a Taylor Swift song for it."

She makes me love being a girl

She makes me embrace femininity

I am a hopeless romantic and I love love and Taylor always reminds me how powerful that is, how beautiful it is to love love.

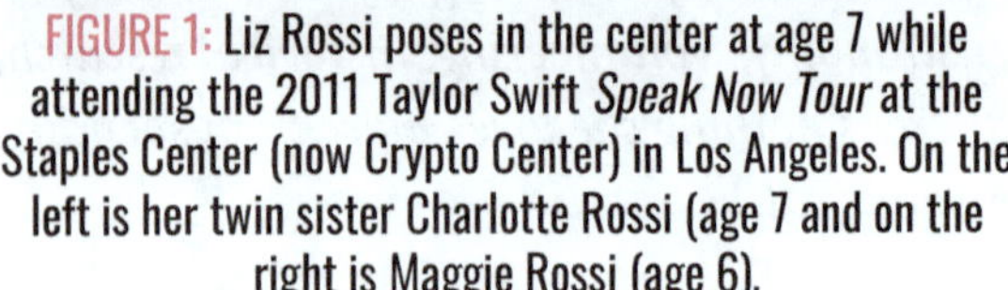

FIGURE 1: Liz Rossi poses in the center at age 7 while attending the 2011 Taylor Swift *Speak Now Tour* at the Staples Center (now Crypto Center) in Los Angeles. On the left is her twin sister Charlotte Rossi (age 7 and on the right is Maggie Rossi (age 6).

FIGURE 2- This photo was taken in August 2023 at the *Eras Tour* at SoFi Stadium in Inglewood, California with the sisters in the same order: left- Charlotte Rossi (19), middle- Liz Rossi (19), right- Maggie Rossi (18). They are wearing VIP concert badges around their neck and interactive LED bracelets about which Liz says: "The LED configurations using the fans in the crowd was absolutely exhilarating and was just another thing that gave you full body chills and made the fans and the art come to life in unison with Taylor, because she created this experience to make us become part of the production and it was just incredible!!"

In a society that tells women what they can and can't be, and frames them in a box with all the assumed right settings, Taylor shows me to destroy that box and say how dare there be a box. I will feel anything I feel and I will be proud of it.

She reminds us that no amount of emotion and pain will ever take hold of where you stand in this world.

There are times where I've felt so alone and like no one could understand but Taylor always did, and she put in a song the exact way I feel and the words I couldn't find.

I started listening to her when I was 4 years old- my dad would play her music videos on the Dell desktop in his home office. I loved her as a little girl because she made me feel like a princess and 17 years later that feeling hasn't changed.

She's been there with me through every stage of my life and she's always had a way to explain it.

I don't think people understand how important it is to feel understood on such a deep and intimate level

I dm her all my diary entries.

She writes the story of our lives, women and girls.

For 17 years, Taylor swift has been incredibly vulnerable with every single facet of her life- dating, friendships, personal life, body image, having people put you down and having to overcome it, literally absolutely everything.

She gets incredibly vulnerable in her lyrics and they get down to tiny nitty gritty details. Most artists today are not that open about their personal life through their music.

A lot of artists today do not write their own music; they just sing. So for 17 years, all of us who are obsessed with Taylor Swift have been able to find our story in hers because she is so open and honest and vulnerable about all these different little pieces of life.

All of us are able to listen to a song or listen to an album and find parts of ourselves in her. She has this magical way of taking something that can be heartbreaking and turning it into a joyous thing by the end of the music. For 17 years we have been able to use her music as a soundtrack to our lives.

When her first album *Debut* came out in 2006 I was 3 years old, and her next album *Fearless* came out 2 years later in 2008, I was just a little girl. She was talking about a day when her friends all ditched her and went to the mall without her. Being that little but having the hardest time with girlfriends I was still able to relate to those songs because they had to do with being a young girl trying to get by in this world. I sang her song *The Best Day* for the school talent show when I was in second grade.

All of us as human beings can collectively agree that dealing with your emotions and going through new experiences and through the trials and tribulations of life is always hard, so to have someone to listen to, someone to look up to, someone to relate to, is incredible powerful.

So as Taylor Swift has aged, so have we and her life experiences and her perspectives on them have also changed just as ours have. But again we can all find pieces of our story in hers.

She is me, I am her, she is us.

We have watched her and related to her throughout our entire lives, we've been through the heartbreaks with her in our own lives.

I heard a woman say "Taylor Swift wasn't born yet and has chronicled my relationship with my first love in the '70s."

What makes us Swifties so obsessed with her is truly watching her continuously bounce back. Taylor Swift has been dragged through the mud endlessly throughout her career, had her success cunningly undermined, and seen herself constantly put down through her entire career- all of us can relate to that, all of us can relate to trying to overcome something or someone that is putting us down and it's inspiring, it is joyful, and it is so so good when you refuse to let it happen. Taylor is a wondrous role model.

I have been in therapy since I was 7 years old, and from as early as I can remember, I have always felt so deeply about everything, and every feeling I had, I gave it my all, and it would encompass me and my world. In my adolescence, I suffered through a lot of sexual abuse and trauma, and was sent to treatment and received intensive care for the majority of my years in high school. When Taylor released *Midnights* I was a sophomore in college, I had fallen in love for the first time in my life, I was still navigating the path of my life and I was still healing. When I listened to the 19th track on the album *Would've Could've Should've* I fell to the floor in tears. It had taken Taylor just 5 seconds and 9 words to explain what I couldn't put into words in 5 years of therapy. "Give me back my girlhood. It was mine first".

When I was 4 years old, my sisters and I would dance to our favorite pop star's music and sing along to *You Belong With Me* and *Love Story*.

We wanted to be princesses just like she was. Girls were always the majority present in my house when I was growing up. I have a twin sister and a little sister two years apart, so the three of us lived in girl world and have always been best friends. We adored Taylor Swift. We idolized her. We wanted to be her. For my seventh birthday in 2011, my mom got my sisters and me tickets to see Taylor Swift live during her *Speak Now* tour. We were so excited and had been counting down the days until we would watch Taylor sing *Sparks Fly* and *Fearless*. I told all my friends and teachers at school who all knew Taylor Swift was my favorite. Everyone had watched me sing *The Best Day* for the school talent show and dance to her radio hits at recess, so they were so excited I would finally get to sing along with Taylor in person. The concert was sensational and secured Taylor's number-one spot in our hearts. My mom took a picture of the three of us smiling in front of the *Speak Now* backdrop before the show, and thirteen years later we re-created the same photo of us at the Eras Tour.

Taylor has been there with me through every stage of my life, and she's always had a way to explain it. I was singing *Enchanted* dressed up as a princess in my room when I was a little girl, and then I was singing *Enchanted* in the car with my first love at 2 a.m., windows rolled down, volume full blast, driving through our college ghost town. We find new meanings in the same songs we've always listened to as we grow up. She writes the story of our lives, women and girls.

Fortnight Gets Steampunked

By David Soren

Note: For this article please first view the publicly available video of Fortnight by Taylor Swift on a media source such as YouTube. After you have read the article please view the video again to see if it breaks differently for you.

This chapter deals with what is probably the most complex video that Taylor Swift has ever made and we have saved it to near the end because it requires a more complex discussion than anything we've offered up to this point in the book. I've tried to make the language as clear as possible and avoid excessive jargon.

PART ONE: ABOUT THE VIDEO

In 2024 Taylor Swift was arguably the most famous woman in the world and her Eras Tour was and currently is the biggest grossing tour by any musical artist or group in the history of the music business (Atwal 2023). And it had a running time of well over 3 hours (and by the time of the later version of the tour sometimes reaching 3 ½!), during which time the main attraction was on stage except for quick costume changes without anyone else taking

FIGURE 1: The weekly Spanish newspaper *El Especialito,* Ed. 1474, published an article: "Taylor Swift makes $10,000 000 a day" - "Taylor Swift hace $10 millones por Dia."

over. This show was a remarkable test of human endurance for its principal performer, and it was a huge success all over the world .

Anticipation grew to a fever pitch among Swifties for the arrival of the new release *The Tortured Poets Department* and speculation arose on what would be the first song out to be promoted, which, no matter what it was, was guaranteed to burst into the top spot on the charts due to the pent-up energy and emotion of the anticipating fans (Bernabe and Berkowitz 2024). The album was also, according to Taylor, a total attempt at exorcism of one of the most difficult periods of her life:

> "There is nothing to avenge, no scores to settle once wounds have healed. And upon further reflection, a good number of them turned out to be self-inflicted." (Perez 2024)

Fortnight became the first hit single from The *Tortured Poets Department* and was the basically simple story of a young married man and woman who slipped into an affair that lasted about two weeks (a fortnight or fortnite), was extremely intense and ended apparently because the man felt he needed to walk away from it more than the woman did. We learn in the song that the woman discovered that her own husband was having an affair which no doubt contributed to her original malaise. She was also undergoing treatment for this and had suffered from alcoholism. In addition pills she was taking did not work effectively for her and judging from her fragile state may have been causing dangerous side effects.

All of this WOULD be quite straightforward except for the fact that this is Taylor Swift's mind, based on a real-life story she said inspired her from the tv show *Dateline* as was the song *Florida* which sent her imagining this song and video about people doing unorthodox things and then all fleeing to Florida (Brockington 2024)! Since it is part of the *Tortured Poets Department* era imagery, and therefore needed to be totally cohesive (a word Taylor likes to use a lot), the video was made in black and white which gives an immediate retro feeling to the proceedings.

Taylor has given us some hints as to what is happening in this strange work. She says that the woman is being treated at a "government municipal building where they study the behavior and minds of poets" and we see also that she has imagined herself in this strange situation (Chan 2024). She is just waking up here when we first meet her but even before that the video is introduced by having its title, *Fortnight*, presented on typical silent movie lobby cards, the kind that were used to introduce and title scenes beginning in the early part of the 20th century, a craft which by the way was the first job given to Alfred Hitchcock when he began in the silent film business in England (Fritz 2020). Right away then we are shown a pre-modern world but with unsettling other-worldly overtones about to appear.

FIGURE 2: Silent movie title card from *Dr. Jekyll and Mr. Hyde,*
Paramount Artcraft 1920 silent film.

We next meet Taylor who is made up in a manner similar to a silent movie heroine with short heavily pinned down hair ca. mid to late 1920s, and heart-shaped "bee stung" full lips which evoke such silent film stars as Clara Bow (also featured elsewhere on the *Tortured Poets* album) (Aesthetics 2021), along with intense dark eye makeup and a choker necklace. Immediately, as we pull back from a closeup of Taylor's face, we notice one detail after another in the room. She is chained to a bed which is hanging on a wall (!) and furthermore it is deliberately placed at a diagonal angle, the famous type of disorienting diagonal or tilted look that was used centrally in Edvard Munch's painting *The Scream* and also commonly used in Expressionist and Expressionist-Cubist German cinema of the silent era. In post World War I Germany such a bizarre scene would immediately suggest madness as in the 1919 German film *The Cabinet of Dr. Caligari*, discussed elsewhere in this volume in connection with Taylor's direct reference to it in *Who's Afraid of Little Old Me*. As Taylor has said regarding Post Malone's look in her video *Taylor Swift Fortnight (feat. Post Malone) (Behind the Scenes)*:

"Nothing says crazy like a slight tilt to the head."

FIGURE 3: Clara Bow in the silent film *Wings* (1927). 1972 stamp from the Middle Eastern emirate of Fujeira.

FIGURE 4: Stamp from Ghana commemorating the 1893 Edvard Munch painting *The Scream* showing the diagonally placed railing along the walkway.

Not only is this world disorienting to the viewer and set back in time to the later 19th or early 20th century (with later incorporated more semi-modern computers) but at this point in the video an attendant wearing black surgical gloves appears bringing Taylor medication. He enters through the door to this room upside down, walking across the ceiling in order to insert a pill from a container labeled "Forget Him" on Taylor's tongue and she dutifully swallows it (the seeming counterpoint to the heart candy she puts on her tongue and swallows in her earlier *Blank Space* music video).

We see that she is wearing what appears to be an old-fashioned white wedding dress but with strange sharply pointed material at the top that gives a hard-edged disorienting angular look. We can also see that there is a bathtub on the ceiling and at the upper left a metal-legged stool that is somehow successfully placed upside down. On the right is a waste basket with a pop-up lid sitting half-way up the wall near a small mirror. A sink appears in a normal position but with a chair tilted back to form once again a powerful disorienting diagonal next to it (Borland 2024).

The attendant now releases her from bondage and she then goes to a mirror where she gently rubs her face, revealing on her face the exact extensive tattooing of Post Malone's face in real life (he plays her great fortnight passion in the piece). We can clearly read "Always Tired" below her eyes, quite appropriate to this situation, as well as "Stay Away" and even Post's daughter's initials DDP. The idea seems to be that the Taylor figure is so obsessed with the Post character that he becomes one with her, symbolized by the tattoos, and obviously the Forget Him pill that she was given has not worked.

There is the suggestion that we are looking at a clinic perhaps of the pre-Freudian period which we are experiencing from the mind of a disturbed patient i.e. Taylor herself. We will come back to this subject in a little while but first let us finish with our visit to this strange "asylum".

The clinic has another room, its main room apparently, devoted to probing the mind of their troubled patients. In that room there is no sophisticated laboratory equipment. It is instead what someone living back in the Victorian Era or sometime soon thereafter would be able to imagine as a super-advanced future clinic and what it would have available to it: what we might call retro-futurism. It is as if time had not gone by as it actually did but instead changes in technological development and psychiatric thinking went down some other strange path or into some parallel but alternate universe. In this room, since it seems to be a Victorian era setting, nobody is thinking yet about a laboratory with computers and

there are only early manual typewriters and vast amounts of shelv-
ing everywhere necessary to file the
enormous amounts of paperwork
the typewriters generate. In its day
of course the typewriter seemed
miraculous and it helped revolu-
tionize what people thought might
be possible in the future and that
appears to be the idea taken in this
video, imagining from the viewpoint of this early time the potential capabilities of this remarkable
transformative machine (Adler
1973).

In *Fortnight* there is a "staff" of seat-
ed black-masked typists stretch-
ing out as far as the eye can see
and they all appear to be male and
wearing top hats as was the fashion
of the time. Two iconic symbols of

FIGURE 5: A 19th century Caligraph typewriter of the series New Century, produced by the American Writing Machine Company of New York City.

the pre- modern era were top hats and typewriters, the latter having been sold first commercially in 1874 and top hats having become a symbol of respectability and style from
about 1850 to 1900 and even a bit beyond (Moore 2023) but of course one did not normally
wear a top hat to type!

As Taylor moves into this heart of the clinic her dress suddenly changes from the strange
white wedding dress to what appears to be a black Victorian mourning dress; it used to be
the custom for women losing their spouse to go into a lengthy or even permanent mourning for their husbands (as England's Queen Victoria herself did) by wearing such dresses
(Celiberti 2021). Women were expected to follow a certain etiquette for mourning in those
days, although the rules could vary from place to place. Here is a typical example from
England:

- 2 years of mourning for a deceased husband

- 1 year of mourning for deceased parents
- 1 year of mourning for deceased children
- 6 months of mourning for deceased grandparents
- 6 months of mourning for deceased friends when the mourner received an inheritance
- 6 months of mourning for deceased siblings
- 3 months of mourning for deceased aunts and uncles (Carmi 2022)

Once entering the heart of the clinic Taylor sits down at a vintage typewriter and prepares to insert the pages on which to type while across from her is the object of her affection (Post Malone) with all of his facial tattoos back. Both of them begin furiously typing, as if this will generate some sort of supernatural contact between them. His typewriter lacks the number 1 on it so apparently he cannot write definitively about the number 1 love of

FIGURE 6: Woman in typical 19th century black mourning dress.

FIGURE 7: Details of a Victorian dress: corset with black lace and lace gloves similar to those worn by Taylor Swift in *Fortnight*.

his life, and when she types the typing spaces out over the word *ruining* and emphasizes the song's lyric "you're ruining my life". So for her there is the literal *rui ning* of her life in the breaking apart of the word and for him there can be no number 1 in his life-- except that such early typewriters did not have the 1 and used the diminutive of the letter L instead (Bloch 2024), so we are left to wonder if this is a Swift Easter Egg or a quasi-Easter Egg or a joke on the Swifties to trick them or have fun with them or prank them which Taylor of course would not be above doing! (Lewry 2024).

As the lovers sit across from each other and type, a pink smoke (perhaps symbolic of their passion and the only other color in this black and white video) emerges from her typewriter and a black one from his and they rise up to a point where the pink and black merge together and suddenly the two protagonists are apparently thought-transferred by the magic of these super-advanced retro-futuristic typewriters and the resulting paper calculations transport them into another realm where they are reclining together and she is reading a book entitled "Us" which is also an apparently deliberate future projection of a song Taylor would write with one of her young protégé singers Gracie Abrams in the future along with arranger-deluxe Aaron Dessner!

As Taylor and Post stare at each other on the blank background with oddly jagged jutting edges the camera pulls back to reveal that all of this background is what is going on in Taylor's head (including the actual "Us" projection). She is thinking about meeting him on a long, deserted road but it is menaced with threatening skies and all around them swirls paper presumably containing information generated by the super-typewriters at the clinic about the "case". Now the tattoos are gone from his face; they embrace for an instant only to be separated again as they reach out to each other, while the typewriter paper tornado is swirling about them with all of the generated data from the clinic, and we see that after this transformative session we have now arrived in another special room in the clinic with an elaborate retro-futuristic device attached to her head no doubt to process the inner workings of her mind.

The room seems to be a computer lab with all sorts of machines with lights that seem to be doing something. My late friend Harry Lange, who was the production designer for the first two *Star Wars* films, and about whom we will say more later on, used to call such things "machines that go ping." He would say that these machines such as the Millenium Falcon space ship interior he designed

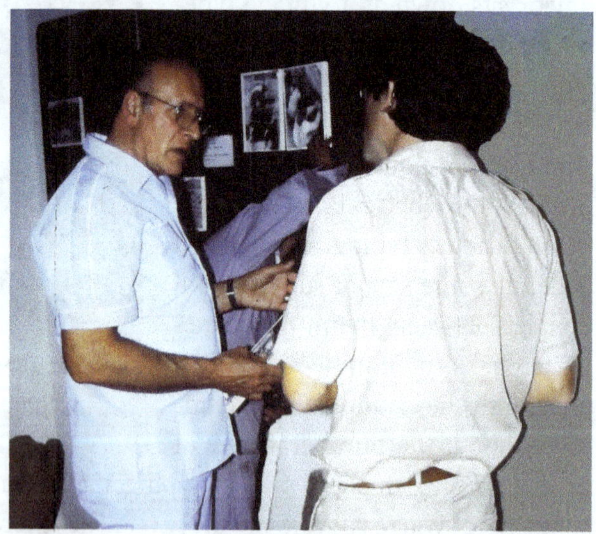

FIGURE 8: Harry Lange on the left discusses with David Soren designs for a museum installation in Santiago do Cacem, Portugal in 1983. Lange was chief production designer for *Star Wars* (1977) and *The Empire Strikes Back* (1980). David Soren Collection. Photo by Noelle Soren).

had to appear to the viewer that they were doing something important even though they were just facades with flashing lights inside. He would design his computerized dashboards and labs so that the viewer would believe that something significant was going on.

The experimental lab is being run by Ethan Hawke and Josh Charles who had starred in the movie *Dead Poets Society*, a 1989 film about an English teacher who together with his students re-established an old poetry club that dealt with the need to break free of society's expectations and strict rules to find truth and happiness or at least seek a way to manage one's life imaginatively. In this more modern environment Taylor is strapped in as a black dog walks diagonally through the frame, a reference to the pub in England where she and her long-time real-life love the actor Joe Alwyn supposedly hung out and a reference to a song called *The Black Dog* on the *Tortured Poets* album (Alwyn denies they ever went there) (Tannenbaum 2024).

In this newer computer-rich environment data can be generated much more easily by probes of Taylor's brain, using a little Geiger counter-like device, and by simply writing down notes based on what seem to be electrical impulses. However, if you study the pulses carefully each row spells out "I love you. It's ruining my life" over and over again! Next we learn that incredibly her true love played by Post Malone is actually another one of the lab's technicians, suggesting the confused state of Taylor's mind.

After taking their data the two principal technicians engage in shock therapy (electroconvulsive therapy or ECT) to Taylor. Such "therapy" was a technique known in a primitive form to deal with syphilis since 1917 and in a more sophisticated form in Italy since the later 1930s. It was used in dealing with extreme depression or manic behavior and was often repeated multiple times weekly until a positive result might be achieved. It was for a very long time used to treat schizophrenia but it was also used at times to silence "uppity" women from getting outside of their "place" as in the famous case in Washington State of the shocking institutionalizing and shock therapy done to Frances Farmer, the film actress of the 1930s whose own mother turned against her. The claim however that Farmer was also lobotomized has now been proven to be false (Shelley 2010).

The *Tortured Poets Department* video is more than just a reference to a similar sounding film name (*Dead Poets Society*) and indeed Taylor has even used two of the key actors from the 1989 film. One can imagine that Robin Williams, the motivating risk-taking teacher in the film, would have been asked to participate had he not taken his own life, himself qualifying in real-life as a tortured poet who reached the highest levels of fame and success and could not remain there due to, it was said, psychological imbalances, Lewy body dementia, and extreme stress which triggered unbearable depression (Rogers 2022).

The 1989 movie, set in an unspecified New England elite boys school in 1959, won an Oscar for best screenplay by the always fascinating Peter Weir. The film reference is inserted here in the video because in the laboratory, filled with strange blinking early-looking computer things, the search continues in order to bring forward again to us the message of that feature film, namely that "poetry, beauty, romance and love are what we stay alive for" and that you have to "*carpe diem*" (Latin for "seize the day") to make the most of your limited time on earth-- and sometimes that pursuit is painfully hard (Gentry 2017).

The feature movie is urging you to constantly look at things in a different way and avoid conformity but realize that the pursuit of beauty—of poetry in the broadest sense—is fraught with danger and can even destroy you (as it did to many of the protagonists in the film) although it can also propel and release you into a freedom to explore new worlds of the mind. This is a feeling expressed by many artists and poets especially during the later 19th century and we

Featureflash Photo Agency/Shutterstock.com

FIGURE 9: Peter Weir at the 56th Annual Directors Guild Awards in Century City, Los Angeles, CA. February 7, 2004.

witness Jean Cocteau, the famous French poet, artist and filmmaker, expressing this same idea in his 1930 movie, the aptly named *Blood of a Poet* in which we are treated to a series of Surrealistic experiences which are supposed to be a short period of time in the mind of a poet who suffers for his pursuit of artistic perfection. Cocteau was fascinated with mirrors and even penetrates one in his film in order to view the world from the other side of it, engaging in constant self-reflection, self-confusion and inspiration not unlike our Taylor Swift video. But more about Cocteau later on. Suffice it to say for now that this Cocteau film is an appropriate counterpart to *Fortnight* or to the *Tortured Poets Department* in its entirety.

We quickly learn after this shock therapy in *Fortnight* that technician/ lover Post Malone is now surprisingly appearing in the lab and he seeks to pull the plug on Taylor's torture in the scene. She is then seen being mentally driven back to the typewriter room looking through the file cabinets and rifling through the billowing typewriter paper perhaps trying to find a solution to her tortured state. At this point we seem to be seeing everything here from Taylor's perspective as the depressed and obsessed fortnight lover, detailing what has been done to her in the pursuit of examining her and in part giving us her surreal reaction to her ordeal.

Finally we see Post Malone talking on the telephone inside an old-fashioned phone booth such as used to appear all over American towns. There is in the video a furious rainstorm outside and the phone booth is bizarrely placed on the top of a sheer precipice around which are other huge mountainous areas—not a zone where one would expect to require public phone service but the zone of a nightmare or bizarre dream. He is reaching out to Taylor and she is ever close to him or at least to his thoughts as she sits perched above him on the phone booth like a sphinx, a mysterious symbol of wisdom in ancient Egypt,

FIGURE 10: Stamp from Czechoslovakia, showing French Symbolist and Surrealist poet and filmmaker Jean Cocteau.

FIGURE 11: Old-fashioned now-removed public pay phone from Alicante, Spain.

Greece and Rome, oblivious to the weather or the location. He discovers her above the phone booth and they reach out and connect as the song ends.

This last section of the video, encompassing the melodic change and musical crescendo, is accompanied by the scene of Taylor frantically ransacking the "clinic" for relevant papers and links that will lead to a union with her beloved, but she cannot find anything. He, for his part, attempts to call her from the outmoded pay phone booth but she doesn't answer. We learn that the fortnight lovers hope to get a car and move to Florida (!) but the car won't start unless the two of them can spark it by his touching her. He phones her but cannot see that she is perched directly above him until he leaves the phone booth and they finally touch once again leaving us to conclude perhaps that at least in her mind she has reunited with her beloved.

FIGURE 12: The mythical Sphinx of Naxos statue stands on the pedestal in the Archaeological museum, Delphi, Greece.

FIGURE 13: The Sphinx of the Naxians or the Sphinx of Naxos stood on a tall Ionic column next to the Temple of Apollo at Delphi. It served as a symbolic guardian within the sanctuary.

Deliberately enigmatic, the video encourages the viewer to follow some of the precepts of the *Dead Poets Society* movie, including the phrase of Robin Williams that "only in our dreams can we be totally free. 'Twas always thus and always thus will be' " (Neese 2015). To be a tortured poet in the Robin Williams style one must view the world with a new perspective and have a reverence for constant learning, excellence, self-expression, and the desire to discover as many layers of meaning in a situation as possible. I find this video particularly inspiring in my own work for that is what an archaeologist examining an ancient site must do in order to fully immerse oneself in the character of an ancient world and people.

As an archaeologist you are presented with a vast field of ruins and your assignment is to reconstruct what happened at the site often many centuries or even more than a thousand years ago just as in this video where you are presented with a great deal of information that you must sift through by analyzing it and attempting to experience it through the minds of the protagonists. In Italy I was presented with a cemetery site that was 1500 years old, full of strange offerings such as raven's talons, toads and cauldrons and it contained graves of infants buried with stones forced into their mouths and placed on their bodies to weigh them down, evidence of witchcraft (Soren 2024).

FIGURE 14: Robin Williams in the film *Dead Poets Society* (1989)

Credit: Alamy Images.

I spent more than 30 years detailing and examining the site from every perspective I could think of but I was constantly afraid that I was missing something, some clue that would bring me closer to the terrified people who died or lost loved ones here. I finally discovered that the mass infant deaths were from an ancient epidemic. There were numerous possibilities as to what actually had occurred but I had to create the most plausible explanation from the artefacts recovered and from the laboratory analyses we could do and the most logical conclusion was that the late Roman village had been exposed to a deadly type of malaria known as *Plasmodium falciparum*.

Sifting through the clues was like researching a Taylor Swift video such as this one. It was as if I had my own personal time machine to go back and rediscover what an ancient world of the fifth century A.D. was really like. My goal in my research is always to gain an overall impression or idea based on factual input which can be used to elucidate the past and that is how I view *Fortnight*. The approach and technique of this *Tortured Poets* video are never far from me and it colors my view of how to approach my work. Recreating and understanding the past has to be done by understanding and extracting layer upon layer of meaning and those layers make up the "stratigraphy" of the ancient site and world you find yourself being drawn into, slowly peeling back the layers of meaning as best you can. Each layer has to be understood and evaluated until a synthesis may be reached. The synthesis you draw from your work could be wrong but it is I always say "a reasonable attempt to explain what other people thought at a given time". That is one defininiton I like of archaeology.

Taylor Swift's body of work is often just that way, including this video. There are layers upon layers of meaning here to sift through which don't make understandable sense in terms of our world because it is a world from within the mind that Taylor has sought to exteriorize and exorcise. There is also a major message within it to the creative artist Swifties of the future. Do what Taylor did. Take a given situation and appraise it to the best of your ability, using it as your starting point or inspiration. Then use it creatively to help you to document your dreams or visions, and focus on presenting them. She's been doing that since she was at least 11!

If you want to be a poet, this video challenges you to suffer, struggle and expect to take the shocks and the hits just as Jean Cocteau or Taylor did and to use these occurrences big and small to find the words and images that form the inner workings of your creative mind which you then present artfully. Use all this to make your life extraordinary because this is the only life you will get. Even though you are suffering inside from whatever it might be, you have to be able to use your input, drive and focus in your work even "with a broken heart" because "it's an art" as Taylor says in her *Tortured Poets* song *I Can Do It With a Broken Heart*.

Part of the poet's makeup is self-loathing and even self-destructive behavior when you realize you can never be all that you hope to become and you can be constantly limited by fate and time. Taylor has reported on numerous occasions about her self-loathing tendencies with regard to her own body and in regard to some of her actions in the past (see my comments on *Anti-Hero* in this volume). Best-selling writer Jonathan Franzen has stated something that seems to apply to Taylor quite well:

> "I love the idea of the writer taking refuge from who he is by putting words on the page. Writing, in fact, provides a much needed escape or confrontation with our

worst emotions. It's just so hard to get to that blissful place where the words are all that matters." (Filgate 2013).

This idea was a good part of the message of the 1989 *Dead Poets Society* movie (the year of Taylor's birth incidentally) and obviously Taylor has found it extremely meaningful and applied it to her own life. You can be like Todd (Ethan Hawke in the movie) and be shy and unsure of yourself and self-critical and you can still become a talented poet by using who you are. But realize that as Taylor has said "one of the stereotypical things that was said about poets over the years is that they were crazy (Daniels 2024)."

PART TWO: THE MEANING OF TAYLOR SWIFT'S *FORTNIGHT* FOR ME

A final thing to consider about this video is something that the taciturn Post Malone stated during its making, namely that it felt "steampunked" to him (Tousignant 2024). This is a term that I first encountered when I was working for eight years with Director Tom Nicholson at the *American Museum of Natural History* in New York City (1980-1987) designing an exhibition of the archaeology of ancient Carthage (in Tunisia, the North African country) which became a multi-million dollar world traveling museum show (Edwards 2017).

While living sometimes with friends in Greenwich Village during my stays in New York to curate the show in the early 1980s, I became aware of a growing trend in the East Village called the Steampunk Movement. The term was first coined by the science fiction and dark fantasy writer K. W. Jeter in 1987 and supported by his fellow travelers James P. Blaylock and Tim Fowler, but elements of the movement had already existed since the 1960s as a major retro and Hippie trend, although the 1980s

FIGURE 15: David Soren at *The Carthage Show* in 1987 at its opening at the American Museum of Natural History in New York. David Soren Collection; Edwards 2017

combined this love of things Edwardian, Victorian and even Frankensteinian with the Punk movement which had been getting very big in the mid 1970s.

The Punk Movement as I remember it had grown gradually out of the Beatnik movement of the 1950s which eventually had morphed into the flower children of the Hippie Movement which had been so big in the Haight-Ashbury neighborhood in San Francisco ("If you go to San Francisco, be sure to wear a flower in your hair" Scott McKenzie sang to us in 1967) (Campbell and Szatmary 2023).

FIGURE 16: Street Scene/painted store from Haight Ashbury in San Francisco California in 2016. Haight Ashbury is a district known as a center for the 1960s countercultural hippie movement.

The Hippie movement was against the war in Vietnam which had taken so many lives and had as a popular theme to "make love and not war" (Moretta 2017). A variety of drugs (especially L.S.D. and mescaline derived from peyote cacti) became popular along with anti-establishment views as well as the use of the word "man" all the time in most sentences ("How ya doin', man?"). I remember this all well because I fronted a rock band called *Sphinx* which played fraternities, had a lot of beer thrown on us, and featured psychedelic music of our own composition plus covers of The Beatles, Donovan, Rolling Stones and even Wilson

Pickett thrown in for good measure. We even purchased fake long hair for 5 dollars at a local discount store that made us look like The Beatles but unfortunately it came down over our ears and we had trouble hearing our own music!

FIGURE 17: The rock group *Sphinx* rehearses at Dartmouth College in 1967, featuring Gene Mackles, Steve Giddings, Dave Seidman, David Soren and Eric Ebbeson. Note the Naxian Sphinx at the lower body of my guitar! David Soren Collection. Photo by Noelle Soren.

Our band even had some groupies, very fashionable at the time and some even wearing their hair super long down the back, and I know this because I became engaged to one and almost married her! The era in my mind is still one of the richest and craziest in my life, a memory of mini-skirts, Marianne Faithful, The Beatles of course, life in the Ivy League, and, for me, watching a movie nobody remembers called *Having a Wild Weekend* (1965) starring a London rock group that early on in 1963 to 1965 at first rivaled the Beatles and was called the Dave Clark Five. Their movie was supposed to be the Five's response to the Beatles' *A Hard Day's Night* except young people neglected to go see it when it came to the states because it was serious and quite sad and wasn't *Help* or *Hard Day's Night* but was more of an art film that pleased a few critics in New York.

In that Dave Clark Five movie which only I and several film critics liked I immediately became enamored of the female lead Barbara Ferris and decided then and there at the age of 18 that I had to go off to England where the film was made, find her and marry her or at least meet her and I would learn to do professional field archaeology at the same time through the Oxford University training program I'd been accepted to. Honestly, this was the full extent of my thinking at the time; I was your basic airhead. But you have to understand that

England was more than just a country then to many of us. It was Swingin' London, British flags and Carnaby Street with fashions modeled by a super thin blonde model named Twiggy, plus the Beatles and London was "where it was at". Mind you, none of us knew what "it" was but we knew it was in England which even was the center for avant-garde comedy with its *Monty Python's Flying Circus* comedy troupe within which group I later became friends with Terry Jones and wound up years later with all of their rehearsal tapes from their movie *Monty Python's Meaning of Life* which Terry gave me one night down in the basement of his Chelsea London home when he was seriously inebriated. Anyway, it took me two years at ages 18 to 20 to earn enough money milking cows on a local Newtown, Pennsylvania dairy farm to pay to go abroad and at age 20 I set off to join the archaeological dig at iconic and beautiful Winchester Cathedral which was attractive to me because of the song *Winchester Cathedral* that was enormously popular at the time and was part of the big retro song movement that was trending in the 1960s where earlier times and its technology was already being embraced. *Winchester Cathedral* both song and place were another seminal influence on my later teenage years.

FIGURE 18: The Beatles were one of the big reasons young people wanted to go to England in the mid to late 1960s.

FIGURE 19: Winchester Cathedral, Winchester, Hampshire 2024 by drone.

In an era before microphones were popularly used at common venues, people could not hear the singers who were becoming popular on the radio when they performed live because they had soft radio voices. In those early days of the 1920s radios used vacuum tubes which were sensitive to shouting or loud voices and a type of singing called crooning became popular where the lyrics were more purred than shouted (Gorvett 2023).

Early crooners who became enormously popular were Bing Crosby, Rudy Vallee and Russ Columbo. But crooners were not able to be heard live for their fans early on so it became typical for the crooners to employ megaphones such as those used by cheerleaders to make their voices carry and Rudy Vallee was particularly known for this, until better quality microphones were developed and more commercially available circa 1932 which helped to turn Bing Crosby into a superstar.

FIGURE 20: Crooner Rudy Vallee with megaphone about to croon in 1929. University of Arizona School of Anthropology Vaudeville Collection.

Everett Collection/Shutterstock.com

FIGURE 21: Group of men and women listening to an Atwater Kent radio with an enclosed speaker ca. 1930, made in northwest Philadelphia.

The song *Winchester Cathedral* was a concept song by English record producer Geoff Stephens using a megaphone to voice the lyrics with studio musicians he called the New Vaudeville Band, suggesting that the early American entertainment form vaudeville was being revived. The concept was to employ in modern times a retro sound and look that emulated the show business/English music halls of the later 1920s and the band dressed appropriately in the jazzy college clothing of that day even though it was actually 1966. Paul McCartney of the Beatles also enjoyed this kind of retro look (old Hollywood or English music hall) and music and in 1967 songs such as *When I'm Sixty-Four* from the Sgt. Pepper album and *Your Mother Should Know* from the *Magical Mystery Tour* and these tunes offered a similar feel, dress and sound. McCartney actually wrote the former song in 1956 when he was just 14 years old and it was retro even then!

I was quite taken with retro costumes and music at the time since I had grown up as a performing child myself in the last dregs of American vaudeville where I found myself on shows with a lot of old timers in the profession. Vaudeville consisted of short variety acts strung into a show, usually with an emcee (Soren 2020). The acts could be singers, dancers, opera stars, actors, jugglers, bicycle trick specialists, actors doing mini-plays and many other talents too and the vaudeville theatres were often built like exotic palaces of escape from the cares of the day.

Rosemarie Mosteller/Shutterstock.com

FIGURE 22: Santa Fe, NM - The Lensic Performing Arts Center is a "Spanish-Moorish" style building originally built as a theater and vaudeville stage in 1931.

When I was 9 I was in early television as a performer on the CBS show *The Horn and Hardart Children's Hour*, where I was the youngest cast member at the time (1954-1956). Shot in Philadelphia, this show was filmed next door to the world's first (and only ever!) live soap opera western called *Action in the Afternoon*, which sometimes "borrowed" kids from our show and used them in the western. That soap opera show was directed by Richard Lester who eventually left Philadelphia's City Line Center where this was all shot and he too, just like me much later on, headed for England where he met Peter Sellers, Paul McCartney and John Lennon and ended up directing The Beatles in *A Hard Day's Night* and also the movie *Help!*

Despite my forays into the glittery world of entertainment and retro culture, I never became a full-fledged Hippie (I came close and my college roommate got arrested and put away for a while) but I certainly became a fly on the wall to some of the biggest movements of the time and to some of the most important movers and shakers of what led to the retro movement and eventually the Steampunk concept and even *Star Wars*, so let me tell you the rest of the story and why I find Taylor Swift's *Fortnight* so fascinating. I should add that I did get to dig ruins in England with the Oxford team but I never realized my dream of meeting Barbara Ferris or even Marianne Faithfull because when I got to Winchester Cathedral I immediately saw a young lady who seemed to have stepped right out of my Dave Clark movie fantasy. I could hardly believe it and I immediately asked her out and, having developed a total-immersion immediate crush on her, proposed to

FIGURE 23: David Soren performing live in vaudeville at the Greater Philadelphia Kiwanis Club with tackle Jesse Richardson of the Philadelphia Eagles football team in 1955.

FIGURE 24: The Beatles Original Motion Picture Soundtrack *Help!* music album on vinyl record LP disc.

Blueee77/Shutterstock.com

her 3 days later (she insists it was 5 days). That was the remarkable feeling of love that was in the air around England at that time and what was even more amazing she accepted my proposal immediately and we tried to get married in England and Spain but were too young. We finally got married at Christmas time that year in St. Louis where her family lived. We are still married and happy 58 years later!! Ultimately, it didn't really matter at all that she wasn't British and turned out to be from Saint Louis!

San Francisco's Haight Ashbury and London were where things were happening in 1968 as we have seen. But Harvard University where I had just become a graduate student was a major center for the Hippie movement as well, on the east coast, and I can remember studying for my Ph.D. and hearing about Timothy Leary not long before promoting L.S.D. there and having virtual seances while wearing Nehru jackets (Jawaharlal Nehru had been the trend-setting Prime Minister of India; Fraquoh and Franchomme 2016), burning incense which seemed

FIGURE 25: David and Noelle Soren at their engagement in Winchester, England while working on an Oxford University archaeological dig and housed there in an abandoned chocolate factory on St. Thomas Street, June 25, 1967.

to be everywhere and eventually attracting so much attention (even Cary Grant came!!), much of it from outraged Conservatives, that Leary got fired. I had to drop my band and devote all my time to study but I kept admiring rock, folk-rock and so-called psychedelic music by Donovan, Tim Buckley and especially the inventive Raymond Douglas-Davies and his group The Kinks.

FIGURE 26: Timothy F. Leary (1920 - 1996), an American writer, psychologist, campaigner for psychedelic drug research and use and 1960s counterculture icon, with Laura Huxley, widow of Aldous Huxley, author of the 1932 novel *Brave New World*, a book dear to the heart of every Hippie and dealing with a dystopian future society).

The Kinks were highly influential on me because during one of their media incarnations they dressed in Edwardian Suits and when I finally got enough money to buy a suit I bought what we called a Kinks suit after which I realized unfortunately that by wearing it I was making the generational statement that I was considering myself a "head" or a counter-culture retro person. At that point I didn't want to go that way and instead really hoped to get employed as

FIGURE 27: Pop and rock band, The Kinks, music album on vinyl record LP disc. Titled: *You Really Got Me* album cover, 1964.

a professor somewhere after I (hopefully) graduated without somehow pissing off the Harvard establishment at the Fogg Art Museum which was supportive of me but wasn't very Hippie or "happening" at all and wasn't plugged in at all as to what was going on in the street.

After I left Harvard I found employment for 10 years at the University of Missouri in Columbia and later became an Art History department head there and finally a head of Classical Studies at the University of Arizona in Tucson. But while I was doing those things I was also working for large blocks of time as a Guest Curator at the *American Museum of Natural History* in New York at 79th Street and Central Park West and commuting periodically for 8 years as well as directing field archaeology operations for the Smithsonian Institution in Tunisia.

The Punk culture had not been that big at Harvard but I found it to be much more of a trend in the East Village in New York where I first began working around 1980. Young people in the East Village resembled those of the Hippie movement I was quite familiar with, but the East Village movement had a harder sometimes nastier edge. It was again fueled by rock music, often still British, but its stars had names like Sid Vicious who became a counter-culture legend with his group *Sex Pistols* despite ending up dead at age 21 of a drug overdose (Cook 2006)!

FIGURE 28: Urban graffiti near Camden Lock Market in London depicting Sid Vicious.

The Punkers in the East Village as we referred to them at the Natural History museum up on 79th Street were anti-establishment when I was there but the flower child aspect of it seemed gone and there were a lot more street drugs including most especially heroin replacing the LSD (lysergic acid diethylamide) and the peyote (a cactus derivative which contained mescaline which was known for its calming effect) and of course the ever present marijuana which were the main stimulants of the Hippies I knew (Grob and Grigsby 2022). Now with Punk there were more piercings which scared the hell out of me even involving safety pins and a feeling of hopelessness and nihilism which had been to a great degree fueled by the Vietnam War (1955 to 1975 but mainly 1965 to its conclusion), and increasing polarization in America often between young and old. But there was also a side of the movement that pushed the boundaries of acceptable art as well as dance and fashion (I recall paintings by Piero Manzoni being exhibited featuring actual human excrement; Ebbett 2015).

The Punk movement was already well under way in the Village when I got there and I was invited to parties where people enjoyed the retro fashion look that they often "modernized" with face painting and tattooing of extreme sorts. It was also pointed out to me at the time that other cultures tattooed the body and face extensively, such as was evidenced by the Sak Yant tattoos of Thailand which feature intricate geometric designs and a background of religious symbolism. It was recommended I should look into this. It didn't convince me to try it although Post Malone apparently has no problem with this sort of thing.

FIGURE 29: Man in Bangkok, Thailand with tattooed face

Mehendra_art/Shutterstock.com

The celebration of past looks interfacing with 1980s contemporary counter-culture (anti military-industrial complex) attitudes came eventually to be cleverly coined as Steampunk, a blending of the Punk movement with primitive 19th century dynamic energy made possible through the influence of the technology of steam power, but the roots went back so much earlier than Jeter's naming of the movement in 1987 and the movement also included so much more by that time than just Punk and Retro.

For example, the movement as it had developed by 1987 also embraced really frightening horror and science fiction often set in scary dystopian future worlds, as fueled by Jeter and his colleagues and initially set in motion by Aldous Huxley's *Brave New World* back in 1931 to go with the wild retro clothing, accessories and anarchic attitudes. For many it was a chance to dress Victorian and enjoy a look at the past through mad scientists such as Victor Frankenstein and grim and eerie Victorian decors such as medical laboratories, and there was a love of strange inventions that seemed to come out of the industrial revolution and the age of steam-generated apparatus. This means the use of water as a gas to power mechanical devices, as in the 19th century when it was the main power form for transportation vehicles and steamboats.

FIGURE 30: Victorian style medical office with operating table.

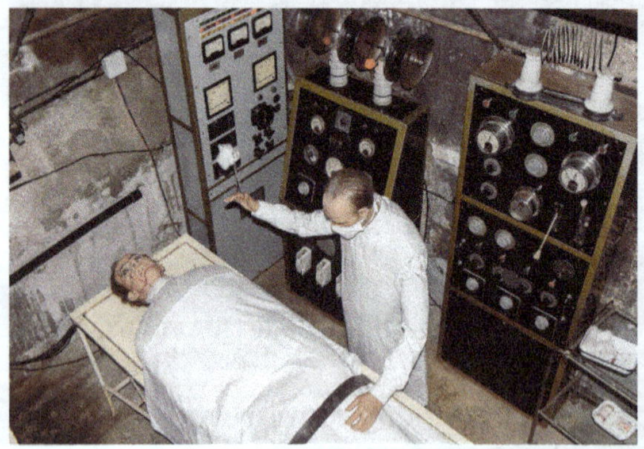

FIGURE 31: Doctor Frankenstein as presented at the wax museum of Barcelona, Spain and resembling the computer room in *Fortnight*.

FIGURE 32: Steamboat Natchez docked at port in New Orleans, Louisiana.

In the 19th century this newly developing energy source was also fuel for the imagination of writers such as Jules Verne who offered a future when all sorts of amazing things were possible due to advances in science and technology (Butcher 2006).

Mary Shelley's prescient 1818 novel *Frankenstein* imagined experimental devices which might harness lightning and be able to regenerate the dead, based on experiments she had personally witnessed by Luigi Galvani (1737-1798), the famous Italian physicist and pioneer in electrophysiology, where a simple battery or a generated spark could make a dead frog's leg twitch and appear to be alive due to electricity. This belief in the power of Galvanism as it was called and a fascination with the power and energy of lightning led to Mary Shelley's horrifying creation that foreshadowed the science fiction of today and can fall under the category of steampunk even though steam power in particular wasn't involved (Fowler and Galvani 2022).

Steampunk by 1987 then often came to mean anything that was trendy, looked old, especially 19th century and British, and yet involved creations that were fantastic and beyond the capabilities of that older time such as H. G. Wells' *The Time Machine* originally written in 1895 wherein someone using parts from Wells' own time was able to travel into the distant future (including in his novel the use of a mysterious transparent crystalline substance) (Beckford 2024). This development is sometimes referred to as Retro-Futurism (Corn and Horrigan 1984; Guffey

FIGURE 33: Portrait of Jules Verne from his house and now museum in Amiens, France where he wrote several of his famous works.

FIG. 34: Italian postage stamp showing Italian scientist Luigi Galvani and one of his static electricity methods to generate "life" in a deceased frog using "animal electricity."

2006) and one could take as an example a city in the 19th century which, if one was imagining the future back then, might look like something full of intricate steam-generated machinery and wheels and pipes strangely fit together and would look nothing like what eventually happened by our time and would not have made many of the discoveries we take for granted today.

The Steampunk Movement had a major injection of graphic shock and horror to go with its fascination for British 19th century fashion, high hats, typewriters and exotic steam-driven clanking inventions. Some of this, although largely uncredited, was the result of a small outfit known as Hammer Films which produced gory (at least gory for their glory days in the later 1950s through the 1970s) horror films about the Frankenstein monster, Dracula, the Gorgon, the Mummy, a werewolf, a reptile woman and the like (Maxford 2018).

Once again I was like a fly on the wall because while I found myself working for the Smithsonian Institution in Washington

delcarmat/Shutterstock.com

FIGURE 35: Image of H. G. Wells surround by images of his famous works *The Island of Dr. Moreau, The Invisible Man, War of the Worlds* and *The Time Machine.*

LoveHex/Shutterstock.com

FIGURE 36: Steampunk or Retro-Futuristic city street. Imagined contemporaneously as a 19th century prediction of a futuristic street. Submitted by LoveHex.

in the country of Tunisia for some years at various sites I made it a point to go to London on my flight back to the states every summer and look up horror film Hammer actors to interview, among them the wonderful Peter Cushing who played Dr. Frankenstein in a number of these films such as *The Curse of Frankenstein, Frankenstein Must Be Destroyed* and *Frankenstein Created Woman*, to name just a few. He told me about the obsession Hammer had through their brilliant set designer Bernard Robinson to create period 19th century sets and how the films normally were set in the Victorian period in Gothic Revival style with appropriate costuming. They were mostly filmed at Bray, England, outside of London at Oakley Court in Berkshire County.

FIGURE 37: A stamp printed in United Kingdom shows Peter Cushing (1913-1994), actor, from the postal series Great Britons, circa 2013.

FIGURE 38: The Oakley Court, Windsor, featuring the Victorian Gothic Revival country house built in 1859 overlooking the River Thames at Water Oakley in Bray in Berkshire County, used as the principal film set for the Hammer horror movies.

Many young people loved the Hammer films which delivered a lot of quality cinema at a low budget but the Hammers had a major effect primarily because they did some things never done before in a horror film: beginning in 1956 with *Curse of Frankenstein* and followed soon thereafter by *Horror of Dracula*, they showed blood in color and allowed it to gush from wounds and goo up Victorian operating theatres, and they put in as much sex as they could get away with, especially with bosomy women thrust into super-tight-fitting low-cut dresses. Young people thought that all women dressed like this back in the day! This, and taut direction from Terence Fisher, who had a brilliant feel for crystal clear narrative story-telling, became their formula for success, along with the Bernard Robinson Victorian sets, mad laboratories and of course the monsters. Cushing was the perfect Dr. F, whom he played earnestly but on the edge of sanity and he did his creature resurrection operations with meticulous detail and retro-futuristic technology.

He told me that he had to wear gloves constantly because of the enormous closeups of his hands when he was using his experimental machines and 19th century surgical instruments to create the monster. He liked to smoke and feared getting nicotine stains on his fingernails that would show up enormously on the giant screen! My interviews with Peter Cushing and Christopher Lee (who usually played Count Dracula) were among the first in American magazines.

A big influence in the East Village in the 1980s also were two young men out of Syracuse University named David McDermott and Peter McGough who, inspired by the Victorian era began producing retro art, movies and photographs, the latter using early production methods. They even took their passion a step further and began to dress and live their lives

neftali/Shutterstock.com

FIGURE 39: A stamp printed in Great Britain shows the film *Curse of Frankenstein* (1957) featuring Christopher Lee as the hideously scarred monster at the top, Peter Cushing as Dr. Frankenstein at bottom left, horror film star actress Hazel Court at lower right and the Victorian fantasy laboratory at bottom.

in this period, being known for their Victorian dress and especially their elegant top hats that appear to have stepped right out of Taylor Swift's *Fortnight* (McGough 2019).

Another big influence on the Steampunkers in the 1980s was of course the 1974 film *Star Wars* and its sequels which were full of futuristic paraphernalia (envisioned from OUR time!) that impressed people such as K. W. Jeter and his friends. It was the film series' incredible production design by Harry Lange (about whom we have spoken previously) and once again, without really realizing it at the time, I was the proverbial fly on the wall. I had been working on the island of Cyprus in the eastern Mediterranean when a Warrant Officer for the British RAF at Episkopi approached me. His name was Harry Heywood and he wanted to know if I could train a young man in his later teens who wanted to learn ancient Roman archaeology technique. I agreed to do it in exchange for some free helicopters to do aerial shots of my excavation site and which I could use to transport some ancient bodies I had found and had cocoon-wrapped in plaster!!

The boy I agreed to train in archaeology on Cyprus proved to be very good at archaeology and was in fact Harry Lange's eldest son. At the end of the digging season, I and my wife were invited to be a guest at the

FIGURE 40: David Soren (in background second from right) supervises the installation of the team's archaeological work on Cyprus. The famous family of 3 buried in the earthquake of A.D. 365 is being prepared for the installation in the foreground after it had been blessed by the Bishop Anthony of San Francisco and cleared for restoration and presentation.

Lange's London area home where we became close friends with Harry and his wife Daisy and ultimately I brought Harry to Santiago da Cacem, Portugal where I had been removing 1st century A.D. Roman wall painting from a building and installing it in the local archaeological and art historical museum. I asked Harry to do the wall background for me and we discussed doing something evoking *Star Wars* so he chose the background of the dashboard of the Millenium Falcon space ship from the film as the framework in which he placed our Roman wall paintings and he came personally and installed it all!

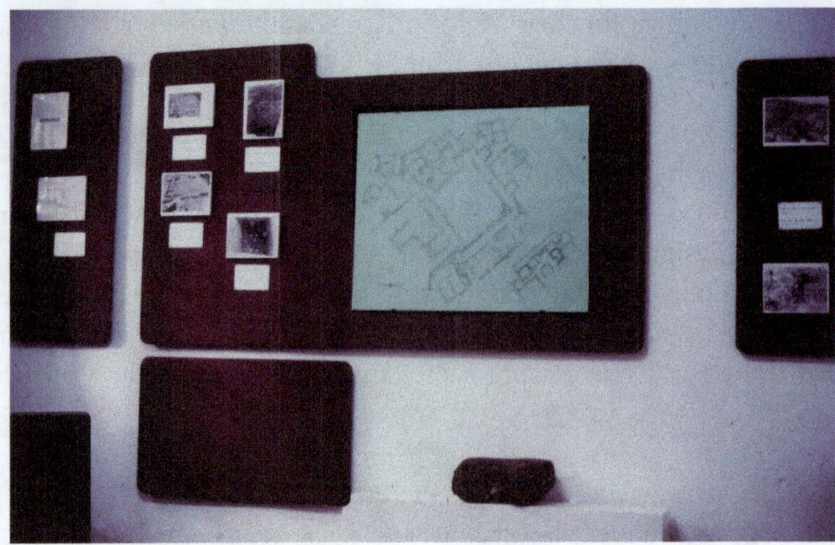

FIGURE 41: Harry Lange's simplified Milennium Falcon style backdrop installation at Santiago do Cacem Portugal's Art Museum in 1983.

Harry and I also concocted a plan whereby the technicians after making *The Empire Strikes Back* in 1980 would come to my site at Kourion, Cyprus and use our reconstruction blueprint of the ancient Roman Temple of Apollo there and would actually build it full size out of fiberglass. This fabulous plan I pressed with full force to the leaders of Cyprus, arguing that the Cyprus government would have a fabulous tourist attraction if they had a rebuilt ancient Roman temple, done with accurate restorations we could document, and made by the people who had literally created *Star Wars*. However, the Antiquities Director Vassos Karageorghis told

FIGURE 42: David Soren poses below the final and not quite correct reconstruction of the Temple of Apollo at Kourion on the eastern Mediterranean island of Cyprus. David Soren Collection.

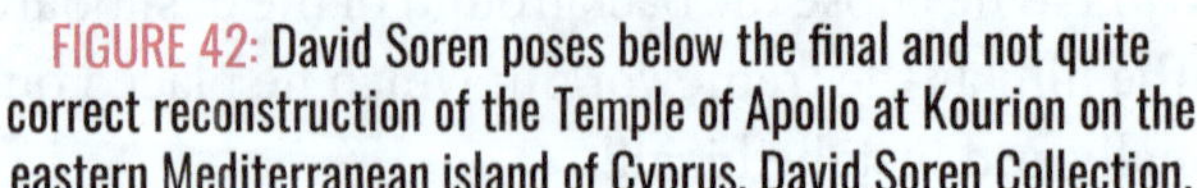

me in no uncertain terms that this "travesty" was never going to happen on Cyprus and I was free to do the rebuilding of the temple at my expense using stone from its original quarry nearby and not textured fiberglass. So I started doing that, fell gravely ill from a coxsakie virus which affected my entire body and spent the better part of a year recovering while another architectural specialist was called in to replace me, didn't use all of my work and screwed up the reconstruction which still stands to this day as a major tourist attraction! (Soren and James 1988.)

Mister Lange, his family and I spent a lot of time together in London and eventually he came to the University of Arizona and I produced a show of his drawings and his model work which included the original table models for *Dark Crystal* provided to me most graciously by Jim Henson (of *Muppet* fame). The show traveled to the Hayden Planetarium in New York and Mr. Lange co-taught a course with me at the University of Arizona in motion picture production design in which he explained how he did his other famous film designs, among them *2001: A Space Odyssey* (when Hal the computer winds down it sings the retro song Daisy in honor of Mr. Lange's wife Daisy, a little gift to Harry from Stanley Kubrick in appreciation of his designs for the film). Harry also designed *Moonraker*, the James Bond film, *Monty Python's Meaning of Life* (his favorite creation in the film was the imploding gourmet Mr. Creosote), and other little known gems such as *Hypersapiens*.

The *Star Wars* futurism of Lange's had a steampunk quality to it of course. He told me that he was interested in films such as *Dark Crystal* and *Star Wars* which could be made to show a technology which might be devised by an alien culture in another world. They might have the same problems as our life forms but how they solved those problems might look a little different from how we attempted to do so. He loved retro-futurism as well but in his sci fi work he specialized in imagining the distant future from the viewpoint of other worlds. Perhaps we might call this parallel universe futurism or other world futurism! He loved the look of computers so that a rocket dashboard could be full of blinking lights and strange language and things that hadn't been seen commonly before and he said he was influenced in his Millennium Falcon spaceship dashboard by the Dutch 20th century artist Piet Mondrian and his colorful minimalist geometrics known as *De Stijl*. I certainly miss the many evenings I enjoyed just sitting in the Lange living room with Harry, Daisy and different family members discussing how he produced the imagery for some of the most important science fiction films ever made. His son even married one of my graduate students when the Langes asked me to "find one of your nice students for our son" and I did!

FIGURE 43: Posters from the 1971 Guggenheim Museum Mondrian Exhibition.

There was also one other element of steampunking which was quite important and that is the role of Surrealism as popularized by Salvador Dali. Combinations of things that were impossible and radically illogical were nonetheless presented by artists and provocateurs such as Dali, images that could shock and disturb the viewer such as his painting *The Great Masturbator* or the fact that he'd take off a tie to reveal he was wearing another tie under that one. Thanks to The Beatles in particular and movies like *Yellow Submarine* and *The Magical Mystery Tour* and of course the drugs of the Hippie generation (especially LSD or *Lucy in the Sky With Diamonds*) fantastic visions became routine.

FIGURE 44: *Magical Mystery Tour* is a double 33 rpm record by the band The Beatles released in 1967.

At Dartmouth College when I was there as an undergraduate during the height of the Hippie movement, a friend of our group (nameless for this writing) earned money as a male model, naked, for an art class in Dartmouth's beautiful Hopkins Center. Our friend enjoyed a phenomenon of the time called a Happening in which in the later 1960s one could sit with friends and contemplate the universe while admiring a lava lamp (look it up!) and seeing reality stretched and deformed into something impossible (Henderson 2023). Art could be declared from what was around you and didn't even have to be made, embracing a kind of nihilism that became associated with something called Neo-Dada, where you were against everything including what you stood for. Unfortunately, before posing for the art class, our friend had ingested a substantial quantity of LSD and in about half an hour he became convinced that he was a tree and had sprung roots. When he had finished 75 minutes of posing he couldn't move or speak and the campus police had to be summoned to cover his nude form with a blanket, remove him by carrying him out horizontally, despite his being stiff as a board, and take him in for medical attention. He soon was encouraged to leave school which he did and joined a local Buddhist commune.

FIGURE 45: Retro lava lamp neon light graphic set. Psychedelic magma luminous illustration with pink, green, red and purple shining float bubbles.

So when all of this retro-futurism, steampunking, Hippie and Punk and Buddhist culture, Neo-Victorianism, *Star Wars* parallel universe futurism, Surrealism, Neo-Dada, Mondrian-esque *De Stijl* art and of course Harry Lange's machines that go ping were going on around me in the East Village, Greenwich Village, Dartmouth, Harvard and London, as you see from what I wrote above, I was there as that fly on the wall in the 1960s through the 1980s and I was interacting with some of the movers and shakers of the time and the drivers of creative movements even though my actual contributions were minimal. One of my students, reading through all of this and realizing that I was personally present for so much of it, described me as "a borderline celebrity" to which I replied "underline borderline".

All of these memories bring me (and I know you thought we'd never get there!) to *Fortnight*, the video. For someone my age (79) and background, Taylor's video feels like something made by someone with wisdom far beyond her years. It centers around a variety of outmoded items which were once considered emblematic of their era and the very latest thing in scientific and technological advancements, such as telephones, electro-shock therapy, top hats, Clara Bow, and mourning dresses, just to name a few of the attractions. The video is largely conceived as if it were made by someone living in the 1910s or 1920s, as witnessed first by the silent movie type art credits and loud simulated old-time movie projector noise which opens the video. But it also has the feel of having been created by humanoid aliens living in a parallel universe in an earlier time who were seeking an experimental future path different from our own and whose technology is ultra-modern and yet somehow strangely retro and also different from how we eventually evolved our techno world: the not quite fully modern computer lab, the lab coats, and the weird printouts that look like encephalograms but contain writing (!). The heart of the clinic features the old-fashioned typewriter blended with the retro-futuristic notion that the typewriter could produce innovative data, hence the room with hundreds of typists seeming to trail off into infinity all doing the same thing (retro-futuristic robots?). Accompanying this is the production of huge amounts of paper with data giving information which then requires a vast storage space and which leads to a sharing of thoughts or thought transference between the shock-revived Taylor and the enigmatic Post Malone. And let's not forget their bond signified by the sharing/transferring of his exotic, mysterious tattooed face with her and the pink smoke jointly resulting from their tandem typed efforts.

This leads to the 1989 *Dead Poets Society* sequence featuring two of the actual stars plucked (time-traveled?) from that movie and they now are lab technicians storing data received in brain scans from the shock treatment given to Taylor. The lab they are in is computer run but the background computers take up a lot of space as if they are old-fashioned computers, although they appear now to be intended to replace the data room of the old lab full of typewriters. The computers blink and flash (Harry Lange's machines that go ping) looking like a bulky retro computer lab more akin to the 1970s.

The horrible electro-shock treatment imposed on Taylor to achieve dramatic results is something that is not in common use today but had a vogue in the 1940s and a rejection in the 1960s. It however had a resurgence in the 1980s and in fact, has defenders of more selective application even today. The video calls to mind the kind of nightmare treatments/experiments performed in mental institutions such as the notorious "Bedlam" in England (Chambers 2019; Kneeland and Warren 2009).

Finally we encounter that retro phone booth with Post trying to reach Taylor who cannot pick up and who remains isolated from him as the lyrics talk about getting a car that won't start until they touch again, but they do finally touch as Taylor manages to break through the treatment and Post rescues her from the shock therapy. Perhaps they live happily ever after somewhere at least in their or his or her mind and the viewer is left to piece the fragmentary surreal logic together. It being Taylor's video, we have to assume that love will find a way. The concluding sequence is extraordinarily visually arresting with the sphinx-like Taylor sitting on the phone booth/statue base in the middle of nowhere amid the storm and the eerie mountainous backdrops.

The video is then a compendium of dreams and thoughts within Taylor's mind, probably occurring at night when she has reported having a great number of her most intense experiences (Watts 2022). While the video remains enigmatic, there are certain things that strike me about it that I would like to highlight.

First, I am amazed at how many different aspects of the video touched my early life and places where I had worked and enjoyed intense experiences. Her ability to communicate her own ideas and feelings to others is at this point legendary and it shows her remarkable talent as a poet who can transfer her feelings to us through her words, her mood-instilling still images included within her sold recordings, the musical tone of each song, the emotional quality of her voice and finally her amazingly detailed self-directed or co-directed videos. These are the things that Swifties relate to and that have made Taylor unquestionably the number one musical star in the world. We feel we can see inside her mind and feel something of her emotions while at the same time we (even old people who have lived most of our lives before she was born!) can feel things in our own lives that she embraces through the intensity, profundity and beauty of her vision.

Secondly, the video itself is head and shoulders above other music videos because it is a work of art which can mean different things to different people, and it manages to incorporate a variety of different cultural movements within it to extraordinary effect, among them Surrealism, Retro-Futurism, Steampunk, Neo-Dada, Neo-Victorianism and alternate/parallel universes.

Third, there is a strong connection to the *Dead Poets Society* movie and book that should not be overlooked. Taylor took the trouble to include actual actors from the film in this video which should send a message that the themes of that film and even its title were important to her. The quest of the poet through the minefield of life and the search for freedom of thought and expression and the self-loathing and insecurities of the poet are what leads to the creation of an artistic work which only through having the artist suffer can achieve true beauty…or lead to self-destruction or both.

Fourth, it is no coincidence that she has chosen a work directed by Peter Weir who has been a specialist in enigmatic cinema. Taylor's video in fact strongly invites comparison to Weir's *Picnic at Hanging Rock* (Australia, 1975), on the surface a movie about three young girls and their supervisor who disappear during a girl's school mountain outing in Victoria, Australia in the year 1900. It is a film which works on many levels but is also about the search for pure beauty and perfect love, a striving for the ultimate beauty.

This is a concept which shows in Taylor's work ethic. When something has been produced that cannot be improved upon and shouldn't be altered, it is then that the artist knows that a work is complete and Taylor has expressed the need to polish up and refine her work, her words, and her visuals up to the point where they need nothing more and yet nothing can be taken away. Raymond Loewy the famous French and American designer in the 1930s once said that a modern airplane wing was the most perfect artistic creation because "nothing needed to be added to it and nothing could be taken away"(Haeberle 2015). This is the approach Taylor uses before she releases a song and she normally records songs for albums that never get released because they don't meet her standards so she puts them in her so-called vault, sometimes never releasing them and sometimes delaying release for as long as 13 years (e.g. *Mr. Perfectly Fine*).

Fifth, Fernand Khnopff (1858-1921), the Belgian Symbolist artist, did a famous painting often studied in introductory art classes called *Des Caresses ou L'Art ou Le Sphinx* (Caresses or Art or The Sphinx) in 1896. It shows that ancient Greek monster The Sphinx , a creature that is often depicted with the head of a woman, the body of a lion, and sometimes wings, who is caressing a poet (?) with an elegant winged cane or sceptre emblematic of his exalted position. The love of the sphinx appears to inspire him but also to be about to wound him with her sharp claws as if to destroy him at the same time. The poet's body is so delicate it is impossible to be sure if he is a man or a woman or an androgyn, a sort of man-woman usually depicted as thin and featuring an elongated body. The sphinx is itself a monster who sits in a pose remarkably like that of Taylor sitting on the phone booth at the end of *Fortnight* and Taylor's touch will of course inspire Post Malone in the video but can also destroy them both and their domestic lives and the ominous atmosphere around them reflects this danger. It is the nature of a sphinx to grant wishes but also to cause death and destruction at the same time (Greenberg 2021). Thus the ending of Taylor's video has strong ties to the Symbolist Movement of the later 19th century in which Khnopff played a dominant part.

FIGURE 46: Fernand Khnopff, *Des Caresses ou L'Art ou Le Sphinx* 1896 Oil on canvas, 50.5 × 150 cm. Brussels, Royal Museums of Art and History.

As in Jean Cocteau's *Blood of a Poet* (1930) film, we have witnessed a view inside the mind of Taylor as she half dreams about a forbidden relationship that ended with nearly disastrous consequences for her protagonists. In *Blood of a Poet* (1930), the poet/filmmaker is inspired by a Greek statue who is a symbol of beauty (the Venus de Milo) and at the same time a Muse, one of the 9 goddesses who were said to be able to inspire poets of old.

FIGURE 46: Roman marble relief featuring a Muse, perhaps Terpsichore, goddess of the dance and the Greek chorus, playing a cithara, a kind of lyre, from the Istanbul Archaeological Museum. It dates perhaps to the first century B.C..

After suffering a wound on his hand from the living statue, Cocteau has his poet (Enrique Rivero) in *Blood of a Poet* break through a mirror and find himself in a special world reserved only for those with the gift of imagination. All of this is intended to be but a moment in the mind of a poet. In the beginning of the film a huge chimney is falling and at the end of the film it falls completely. Only a moment of time has elapsed in a world that is not bound by time. It is a perfect companion for Taylor's video and it shows that tortured poets have existed for a very long time, since Cocteau's film dates back to 1932.

Taylor's video is significant because it is a trip inside her mind just as each poet's voyage to discovery must be. We see in this video its focus on the shocking treatment of women in society which is a theme Taylor has long pursued and is literally shocking in her video. Her long-time fascination for history and antique art is evident in the movie along with its confounding of bygone eras of time, and the fascination with Steampunk and Retro-Futurism which allows the mind to redefine the history of the world as if it were governed only by her desires, fascinations and fears. There is in *Fortnight* the attempt to define the struggle of a poet in her pursuit of true love despite physical suffering, societal and physical constraints and gender discrimination. In the simplest terms this might be seen as the difficulty of achieving a long-term relationship when every movement you make is scrutinized by a dystopian world and there are daily updates on every single place you and a lover actually go or might go or think about going. It sounds like Taylor's daily life more and more today!

On another level paralleling Taylor's personal life there is the constant attention to and criticism of what you wear, the backlash against your opinions or even your right to have an opinion and of course the constant threat of violence to yourself. And in Taylor's actual personal life there are even deadly threats to her supporters even if they are young children! (Deliso 2024; Dazio 2024). It's not a life for the faint of heart and maybe as Taylor has sung: "You wouldn't last an hour in the asylum where they raised me" (from her song *Who's Afraid of Little Old Me?*). Taylor has stated that as a society we tend to put our writers, artists and creative people through hell, watch what they create and then judge it, enjoying particularly watching artists in pain and even making up things to provoke the pain so they can watch it with even more enjoyment (Richardson 2024).

In the 4th century B.C. the Greek philosopher Plato in his work *The Republic* wrote of the need to pursue divine love which he said man could aspire to but never quite attain. It was a mystical area of the gods known as the *logos* which could only be reached by a step by step appreciation of beautiful things, then an appreciation of beautiful ideas, then the leading of a beautiful life and then finally just a taste of what it is like to experience divine love. Although it is in fact unattainable, one must pursue it to find true beauty and love. This is the pursuit that Taylor appears to go through in *Fortnight*, a goal through eras of time and terrible adversity, step by step towards the unattainable *logos*. This is the poet's choice and tragic fate and perfect love may be attained (if only briefly!) in the mind. "I love you," she says. "It's ruining my life".

Katarsis Stock/Shutterstock.com

FIGURE 48: Projection of what Plato looked like based on comparison of multiple images.

One of Taylor's obsessions in life seems to be using every day you have to the fullest ("I'm so productive" she sings in *I Can Do It With a Broken Heart*) and being all you can be because your time at your peak may be very limited and you should take mental pictures of your most wondrous moments and never forget them. She has as we have seen admitted to a mental block about looking too far ahead and knowing what the next step will be, and it is particularly hard when you are the most followed woman on the planet and your every single day is carefully chronicled and scrutinized as good AND bad by the media. You may not be able to do math or play the guitar like Segovia or read music at sight, but you may have an ability to follow the precepts of the *Dead Poets Society* and achieve greatness and indeed in that film one can definitely argue that all of the boys ended up standing up for what they believed in but paying a heavy price or sometimes the heaviest price-- their lives. Life is short and youth even shorter and the roadblocks to great achievement can be many. With her music, poetry and video imagery such as *Fortnight*, her anxieties, fears and depressions are laid out for us just exactly as she feels them, a surrealistic diary but also for her a process, self-proclaimed, of mental exorcism.

Perhaps the best explanation of the meaning of *Fortnight* is Taylor's brief poetic recitation at the end of one of my favorite songs of hers of epiphany: *Daylight*:

> "I want to be defined by the things that I love, not the things that I hate, not the things that I'm afraid of (*afraid of*), not the things that haunt me in the middle of the night, I just think that... You are what you love".

I'm grateful that I let Taylor Swift's poetry and visual imagery into my life and I am amazed at how much her work helps me to crystallize my own voyage through life even though most of it took place, as I have said, decades before she was born. I have heard over and over again from my student Swifties how Taylor has this remarkable ability to seem to be bringing into focus the story of their own lives over many years, especially through songs such as *Never Grow Up* or *The Best Day* which have influenced entire families! With *Fortnight*, whenever I hear it and especially see it, it triggers memory upon memory of famous people I experienced and worked with and moments of time that I should have taken more mental and physical snapshots of so that my hindsight would be clearer than it is now at my advanced age. I don't get that feeling from any other musical artist that I can think of and it is a sensation that I truly treasure.

EPILOGUE:

Many of my students, especially my female Swiftie students, also enjoy the films of Australian director Peter Weir, who has made numerous films in addition to the *Dead Poets Society* which we have mentioned above.

One that you may like is his second major film, made in 1975 and entitled *Picnic at Hanging Rock*. He was influenced by Richard Lester, the American director with whom I had worked briefly in 1955 when I was a child of 9 in live television in Philadelphia (another time I was a fly on the wall to history). Lester made a series of surrealist comedies in 1967/1968 and this led to Weir making the surreal and rarely seen *Homesdale* in 1971, a black comedy about the staff and guests at a strange island guest home.

In 1974 his horror comedy *The Cars That Ate Paris* was his first film that attracted some international attention as a horror comedy in which self-willed cars wreaked havoc. The film revealed his own fear of cars and of driving them but it was lambasted by the Melbourne film critics and, although it had its supporters, it was a commercial flop.

But in 1975 he found small funding from David Williams, who was then fronting an Australian exhibition chain, and Weir was able to try again. In an Australian field of generally poor quality films which were often full of sleaze he produced an art house classic that made a little money and has remained one of the most remarkable independent films ever. It also revolutionized the Australian film industry by opening the door to quality films being made there by a variety of young visionary directors both male and female.

The title of the film, *Picnic at Hanging Rock*, suggests both happiness and death, and set the tone for the movie which critics described as hypnotic, eerie, erotic, visually gorgeous, mysterious and deliberately ambiguous. *Variety*, the show business "bible", simply called it one of the most beautiful films ever made while Roger Ebert cited its "haunting mystery and buried sexual hysteria" (Ebert 1998).

I don't want to tell you too much about it and spoil it but I feel that after *Fortnight* it would make stimulating viewing for people who appreciate the subtleties of Taylor's work. On one level it is very simply the story of a group of school girls and their young female teacher in the area of Victoria, Australia around the year 1900 who go out from their remotely set school for a picnic by a rocky crag, get lost and are never found.

But on another level the film appears to be about the collision of later 19th century certainty and pomposity and several girls' desire to escape from the repressive confinement of the era and heed the call of nature. We are shown a host of meaningless rituals that are celebrated at the school (evoking the *Dead Poets Society* film) and like the boys these girls are forced into behaviors by parents who either want them to adhere to ways that won't embarrass their families or else the parents have placed their children out here and forgotten about them entirely which appears to be mostly the case.

Despite the illusion of propriety, this "educational establishment for young ladies" is awash with deception, most stunningly exemplified by the headmistress Mrs. Appleyard (Rachel Roberts) who is beset with financial difficulties and is rapidly becoming an alcoholic. She makes a good parallel with headmaster Mr. Nolan (Norman Lloyd) of the *Dead Poets Society* and incidentally in yet another parallel Norman Lloyd came to Arizona and taught a class with me about his own life about the same time he was making *Dead Poets Society*! He was Alfred Hitchcock's best friend and one of his television producers and of course a star in Hitchcock's famous *Saboteur* film. In real life he was as distinguished and formal about things as the character he played in the Hanging Rock film although he was much more fun to be around! By the way he died recently at the age of 106, the longest lived famous Hollywood actor anyone could remember!

But let me not digress from *Picnic*! One of the teachers is scurrying about getting involved in a clandestine sexual escapade with one of the few serviceable males of the area. The schoolgirls in the meantime are being laced up in body-strangling corsets as the image of Queen Victoria herself menaces them along with disapproving portraits of the pompous remote-looking founders of the institution. Although it is not spoken about, some of the girls are attracted to each other, as is the case of Sara (Margaret Nelson) for the beautiful Miranda (Anne-Louise Lambert) and perhaps the headmistress and her "masculine" assistant.

Hanging over the school are the desperate need of its occupants for escape, the obsessive chaperoning, the need for the young ladies to remain "intact" and the doctor who gets to check them for it, and the rare presence of boys who must remove their hats in their presence.

The picnic expedition to Hanging Rock thus builds up in the minds of the young ladies as a symbol of freedom and fuels their desire to climb higher and higher to soak in the sun-drenched nature of the heights and we watch as they strip off their clothing and free their bodies from their Victorian restraints both mental and physical to seek pure beauty and to find love. As they ascend, the movie is filmed in an ever so slight slow motion. But it is not just physical love they seek in leaving the group, although they can appreciate that too, but it is spiritual love, the pursuit of beauty, the Platonic *logos* or highest plain attainable or at least aspired to by humans which we have mentioned before in this essay.

For parallels to this, one can note Taylor's song *The Lakes*, the crucial final song in her *Folklore* album, a reference to the retreat of the English Victorian poets in the countryside and a celebration of nature as exemplified by William Wordsworth who is referenced in Taylor's song ("Tell me what are my words worth") and throughout the *Dead Poets Society* movie.

This Platonic *logos* which is Greek for "word" literally is the highest level of pure love and beauty possible and is considered in its purest form divine. So the picnic becomes a climb, a search for the highest plain or level possible that perhaps can only be sought in our dreams as beautiful Miranda tells us at the beginning

FIGURE 50: Australian stamp commemorating the film *Picnic at Hanging Rock*.

of the film, roughly quoting Edgar Allan Poe: "What we see and what we seem are but a dream, a dream within a dream."

And we are left to wonder what does it mean when it is discovered that one of the girls, Irma, has her corset missing on the mountain and eventually three girls and their teacher have vanished. The homely and constantly complaining Edith (Christine Schuler in her only film role) attempts to go with them but is not attuned to this higher world, constantly complains and is in the end completely ignored, left behind and totally abandoned. Only she of the five lost females is found.

Picnic at Hanging Rock is the female corollary to the all-male *Dead Poets Society* and a close relative to *Fortnight* that affords Swifties a remarkable visual and intellectual trip if they will choose to take it and reflect upon it. I really invite you to do so!

The *Fortnight* video and *Hanging Rock* both have echoes of a third century A.D. philosophy known as Neo-Platonism. In this a mere mortal can learn to aspire to the greatest heights, to virtually become like a god. Plato (427-348 B.C.) was an innovative thinker and founder of the Academy in Athens where he held his philosophical school and, among many other things, discoursed on how to find pure aesthetic love and beauty in his *Symposium.* In a statement evocative of *Fortnight,* he wrote:

"If man had eyes to see the true beauty….pure and clear and unalloyed, not clogged with the pollutions of mortality and all the colors and vanities of human life beholding beauty, he will be able to bring forth not images of beauty but realities for he had hold not of an image but of reality."(Plato, *Symposium* 183e)

When the girls in the film remove their confining clothing it is as if they are removing layers of consciousness, freeing their bodies from Victorian constraints and seeking the upward "climb" to what Plato termed the *logos.* In their upward search which they seem unable to stop doing for some mysterious reason they disappear into true beauty in which case the movie is completely allegorical just like the ending of *Fortnight* and we are left to wonder whether or not they find true love at that final arrival or if they are all just possessed by the power of nature and an ardent reaction to the oppressive nature of their environment.

For the Neo-Platonists of the post 250 A.D. Roman period the *logos* was shapeless and formless, a divine exalted source of beauty and love which they said exerts a pull and attraction to the intellect for those who will heed its call (its telephone call in *Fortnight*?). Intellect is for the Neo-Platonist group the most beautiful state of mind, the highest point to achieve before the *logos*, for the more that matter can dematerialize and lose its form the closer it resembles its original model: the idea. When the girls peer into the lake in *Picnic at Hanging Rock* and see their reflections dematerialize the more it is a step closer to the ultimate goal.

The Neo-Platonist movement was not only popular among the Romans of the time of the later emperors, especially in the mid third century A.D., but it was, surprisingly, also a big movement in 15th century Florence in Italy and was part of the revival during the Renaissance of the Greek and Roman classical traditions and part of a general movement known as Humanism which encouraged (and still encourages!) the study of the Humanities and the pursuit of ancient culture, as if the Greeks and especially now the Romans (since this took place in Italy) were important thinkers to be learned from.

The Medici family, many of whom were fabulously rich bankers, became the leaders of Florence and promoted this Renaissance Humanism and thought that their beloved city of Florence could be a new Athens of classical antiquity. Cosimo de Medici was a ruler who unlike others in surrounding areas of power actually read the surviving works of Plato (!) and his personal tutor was none other than Marsilio Ficino who was a leading Neo-Platonist!

Morphart Creation/Shutterstock.com

FIGURE 51: Coronation of Cosimo De' Medici in 1569, by Philips Galle, after Jan van der Straet, 1583 In the Sistine Chapel, Cosimo De' Medici was crowned Grand Duke of Tuscany by Pius V in 1569.

Lorenzo de' Medici, the most powerful member of the family and the dominant influence in Florence, lived on a steep hill and often contemplated attaining the *logos* in the stillness of summer. After his death in 1492 Italy entered into an age of warfare with France, Spain and Germany which put an end to this Golden Age of classical (Greek and Roman) revival but before that happened artists labored in the beautiful Medici villas to document the Medici's beliefs and support their restful contemplation.

Lorenzo was the principal patron of many artists, among them Sandro Botticelli and of course Michelangelo. Botticelli (1444-1510) was noted for his mystical creations in Medici villas and his ability to combine Greco-Roman mythology and the Christian love for the new Athens that Florence had become (Debenedetti 1995), reminiscent of a painting of a girl with a guardian angel that is shown in Sara's room in our *Picnic at Hanging Rock* movie.

Botticelli's *Birth of Venus* (ca. 1484-1486) is one of the most famous Renaissance paintings, depicting the goddess of love and beauty as she is born fully grown rising from the sea (Venus *anadyomene* in ancient Greek) off the coast of the island of Cyprus (just a few miles from where coincidentally I used to conduct archaeological excavations!). She is naked, apparently weightless and blown by gentle breezes towards the shore as she perches on a large scallop shell that brings her up from the deep, a spiritual apparition of beauty meant for contemplation. An attendant brings clothing for the goddess at the right). There is a magnificent rocky place on Cyprus traditionally identified as the spot, in between the town of Paphos and my former site of Kourion.

Credit: Alamy Images.

FIGURE 52: Sandro Botticelli (1445–1510). *Birth of Venus* ca. 1482 Florence, Galerie des Offices.

This image when contemplated by the Neo-Platonists would be likely to inspire one to the appreciation of pure beauty and to pursue the *logos* as this painting has inspired viewers to do for centuries now (Wallis and Gerson 1995).

The "Venus" of *Picnic at Hanging Rock* is the beautiful goddess-like Miranda and her "birth" occurs at the start of the film as she awakens at the school for young ladies and is attended to by Sara as if she is a goddess seemingly in possession of secret knowledge and Miranda announces mysteriously: "I won't be here much longer." Miranda seems to be in touch with nature as birds rush about her as she emerges from a carriage amid gently rustling wind, the excessive heat of the area and red flowers. There is even a visual of Botticelli's *Venus* painting used briefly in the film, as reproduced in an art picture book the girls look at and from which they seem to get inspiration for the climb.

Sculptures of Cupid and Psyche flank the steps, an ancient symbol of love and the soul seeking union and a Neo-Platonist and Renaissance symbol *par excellence* (Harrison 2010; Kingsley-Smith 2010). Saint Valentine also appears in the film, for on Saint Valentine's Day the young ladies hold up an image of the saint and attend a ritual meal for him. There Miranda cuts into a heart-shaped cake with a knife, foreshadowing that a sacrifice will

be coming, a death and rebirth, great suffering and the search for true love (reminiscent of the heart sign Taylor Swift gives to and receives back from her fans at her concerts!). It is at this gathering that Miranda says she won't be there much longer and there her devoted acolyte Sara is told she needs to find somebody else to love.

In this film primordial ancient forces appear to have the power to attract the chosen girls and Hanging Rock is described as "magnetic". Mysterious and remote and waiting since "the beginning of time", it is not for the unchosen or uninitiated and it is said to have poisonous ants and venomous snakes.

D-VISIONS/Shutterstock.com

FIGURE 53: Georghe Zamfir in 2019.

The music that accompanies this is rustic too. The main theme is played by Georghe Zamfir, the famous Romanian pan flute musician. The pan flute (or pan pipes) is the symbol of the woodland god Pan who often accompanied mystic rituals in antiquity such as the cult of the brides of the god Dionysus.

There is about the film a sense of impending doom. Clocks tick with amplified sounds and then inexplicably disappear from the sound track. The knife cuts the heart-shaped Valentine's cake. Watches stop at noon, the time of the high heat of a summer's day. The schoolgirls are shot from dizzying low angles, curtains rustle and flies quietly buzz. Later on, ants appear on a giant cake and a swan appears at

Sebastian Schuster/Shutterstock.com

FIGURE 54: **The Greek and Roman god Pan with his pan flute.**

the foot of a bed. Two different young people end up with the same cut on their faces. Much of the dialog is enigmatic. The three girls and their instructor who head off for a further excursion up the rock appear to move behind Miranda in slow motion. A missing girl's location is described metaphorically by one of the survivors of the further trip, chubby Edith, as "about as far away as those dead trees over there". A groundskeeper when asked what he knows says "there's some questions got answers and some haven't" and someone observes that "the end of summer is like someone dying." And of course the very name Miranda, who is the focal point of the film, means marvelous one worthy to be admired.

There is also a sense that the rock may only exert its power under certain conditions, when a variety of things are in conjunction, such as the sun, the summer heat, or an image of Venus and it is observed that "everything begins and ends in exactly the right time and place." There is also the mystique of water which is crossed by Miranda when the climb begins. Reflections in water make reality fall apart and shimmer and distort and forces one to see material things differently.

Picnic at Hanging Rock is about people being driven by powerful romantic urges that influence the young girls' entire surrounding environment just as the lovers in *Fortnight*. As the laboratory probes Taylor's brain her quest for love is revealed to us even as she is constantly aware of the danger that will happen when she trespasses into that territory ("I love you. It's ruining my life") and yet she is drawn into the whirlwind of the fortnight of love and its mystical and overwhelmingly powerful attraction. Taylor's search is similar to Miranda's: irresistible, fatalistic, supernatural, powerful and proceeding hypnotically towards a rendezvous with divine love…or death…or both.

It was noted in our essay *Why Do Swifties Cry?* that Plato was the mentor of another great thinker of antiquity: Aristotle. It was the latter who wrote the now mostly lost *Poetics* which contained significant discourses on the theater and poetry (Burton 2023). As we have seen earlier, Aristotle talks about how literary tragedy uses emotion to effect *katharsis* which means that there is a character or characters we feel sympathy for and want to help because they are in a terrible and fearful predicament, just as Taylor is in the Tortured Poets laboratory.

FIGURE 55: Portrait of Aristotle on old Greek drachma banknote.

Aristotle also mentions something called *hamartia* which involves some kind of terrible thing that happens to a protagonist because of an error made by him, perhaps a character flaw or an error in judgement. In the case of *Fortnight* it is the error of the affair with Post Malone which leads to Taylor being confined, examined and even tortured until a sort of *katharsis* is reached. So *Fortnight* satisfies the essential idea of the pursuit of a mystical *logos* of love as exemplified by Plato's *Symposium* and it also follows the advice of Aristotle, the pupil of Plato, in his *Poetics* to include *katharsis* and *hamartia* in one's dramatic work.

Taylor has also given us a tribute to filmmaker Peter Weir and his movie *Dead Poets Society*. Weir is a filmmaker who has used Neo-Platonic imagery in his *Picnic at Hanging Rock* film, a film that was a kind of predecessor to *Dead Poets*. She has even used two cast members from *Dead Poets* in *Fortnight*. Her fascination with classical tragedy and myth is also borne out in her song *Cassandra* which I discuss elsewhere in this volume as it pertains to the Trojan War and to the Kanye West and Kim Kardashian episodes, but let it be known that Taylor has classical Greek and Roman thoughts in her head quite frequently, enough apparently to state that she does indeed know something about Aristotle.

Where did all this classical scholarship come from? It suggests to me that the six years before with Joe Alwyn (2017-2023) might have been fruitful intellectually and appropriate for pandemic isolation but difficult to navigate socially for her after the pandemic had dissipated. Joe was introspective even from youth, it has been reported, and was not someone who wanted to be in the public eye but who nonetheless contributed to Taylor's erudition (he has a degree in English Literature from a fine school) and he participated significantly in her *Folklore* and *Evergreen* albums as a secret composer, deep-voiced vocalist and pianist under an assumed name. But it appears that he was too reserved and enigmatic for her to get really close to, especially since her concerts were so flamboyant and she is such a dominant public figure. Taylor is constantly learning and it is likely that she would have taken advantage of the isolation with Joe to benefit from his fine education but, typically, she likely sampled what he had to offer and found ways to wonderfully incorporate it into pandemic era music magic.

NOTES

Adler, Michael H). *The Writing Machine: A History of the Typewriter* (Routledge: New York 1973)

Aesthetics 2021. "Clara Bow to Russian Lips: Lip Trends Through The Years," *Aesthetics by Design* 2-2-2021 https://aestheticsbydesign.com/news-blog/2021/1/27/clara-bow-to-russian-lips-lip-trends-through-the-years

Atwal Sanj, "Taylor Swift's Eras Tour breaks record as highest-grossing music tour ever," *Guinness World Records* 12-12-2023 https://www.guinnessworldrecords.com/news/2023/12/taylor-swifts-eras-tour-breaks-record-as-highest-grossing-music-tour-ever-762285

Beckford, Avil, "SummaReview of The Time Machine by HG Wells," *The Invisible Mentor* 1-23-2024 https://theinvisiblementor.com/summareview-of-time-machine-by-hg-wells/

Bernabe, Angeline Jane and Brittany Berkowitz, "Taylor Swift's 'The Tortured Poets Department' double album is out now," *ABC News* 4-19-2024 https://abcnews.go.com/GMA/Culture/taylor-swift-tortured-poets-department-album/story?id=109014004

Bloch, Emily, " No, the missing '1' on Taylor's typewriter isn't an Easter egg", *Philadelphia Inquirer* 4-22-2024 Inquirer.com https://www.inquirer.com › News › Nation World

Borland, Charlie, "The Power of Diagonal Lines in Photographs," *New Photography School* 2-5-2024 https://newphotographyschool.substack.com/p/the-power-of-diagonal-lines-in-photographs

Brockington, Ariana, "Taylor Swift says 'Florida!!!' was inspired by 'Dateline'. Here's why," *Today Entertainment News* 4-25-2024 https://www.yahoo.com/entertainment/taylor-swift-says-florida-inspired-001637652.html

Burton, Neel, *The Gang of Three: Socrates, Plato, Aristotle* (London: Acheron Press 2023)

Butcher, William, *Jules Verne: The Definitive Biography* (London: Thunder's Mouth Press 2006)

Campbell, Robert J. and Szatmary, David P. Haight-Ashbury, *Psychedelics, and the Birth of Acid Rock* (Excelsior Editions, Buffalo: State University of New York Press 2023)

Carmi, Ziv, "Until We Meet Again: Victorian Mourning Practices," *The Gettysburg Compiler* 2-24-2022 https://www.google.com/search?client=firefox-b-1-d&q=ziv+carmi+until+we+meet+again+mourning

Celiberti, Joanne, "Mid-Late Victorian Mourning Dress," *Lancaster History* 10-6-2021 https://www.lancasterhistory.org/victorian-mourning-dress/

Chambers, Paul, *Bedlam: London's Hospital for the Mad* (The History Press: New York 2019)

Chan, Anna, "Watch Post Malone Freak Out Over How Typewriters Work in Taylor Swift's 'Fortnight' Behind-the-Scenes Video," *Billboard* 6-21-2024 https://www.billboard.com/music/music-news/taylor-swift-fortnight-behind-the-scenes-post-malone-video-1235715140/

Cohen, Sandra E., "GOOD WILL HUNTING. Whys of Robin Williams' Suicide, Self-Hate Must Be Healed?" *Characters on the Couch* 9-8-2014 https://charactersonthecouch.com/hunting-for-the-whys-of-depression-and-suicide-what-self-hate-has-to-do-with-it/

Corn, Joseph J. and Brian Horrigan, *Yesterday's Tomorrows: Past Visions of the American Future* (Johns Hopkins Press: 1984)

Cook, Paul, "The Birth of Punk," *The Independent, Online Edition* 4-27-2006 http://enjoyment.independent.co.uk/music/features/article324977.ece

Daniels, Karu F., "Taylor Swift Drops Behind the Scenes "Fortnight" Footage," *New York Daily News* 6-21-24 https://www.nydailynews.com/2024/06/21/taylor-swift-behind-the-scenes-fortnight-music-video/

Dazio, Stephanie, "The plot to attack Taylor Swift's Vienna shows was intended to kill thousands, a CIA official says," *AP* 8-29-2024 https://apnews.com/article/taylor-swift-cia-vienna-concerts-foiled-attack-7e454af63efcff2a3ab0a20c718aba8d

Debenedetti, Ana, *Botticelli: Artist and Designer* (Renaissance Lives) (Reaktion Books: London, 1995)

Deliso, Meredith, "Teen accused of deadly UK stabbing at Taylor Swift-themed event now faces terror charge: Police," *ABC News* 10-29-2024 https://abcnews.go.com/International/teen-accused-deadly-uk-stabbing-terror-charge/story?id=115268460

Ebbett, Kathleen, "Everybody Poops, But These Artists Made It Into Masterpieces," *Global Citizen* 1-30-2015 https://www.globalcitizen.org/en/content/this-art-is-shit-literally/

Ebert, Roger, "Picnic at Hanging Rock," *RogerEbert.co*m 8-2-1998 https://www.rogerebert.com/reviews/great-movie-picnic-at-hanging-rock-1975

Edwards, Roxanne, "Carthage: A Mosaic of Ancient Tunisia (Exhibition)," *American Museum of Natural History* 12-17-2018 https://data.library.amnh.org/archives-authorities/id/amnhc_5000401

Filgate, Michele, "Literary self-loathing: How Jonathan Franzen, Elizabeth Gilbert and more keep it at bay," *Salon* 12-1-2013 https://www.salon.com/2013/12/01/literary_self_loathing_how_jonathan_franzen_elizabeth_gilbert_and_more_keep_it_at_bay/

Fowler, Richard and Galvani, Luigi, *Experiments and Observations Relative to the Influence Lately Discovered by M. Galvani and Commonly Called Animal Electricity* (Paperback) (Franklin Classics: Stansted Mountfitchet, England, 2018

Fraquoh and Franchomme, "The Guide to the Nehru Jacket," *Attire Club* 3-5-2016 https://attireclub.org/2016/03/05/guide-nehru-jacket/

Fritz, Penelope H., "The Master of Suspense: Inside Alfred Hitchcock's Thrilling Film Career," *Martin Cid Magazine* 11-4-2020 https://www.martincid.com/movies/alfred-hitchcock/

Gentry, Alex, "My favorite quote from Dead Poets Society (with a quote from Walt Whitman)," *Medium* 1-13-2017 https://medium.com/@gentryalex13/my-favorite-quote-from-dead-poets-society-with-a-quote-from-walt-whitman-9b6505f0190b

Gorvett, Zaria, "How modern singing was invented," *BBC* 5-11-2023 https://www.bbc.com/future/article/20230511-how-singing-has-changed-over-the-centuries

Greenberg, Mike, "What Was the Sphinx in Greek Mythology?," *Mythology Source* 3-22-2021 https://mythologysource.com/sphinx-in-greek-mythology/

Grob, Charles S. and Grigsby, Jim, *Handbook of Medical Hallucinogens* (Guilford Press: New York, 2022)

Guffey, Elizabeth, *Retro: The Culture of Revival* (Reaktion Books: London 2006)

Haeberle, Rob, "Some of My Favorite Design Quotes," *Linked In* 3-27-2015 https://www.linkedin.com/pulse/some-my-favorite-design-quotes-rob-haeberle

Harrison, Stephen, "Cupid and Psyche" *The Oxford Encyclopedia of Ancient Greece and Rome* (Oxford University Press, 2010), p. 339. https://people.com/travis-kelce-says-he-doesnt-mind-being-girlfriend-taylor-swift-arm-candy-8706796

Hatcher, Kirsty and Dave Quinn, "Travis Kelce Says He Doesn't Mind Being Taylor Swift's Arm Candy: 'It's the Life I Chose,'" *People* 9-5-2024 https://people.com/travis-kelce-says-he-doesnt-mind-being-girlfriend-taylor-swift-arm-candy-8706796

Henderson, Austin, "How Do Lava Lamps Work? The Science Behind Liquid Motion," *howstuffworks* 9-29-2023 https://science.howstuffworks.com/innovation/science-questions/how-does-lava-lamp-work.htm

Johannesson, Asgeir Theodor, "Socratic Irony: What Is It?," *Academia* 2024 https://www.academia.edu/16868322/Socratic_Irony_What_Is_It

Kingsley-Smith, Jane, *Cupid in Early Modern Literature and Culture* (Cambridge University Press, 2010)

Kneeland, Timothy and Carol A. B. Warren, *Pushbutton Psychiatry: A Cultural History of Electric Shock Therapy in America*, Updated Paperback Edition 1st Edition (Routledge: London 2009)

Lewry, Fraser, "Taylor Swift once dressed up as Kiss legend Ace Frehley to prank Keith Urban during a live show", *Classic Rock* 2-1-2024 https://www.loudersound.com/news/taylor-swift-ace-frehley

McGough, Peter, *I've Seen the Future and I'm Not Going: The Art Scene and Downtown New York in the 1980s*, (Knopf: New York, 2019)

Maxford, Howard, *Hammer Complete* (McFarland Books: Jefferson, North Carolina, 2018)

Moore, Steven, "A Short History of the Top Hat," *The English Manner* 10-30-2023 https://theenglishmanner.com/insights/history-of-the-top-hat/

Moretta, John Anthony, *The Hippies: A 1960s History* (McFarland: Jefferson, North Carolina, 2017)

Neese, Joseph, "10 Quotes from Robin Williams That Teach Us Everything," *MSNBC* 8-11-2015 https://www.msnbc.com/msnbc/10-quotes-robin-williams-teach-us-everything-about-life-msna659051

Norwin, Alyssa, "Taylor Swift Flashes Smile Singing About 'Dating the Boy on the Football Team' Amid Travis Romance," *Y Entertainment News* 6-3-2024 https://www.yahoo.com/entertainment/taylor-swift-flashes-smile-singing-095035111.html\

Perez, Lexy, "Taylor Swift Details Meaning Behind 'The Tortured Poets Department' Songs," *Hollywood Reporter* 4-22-2024 https://www.hollywoodreporter.com/news/music-news/taylor-swift-explains-tortured-poets-department-songs-1235878743/

Richardson, Kalia, "Taylor Swift Reveals Meaning Behind Songs in 'The Tortured Poets Department'," *Rolling Stone* https://www.rollingstone.com/music/music-news/taylor-swift-tortured-poets-department-song-meanings-1235008538/

Rogers, Kristen, "What Robin Williams' widow wants you to know about the future of Lewy body dementia," *CNN* 8-17-2022 https://www.cnn.com/2022/07/01/health/lewy-body-dementia-robin-williams-life-itself-wellness/index.html

Schillaci, Sophie, "Travis Kelce Plays 'Kiss, Marry, Kill' With Taylor Swift, Katy Perry and Ariana Grande in Resurfaced Interview," *ET* 9-26-2023 https://www.etonline.com/travis-kelce-plays-kiss-marry-kill-with-taylor-swift-katy-perry-and-ariana-grande-in-resurfaced

Shelley, Peter, *Frances Farmer: The Life and Films of a Troubled Star* (McFarland: Jefferson, North Carolina, 2010)

Soren, David, American Vaudeville: A Celebration (Kendall Hunt: Dubuque, 2020)

Soren, David, Delaney Fisher, Roberto Montagnetti, David Pickel, Jordan Wilson, *What Were They Afraid Of? The Cemetery of the Infants Near Lugnano in Teverina* (Kendall Hunt: Dubuque, 2024)

Soren, David and Jamie James, *Kourion: The Search for a Lost Roman City* (Doubleday: New York, 1988)

Tannenbaum, Emily, "Joe Alwyn Subtly Responds to 'The Black Dog' Rumors in First Comments on the Taylor Swift Breakup", *Glamour Newsletter* 6-15-2024. https://www.glamour.com/story/joe-alwyn-breaks-silence-taylor-swift-breakup-the-black-dog

Tousignant, Lauren, "Post Malone Discovering a Typewriter is my Personal 'American Gothic'," *Jezebel* 6-21-2024 https://www.jezebel.com/post-malone-discovering-a-typewriter-is-my-personal-american-gothic

Wallis, R, T, and Lloyd P. Gerson, *Neoplatonism* (Hackett Classics: Indianapolis 1995)

Watts, Marina, "61 Taylor Swift Lyrics About Midnights and The Nighttime from 2006 To Today, *Bustle* 10-21-2022 https://www.bustle.com/entertainment/taylor-swift-lyrics-about-midnights-night-am-songs-albums

10

When the Devil Rolls Her Dice

By Dave Hahn

(Dave Hahn is an adjunct professor of philosophy at SUNY Geneseo where he teaches intro-ductory classes as well as a course on Skepticism, Conspiracy Theories, and Critical Thinking. His PhD dissertation was a philosophical analysis of the subject of conspiracy theories which he defended via the internet due to Covid restrictions. He is a regular contributor to "The Skep-tic" the UK's oldest skeptical magazine. His writing has also appeared in the Skeptical Inquirer and Open Court's Pop Culture and Philosophy series (including the recent "Taylor Swift and Philosophy"). Dave Hahn lives with his family in Buffalo, NY).

It's difficult to pinpoint why we appreciate certain things. First contact is usually the answer, I fell in love with Swift's music when I heard a certain song. That does not answer how a person ended up encountering it in the first place. You heard a song on a streaming platform, clicked on the "heart," and it gave you another song. I didn't come to her on my own. For that I have a friend of mine to blame (credit). My daughter and I went for a mid-afternoon coffee treat; the worker, a friend of ours, told my girl that she needed to tell me to get the album 1989 to listen to. It was 2014, the café was selling it, and I told my daughter that we would get it on our next trip to the library.

Our very next trip to the library we walked to the music section and began searching for the album which we eventually found…in the section labelled "country." I dislike country music as a genre. It's just not to my taste and I was beginning to think that my friend was engaging in a first strike in some kind of elaborate prank war. It never dawned on me that the library could have placed the album in the wrong section. I was not entirely ignorant of the singer, I knew the various pop-culture things about her but none of that really stuck with me. Nevertheless I made a deal with my kid and slid the CD into the car to hear, on purpose, the first track. The first one that played was "Welcome to New York" which, to be honest, is kind of meh. You can tell me all about the backstory of the song and how this represents a declaration of separation from her strictly country history, whatever; the song is fine. The second track played and I was hooked.

What grabs me about her are the lyrics. I'll skip the more pop-bait songs, for example, I think "Bad Blood" is the weakest song on the album, but I get the metaphor. "Wildest Dreams" on the other hand, is, my favorite song on the album. It does such a wonderful job in delivering a very complicated and sad message. She recognizes that the possibility that she/we may just end up as someone's memory. Then with an almost Stoic acceptance she wishes that the memory be at least a fond one. That's the kind of thematic singing that really hit me.

I was hooked, following up that album with "Reputation" which represented a drastic tone shift that has come to define her "Eras" era. Yet, somehow, I missed "Lover," probably because I was busy wrapping up my PhD dissertation while the subject of my writing seemed to be devastating society.

Am I a "Swiftie"? No. I don't deny this out of some desire for academic separation between pop-culture and my holy ivory tower. I do not consider myself a "Swiftie" because I have made a conscious and active attempt to not get involved in the personal lives of people that I do not know. I had no idea that "London Boy" was about a specific person, and I was completely ignorant that she had even a single date with the actor who plays Loki. For years I held out as long as possible but politics forced my hand.

THE PATH IS TREACHEROUS

The political sphere began adopting a very complicated conspiracy theory surrounding Taylor Swift, President Joe Biden, and the NFL. This meant that suddenly the woman's voice that soothes the rage I feel when grading papers is now going to be the subject of those papers. Now, I had to learn about her personal life in ways that I didn't want to before. From my perspective, I don't see a reason to know any of the intimate details of her (or any other person's life). This isn't an ethical position; it's just a preference.

How I arrived at the point where this article will now be my 5th with Swift as the subject, is intrinsically related to my academic focus: conspiracy theories, misinformation, and pseudoscience. What is important to remember about conspiracy theories is that anyone can make one. They are unsupported explanations of events and phenomena so there is no barrier to making up a theory (Napolitano and Reuter 2020). The barrier for conspiracy theorizing is not creating the theories; it's in getting them the attention that they want.

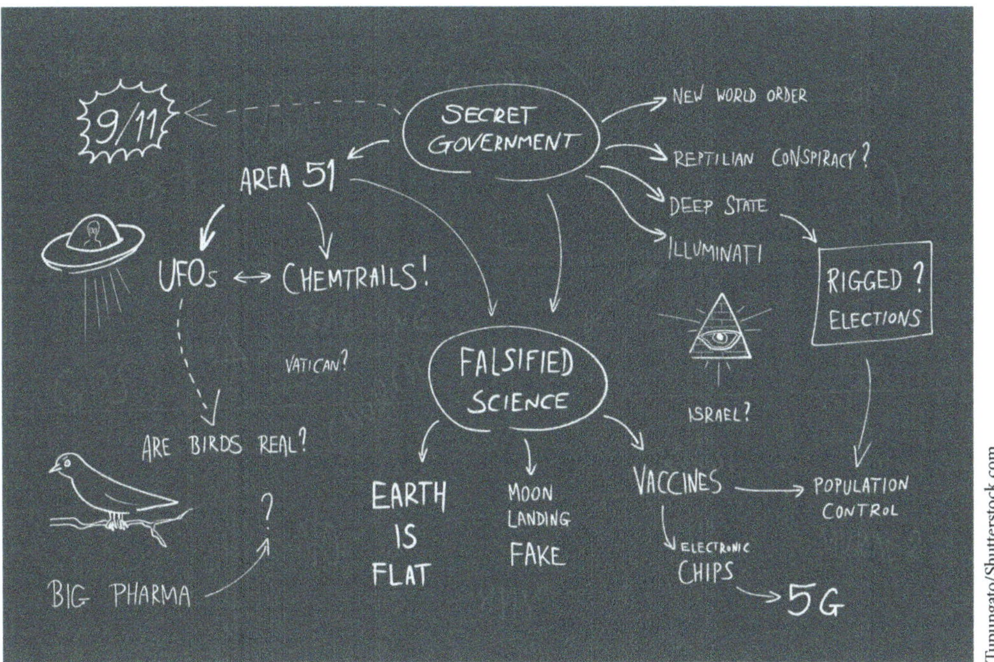

FIGURE 1: Conspiracy theory blackboard chart with paranoia theories about illuminati, reptilians, rigged elections, chemtrails and more.

A conspiracy theory needs a few things: it needs an official story that it can be the alternative explanation for (Keeley 1999). It needs an emotional appeal that "hooks" the audience into it.[1] We think of conspiracy theories as the odd things that estranged relatives believe, but Dentith observes that we are all susceptible to the irrational thinking that causes us to believe in conspiracy theories (Dentith 2014, 2017). If we've ever believed something just because it "felt good" we are falling into the trap of conspiracism. The Eras Tour never came to my hometown of Buffalo NY, but was there a reason for it? It is possible that the tour planners couldn't make it work logistically, perhaps because stops were already in nearby cities so that it didn't make sense to also have a show in Buffalo. The facilities could not have been able to handle the tour's needs; I don't know; this type of thing is entirely outside of my knowledge base. However, because the tour's US dates were taking place during the NFL season, and the Buffalo Bills are a conference rival with Kansas City, there were some that believed this was the reason. She wasn't going to stop in Buffalo because her boyfriend played for a rival team.

It's a silly theory. However, it will grab some people because it's a much easier reason to grasp. Tour logistics are complicated, planning is complicated; this was the first major tour of any musical act since the pandemic, and sometimes cities just get skipped. I have friends that drove to Philadelphia who wished they didn't have to spend the travel money to see her, and I have friends that have tickets to the Toronto show who would rather not have to deal with the border. The other explanation is just easier to accept and just be happy for her, but it doesn't make sense, especially considering Swift left her concert in a different country to fly to Buffalo to watch Kelce's team play the Bills in January of 2024 (although not wanting to have an outdoor concert in the Buffalo winter does make sense, but we do have an indoor arena).

Conspiracy theories feed off popularity, so the hook needs to be something strong to grab people who would otherwise not engage with them. For major political and historical events, the hook is readily available—the conspiracy theory explains an event that is difficult to understand especially in the immediate aftermath or even during it (Prooijen and Dijk 2014). Conspiracy theories concerning the pandemic were easily adopted because it was an emotionally draining time and in the early days there was no scientific consensus on what to do. The constellation of conspiracy theories surrounding events like the assassination of John F. Kennedy and the attacks on 9/11/01 served to provide a strange comfort in

---

1. There many different reasons that people get hooked into conspiracy theories: the need to feel special or unique (Imhoff and Lamberty 2016, Lantian et. al 2017), political paranoia (Bale 2007), the need for order in the world (Brotherton and French 2015); the list goes on and is outside the scope of this chapter.

the face of national tragedy. It's easier to believe that forces "allowed" 9/11 to happen than that the US had no defense against this kind of attack, just as it is easier to believe that the CIA/military killed a young president who was friends with people like Frank Sinatra than some oddball loner that even the USSR sent back.[2] The hook is easy to establish with these events. If you pay even moderate attention to conspiracy theories this should make sense.

I don't mean to claim that the people that believe them are emotional wrecks who can't think straight. I've talked with people who believe in a wide variety of different theories and who legitimately believe them even though it seems absurd. I know a person who earnestly believes that the Earth is flat. My intention is not to belittle conspiracy theorists, but to point out that this emotional attachment works best when the event is big. No one is going to care about your conspiracy theory that the traffic lights are always red on your way home, even if you blame the Illuminati, the Freemasons, the Deep State, or the International Jewish Cabal.

Another way to get your conspiracy theory some traction is to make outrageous claims about the most well-known individuals in the world. It's a cheap way to grab attention in that you just place that individual into an existing conspiracy theory where the only creative thing that the theorist has done is swap out some proper nouns.

Conspiracy theories are not equal (Barkun 2003). Some conspiracy theories cover anything and literally everything, while others tend to isolate themselves to one event. This is important to understand before we dive into the claims about Taylor Swift. This matters because as the theory grows the more parts and people are necessary to make it function (Grimes 2016). Claiming that a particular tour stop, for example, was artificially sold out is much different from claiming that a singer's entire career is inorganic. The former theory is possible, the latter is so incredibly improbable that it borders on impossible. While one can claim that Taylor Swift's popularity is artificial, that claim is not a simple claim. There are so many people affected by this claim that it stretches reason to think that it could be true. Even claiming that the current tour is artificially popular would mean that an incredible infrastructure and bureaucracy would have to exist just to manage it. What happened last year were cheap grabs at attention for theories that were not thought out by the people that were pushing them.

---

2. Also to be clear, because one should never introduce a conspiracy theory like this without immediately debunking it, there is no supporting evidence that either of these two events happened any differently from the official story.

WHAT YOU MADE ME DO

To understand the cultural obsession with Taylor Swift we have to take a step backward. In the years before the pandemic, the pop-music stage was rather empty. I don't mean to say that there were no singer/performers at all; but that pop-music didn't have a "ruler." In the '80s, the clear queen of pop was Madonna, in the late '90s/'00s there was the Britney-Christina rivalry, but for a great while there existed many musical acts that, while popular, never ascended to that level. There was Beyoncé, Lady Gaga, and Katy Perry in the '10s; but no true monarch. Behind their "game of thrones" were singers like Rihanna, Shakira, and a young woman coming up in the country music genre.

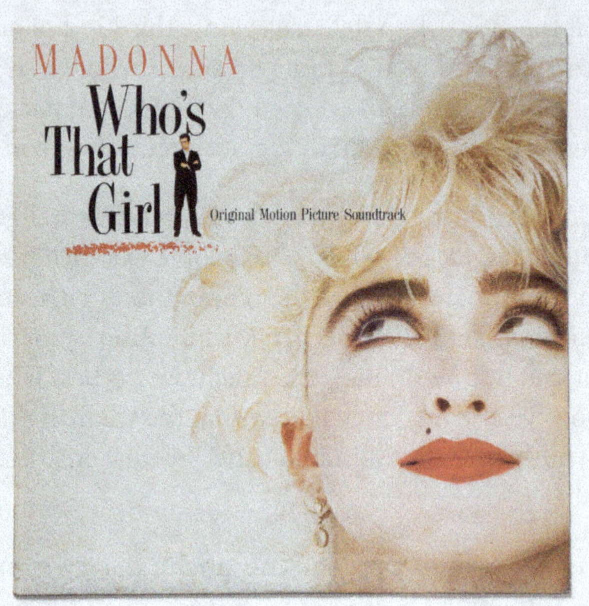

FIGURE 2: *Who's That Girl* by singer Madonna is a soundtrack, released in 1987.

In the above section, I mentioned that I don't like country, so I had no idea who she was and only saw the headline about Kanye West's stunt well after it happened. In that group of performers there are some pretty solid albums and some great performers. Maybe the era of the music monarch was over…and then the pandemic hit. As someone that studies conspiracy theories, the pandemic was a "gold mine" for material but an absolute disaster for society. Prior to the pandemic the album releases from the would-be contenders weren't as well received. Lady Gaga's follow up to Art Pop was a country inspired album "Joanne" (2016—I'm not counting the soundtrack to "A Star Is Born") which had favorable reviews but nothing like her previous releases. Similarly with Christina Aguilera's "Liberation" (2018) garnering favorable reviews but not in comparison to her mega-popular efforts.

Swift on the other hand, seemed to have a steady increase in both popularity and critical reception leading up to the pandemic. "Lover" (2019) is followed by "Folklore" (2020) and then "Evermore" (2020). In the span of a year and half she released three full albums and a musical documentary about one of those albums within the same span of time that people were in their homes because of the pandemic. What the "haters" fail to understand is that while everyone took the time off, she put the work in and created a pressure cooker situation that would directly lead to the record-annihilating Eras Tour and a steady stream of album releases. I'm not going to get into the "Taylor's Version" dispute; that's for someone else with a legal mind to do, but I do know that she did her best to keep her fans engaged with releases, "Fearless (Taylor's Version)" is released in early 2021, later that year is "Red (Taylor's Version)," and the next year is "Midnights." This album was promoted by a comprehensive and cryptic series of clues on her various social media accounts. When the tour begins on March 17th of 2023, it's not just that people were ready for the tour --they were thirsting for it. After five album releases in as many years people had her music simmering in their brains. It is not a mystery why the tour was so popular and why Swift is so adored.

So, when I sit down to write about a singer, I'm not writing with someone at the dawn of their career. By 2023 Swift has been in the public spotlight for seventeen years. She's been building her career that entire time. Couple this with her scandal-free public persona that is only marred by tabloid over-interest in her dating life and there is little that has stemmed her popularity. The thought that her tour would be *that* popular was not something that anyone could have anticipated and then the conspiracy theories began.

WILDEST DREAMS

Looking at her current popularity, it was inevitable that someone would begin to claim that "something seems odd about this." Her popularity in the Fall of 2023 was driven by her near omnipresence in Celebrity/Entertainment news and this, as I mentioned above, is a primary motivator in choosing conspiracy theory subjects. The popularity was "helped" by her relationship with Travis Kelce, Kelce is a star in his own right, but he earned the ire of extremist conspiracy theorists for his endorsement of the Black Lives Matter movement, LGBTQIA equality, and serving as a spokesman for Pfizer's Covid-19 vaccine. Kelce, as an NFL star player, does not fit the stereotype that extremist conspiracy theorists have of people supporting these causes. Skinny, bespectacled, long haired, liberal guys are the people that support those causes, not muscular, short-haired, football players with Superbowl rings.

As much as I'll admit that I'm a fan of hers, I'm not really a fan of his. I've nothing against him, I'm not a football guy. The only NFL football I see is when it's on the television at a place that I'm at. This is especially difficult in Buffalo, NY as for the first time in a very long time the Bills are actually good; and I only keep up on it to stay culturally relevant. I'm aware of who plays in the Superbowl, and I'll find out who won, but that's only because it's a news item. Despite this, I did know of Travis Kelce because Amazon Prime had a sports' documentary series about him. I knew who he was, I figured he was good because of the series, but that's it.

It's a troubling thing for the conspiracy theorist to have to watch, and possibly root for, someone that supports the causes that they believe are part of the conspiracy. Then, that person and a singer who had the audacity to make political statements to her incredibly vocal and zealous fan base are romantically entangled—it became too much to just ignore. There must be something else going on. It's obvious that there's more to this story, but what was the "more" to that story…well the conspiracy theories never got into those details. When he links up with Swift, it becomes a little easier to swallow if he's under her thrall, but even then, it made little sense.

FIGURE 3: Taylor Swift, Travis Kelce on cover of National Enquirer Magazine. The international pop star and the Kansas City Chiefs tight end are frequent topics of celebrity gossip.

The conversation in conspiracy circles revolves primarily around the perception of power that Taylor Swift wields. The conspiratorial extremists note that Swift's political endorsements seem to favor people and causes they despise. Her first endorsement was that of a Democratic Senatorial candidate named Phil Bredesen in 2018 when she wrote: "In the past I've been reluctant to publicly voice my political opinions…but due to several events in my life and in the world in the past two years, I feel very differently about that now…"

The post continues stating that "any form of discrimination based on sexual orientation is WRONG"…and that "the systemic racism we still see in this country towards people of color is terrifying, sickening, and prevalent…[3]" She goes on to explain that she cannot vote for someone whose values do not align with hers and that her fans should vote for the individual that aligns with their values.

As far as a statement of political views goes it's clear, direct, and a bit neutral. She tells her fans who she is voting for and why, but then does not go as far as telling her fans to vote for the same candidate. I would not go so far as to say that it is an entirely neutered statement; it's very clear what she is implying or else she would not have said anything. This we can contrast with her contemporaries such as Lady Gaga.

Gaga's advocacy for LGBTQIA+ was extremely vocal. During the tour for her *Born this Way* album she told her audiences to pressure

FIGURE 4: Lady Gaga at the 2016 American Music Awards held at the Microsoft Theater in Los Angeles.

Tinseltown/Shutterstock.com

local and state officials to recognize marriage equality. She even publicly admonished then President Obama about the issue (Zak 2009). Swift has been less vocal but very consistent in her advocacy of candidates that align with the views she expressed in her 2018 post, endorsing candidate Joe Biden in 2020[4], and then Vice President Kamala Harris in 2024.[5] Her main advocacy has thus far been to encourage people to register to vote (Kaufman 2018). Increasing voter registration should not be considered an issue, but for these types of individuals wanting more voters is somehow anti-American. In their dreams, well nightmares really, encouraging her fans to vote is evidence of her evil designs.

3. This was via her Instagram account October 8th 2018

4. Instagram October 7th 2020

5. Instagram September 11th 2024

The main thing to keep in mind is that if she wasn't as popular as she was, the conspiracy theories wouldn't exist, because there is an element of opportunism for these individuals. Attacking Swift, as I wrote for *The Skeptic*, is a cheap way to get attention (Hahn 2016). When Vivek Ramaswamy claimed that Swift's popularity was artificial, and that the NFL season was staged it gave his dying presidential campaign a temporary jolt of publicity. It's cynicism at its best, and when he was proven wrong (Joe Biden was not coronated after the Superbowl), there was no follow up.

The entire point is to grab attention. We can look at the conspiratorial obsession with Lady Gaga as an example of the pattern. Conspiracy theorists focused on her following her mainstream explosion with her debut "The Fame Monster." She was a break from the previous women that captured pop music with her loud costumes, stage show, and regal persona. However, as the culture became accustomed to her the conspiracy theories died down until her Superbowl LI halftime appearance. It never picked back up which is strange because Lady Gaga's 2020 album *Chromatica* is full of the kinds of symbolism that conspiracy theories thrive on; one song is even called *Babylon* which some of the larger conspiracy theories trace everything back to. The apathy is good for Lady Gaga who no longer has to concern herself with it, and for us because it really exposes the theories for what they are.

IF I WERE A MAN…

There is a final motive that presents itself in these kinds of conspiracy theories. Let me list the candidates once more: we start with the woman herself Taylor Swift, but then we add, Lady Gaga, Beyoncé, Rihanna, Britney Spears, Christina Aguilera, Katy Perry, and so on. Other than being pop megastars there is something else these people have in common as well: they're all women, they're gorgeous, and they are in charge. It's the exact type of attacks that Swift writes about in *You Need to Calm Down*, as internet conspiracy theorists throw their darts at the women who are "killing it."

Aside from gaining popularity, conspiracy theorists also attack Swift as a way to deny her reality. Over and over again the conspiracy theories claimed that she was a "psy-op" (short for "Psychological Operation") and what was happening with her was not "organic." The former is a claim based on the myth that fiction has created about what a "psychological operation" by the military or intelligence agency is alleged to be. Psychological operations as a concept evoke the images of the CIA's MK Ultra program that conducted a series of psychological experiments with little to no concern for the ethical safeguards. The point of the "psy-op" claim is to make it seem like her fans are under the control of a brainwashing program.

The parallel claim that her popularity isn't organic is similar but more obviously misogynistic. This accusation means that her popularity is artificial; while the conspiracy theories and news pundits that repeated this claim said it as an off-the cuff comment (Czopek 2024), it actually implies a vast conspiracy theory. What it means is that her tour stops never sold out, the fans of the shows were paid to be there (thus rendering their complaint about the monopolistic practices of Ticket Master very mysterious), the albums are not selling, the vinyl exclusives are lies, and as I type this I am not listening to *Red (*Taylor's Version) but instead a collection of Viking ballads or some such things. It means that every one of my young college students toting some Eras Tour bag or wearing one of her shirts was paid to do so. The streaming statistics, the end of year top ten lists-- these are all fake.

As my colleague in *The Skeptic* writes: "These conspiracy theories often target female celebrities in a bid to rob them of their own hard work, resilience, and determination to succeed. Taylor Swift's success can be fully attributed to her top-tier and unique songwriting skills, her brilliant and borderline terrifying attention to detail, the relatability of her songs, and much more – not to a secret and powerful organization who has bestowed success on her (Ting 2024)."

The author goes on to mention a male rap artist that implies he sold his soul for fame, a claim which was greeted by the sound of silence. Male artists who make loud attacks on the ideas that conspiracy theorists hold dear are never subjected to the type of scorn and derision that non-male artists are. Jay-Z, for instance, holds his hands in a triangle fashion quite a bit but there are not tweets from presidential candidates calling his fame artifi-

FIGURE 5: Conceptual image of money worship. Fingers arranged in a triangle with banknotes inside, evoking symbolism of wealth and the enigmatic allure of the Illuminati, indicating that money rules the world.

Pawel Michalowski/Shutterstock.com

cial or accusing the entire NFL season of being rigged, even if Beyoncé is going to be the halftime headliner for the Superbowl.

I must reiterate that the entire point of these attacks is because Taylor Swift the person and Taylor Swift the singer do not support their worldview. If she was apolitical, I doubt that as much attention would have been thrust upon her by these extremists. They would have turned their eye toward her because of her popularity but because she spoke about issues outside of her profession they feel that all of her work needs to be undercut.

WEAVE YOUR LITTLE WEBS OF OPACITY

In the beginning of this chapter I said that there is no barrier to making a conspiracy theory. You can just make one up, but a conspiracy theory needs some kind of evidence if people are going to buy it. Taylor Swift is an Illuminatus is just an accusation; you might as well just call her a jerk too. However, the theorists tend to do way more pedantic "research" in order to make their claims.

Conspiracy theories thrive on symbolism. They thrive on the little minutiae that we overlook everyday because we know that such nonsense doesn't matter. The problem for a conspiracy theory is that the thing they are trying to prove is usually nonsense, so evidence of substance is hard to come by—but because their point is emotional rather than rational there are a variety of techniques that they employ to convince us. Conspiracy theorists looking for Swift-Illuminati evidence will pour through every frame of one of her videos, every lyric, and social media post looking for some connection to the short-lived reading society of the 18th century.

Here is where our singer does us a disservice: the lead up to her album is a series of cryptic clues. She's got a very famous and well-known "obsession" with the number 13 which has very famous references to superstitions and even has its own phobia—triskaidekaphobia. If you just run an image search for "[female pop singer] + Illuminati" you'll get pages and pages of images with theorists pointing out clues in the background of music videos, public appearances, and award ceremonies which "prove" their claims. It becomes a dizzying affair trying to unknot the waft and weft of the theory but we should keep in mind a few things: the Illuminati no longer exist except in their head, there is no attempt to use the songs of Taylor Swift to brainwash the masses, and everything that she's gained from her career she's earned through tenacity, creativity, and a little bit of luck.

VINTAGE TEE, BRAND NEW PHONE

The message I want to communicate in this chapter is that while the accusations against Taylor Swift are new regarding her, they aren't new as a concept. In Aristotelian terms they are only novel in their accidental nature but not in their essential point. It's an old story that goes back as far as accusations that jazz music was corrupting the children (Hardesty 2016).

It would be hyperbole to describe her music as "subversive" but because she refuses to conform to the ideas that extremists subscribe, she's viewed as an agent of corruption. For an individual whose pen is focused primarily on interpersonal relationships it's quite depressing that her detractors refuse to listen to the themes rather than "discovering" that the inscription at Bohemian Grove (an infamous center point for many conspiracy theories) and Swift's song *Karma* both mention weaving spiders.

As the book *Architects of Fear* observes, conspiracy theories are always about protecting orthodoxy from change (Johnson 1983). A woman leveraging her talent and celebrity to encourage people to vote, to express her disdain for any kind of bigotry—is emblematic of the kind of change that they despise.

I was attracted to her music, after the initial exposure, because she does a sublime job of expressing difficult and often contradictory emotions: enjoying the moment while aware that such happiness is fleeting, pursuing a passion which is thrilling while being aware of how dangerous it could be, or simply just embracing fate as though one has a choice.[6] She's an impressive songwriter and individual, and that is always going to attract the wrong attention. Luckily, we can follow her example and just ignore them.

NOTES

Bale, J. M., "Political Paranoia v. Political Realism: On distinguishing between bogus conspiracy theories and genuine conspiratorial politics," *Patters of Prejudice* 2007 pp.45-60

Barkun, M., *A Culture of Conspiracy.* (Berkeley: University of California Press 2003)

6. For a more Stoic interpretation of her lyrics, see my article in "Taylor Swift and Philosophy" by Open Court Publishing Fall of 2024.

Brotherton, R., & French, C. C., "Belief in Conspiracy Theories and Susceptibility to the Conjunction Fallacy," *Applied Cognitive Psychology* 2014 pp. 238-248.

Czopek, M., *Taylor Swift: Singer, songwriter, psyop? How Conservatives spread a wild theory.* Retrieved from *Politfact*: 2-2-2024 https://www.politifact.com/article/2024/feb/02/taylor-swift-singer-songwriter-psyop-how-conservat/

Dentith, M. R., *The Philosophy of Conspiracy Theories.* (London: Palgrave MacMillan 2014

Dentith, M. R., *The Problem of Conspiracism* 2017 ttps://www.argumenta.org/wp-content/uploads/2017/10/Argumenta-Matthew-Dentith-The-Problem-of-Conspiracism.pdf

Grimes, D. R., "On the Viability of Conspiratorial Beliefs," *PLOS One* 2016 pp.1-17

Hahn, D. , *A Swift Conspiracy.* Retrieved from *The Skeptic 11-15-2023* https://www.skeptic.org.uk/2023/11/a-swift-conspiracy-why-almost-all-major-celebrities-get-accused-of-being-in-the-illuminati/

Hardesty, J., "Moral Outrage and Musical Corruption: White Educators' Response to the 'Jazz problem,'" *History of Education Quarterly* 2016

Imhoff, R., & Lamberty, P. K., " Too Special to be Duped: The Need for Uniqueness Motivates Conspiracy Beliefs," *European Journal of Social Psychology* 2017

Johnson, G., *Architects of Fear* (New York: Tarcher 1983)

Kaufman, G., *Was There an Election Bump in the Midterm Elections? Vote.org says Yes.* Retrieved from Billboard Magazine: 11-8-2018 https://www.billboard.com/music/pop/taylor-swift-bump-midterm-election

Keeley, B. L., "Of Conspiracy Theories," *The Journal of Philosophy*, 109-126 1999 pp.109-126.

Lantian, A., Muller, D., Nurra, C., & Douglas, K., "I Know Things They Don't Know! The Role of Need for Uniqueness in Belief in Conspiracy Theories," *Social Psychology*, 2017 pp.160-173.

Napolitano, G. M., & Reuter, K." What is a Conspiracy Theory?," *Erkenntnis* 2021

Prooijen, J.-W. v., & Dijk, E. v., "When Consequence Size Predicts Belief in Conspiracy Theories: The Moderating Role of Perspective Taking," *Journal of Experimental Social Psychology*, 2014 pp. 63-73.

Ting, J. G., *Taylor Swift Conspiracies owe more to misogyny than to the Illuminati.* Retrieved from The Skeptic 1-10-2023: https://www.skeptic.org.uk/2024/07/taylor-swift-conspiracy-theories-owe-more-to-misogyny-than-the-illuminati/

Zak, d., *Lady Gaga, Already an Icon, Show's She's an Activist Too.* 20-12-2009 Retrieved from *The Washington Post*: https://www.washingtonpost.com/wp-dyn/content/article/2009/10/11/AR2009101101892.html

11

How Does She Do It?

By David Soren

I have talked a bit about how Taylor Swift puts together the look of her Eras Tour and other notable performances. Now I'd like to try to do the speculative and risky task of trying to investigate how her mind works which is of course only my opinion of how she does that special magic that causes such fervent fan reaction. It's only guesswork about this mysterious process and I suspect that to some extent it's almost as mysterious to her but, well, here goes.

I believe that a lot of what happens to her is involved in her creating a song and subsequent visual project has been termed Surrealist Automatism which sounds like a big mouthful but it has actually been around as a concept since the 1920s and basically finds the creative artist (be he/she painter or writer or composer or whatever) in a receptive state of mind to respond to random thoughts or to planned or unexpected outside stimuli (Kramer and Grant 2025).

Sometimes the recipient can respond to an emotional input and have it reflect itself in a particular color such as red for passion and a composer might write a song evocative of various colors and their meaning in the physical world. The song *Red* is a typical example of such a thing and the colors can be more or less intense too, such as comparing her love to someone who is bursting with attractiveness but who is really a cipher. Loving him is said to be like "burning red" and "like the colors in autumn just before they lose it all." And losing him was "blue like I've never known" and missing him was "dark gray."

FIGURE 1: Detail of the cover and CD *Red*, fourth studio album by American singer Taylor Swift.

In the song *Out of the Woods* (2014) on the *1989* album, Taylor wrote about lying on her lover's couch, having him take a Polaroid of themselves and discovering that while the rest of the world was in black and white they were in screaming color.

Seeing emotional input as color is a complex phenomenon known as synesthesia which, generally, involves the stimulation of one sensory or cognitive pathway which causes involuntary experiences in a second sensory or cognitive pathway (Watson 2018). In other words the pathway of deep feeling and emotion can be blended with the body's pathway to color sensitivity and virtually cause you to think and feel in color. And *Red* is a song that reflects such a condition. It's not a harmful state to be in but many composers and artists have it and can use it creatively, such as the great Pharell Williams who has spoken of it in detail in a recent PBS interview (Brown 2024).

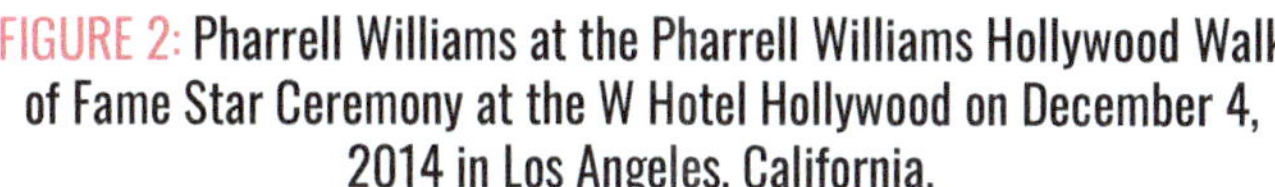

FIGURE 2: Pharrell Williams at the Pharrell Williams Hollywood Walk of Fame Star Ceremony at the W Hotel Hollywood on December 4, 2014 in Los Angeles, California.

FIGURE 3: Taylor Swift before she turns on the Christmas Lights at Westfield Shepherd's Bush, London. 06/11/2012.

Often the automatistic response requires the suppression of conscious control and leaves one free floating at which point the unconscious mind takes over and offers suggestions not limited to the actually possible (such as the *Fortnight* video discussed earlier?). For example, in thinking about Ronan the little boy who died of neuroblastoma cancer at age four, Taylor uses exaggerated language to describe how she feels: "I love you to the moon and back" which is an impossible reality and yet full of poetic meaning. It was a phrase used by the child's actual mother repeatedly and then it was picked up by Taylor as a main phrase in her song. The awful notion that the child is about to die is counteracted by a phrase suggesting that they could "fly away from here" and the child would be miraculously saved, and I find that I am unable to read the article about creating this song and watch the video itself and not be moved to tears at the combined feelings of love and helplessness (Ahlgrim 2021).

This kind of automatism often happens when Taylor is alone in the middle of the night (Watts 2022) and comes in the form of pleasant dreams or night fears and terrors (Dailey 2022), but it also can occur to her at any time that strong impulses are coming into her life.

In this case she was reading about the child and could relate because her own mother had been dealing with cancer. Since Taylor tends to record just about everything significant in her life as a musical diary, her song *Ronan* was a direct and even logical, thoughtful and sweet response to outside stimulus.

In another case, the number one country hit off of the *Fearless* album *You Belong With Me*, Taylor wrote about:

> "Just like all of my songs, *You Belong With Me* is based on a real person. When I write a song, my goal is to confess what happened in a situation ... When I look at the track listing on my album, I can see a face pop out in my mind.
>
> I remember I was overhearing a conversation one of my friends was having with his girlfriend, and he was obviously getting completely chewed out by her! She was just screaming through the phone at him, and I think it was for something really small, like he told her he'd call her in 10 minutes and instead it was 15 minutes later ... something like that.
>
> I remember thinking to myself why does he let her push him around like that because she obviously doesn't appreciate him? But instead of saying that out loud to him, I wrote it down in a song." (Boot Staff 2014)

But Taylor also has what may be called the introspective response that seems even to her to be coming from nowhere. For example she was riding in a car with her friend Claire and listening to Claire talk about her own relationship with her sister, friends and various family members when Taylor got a sudden inspiration which kept repeating "I just want to know you better", which perhaps referred to her friend Claire and, ever keeping her phone on the ready for inspirational phrases, Taylor began to sing what had flashed into her mind instead of just repeating the words to herself rhythmically. The next day she met with friend and fellow composer Ed Sheeran and had already polished the song into a rough version for them to finish composing together and then performing and recording (Couric 2013). Claire met up with her again, heard the song now in a more final state and remarked "so that's what you were doing into your phone!"

FIGURE 4: Victoria's Secret Models pose with performers Hozier, Taylor Swift, Ed Sheeran and Ariana Grande during the show finale of the 2014 VS Fashion Show on December 2, 2014 in London, England.

As a young girl Taylor was rather shy and often mocked or ignored or even bullied, with few friends, and considered gawky and thin and overly tall (CLRN Team 2025). She would also go to great lengths to avoid confrontation with others and by the time she was 12 she preferred to simply log in her feelings diary-style, especially through songwriting. This was a device which was also used by her distant relative Emily Dickinson (1830 – 1886) who confided her deepest feelings of love

FIGURE 5: Image and diary of poet Emily Dickinson.

into an elegant diary that nobody got to see until after her death and which she set down in the strictest confidence about her beloved Susan Gilbert (Popova 2018).

Taylor began responding to stimuli through writing at a very young age. Afraid to go swimming one summer at age 14 because a shark had been found beached near where she would have gone in, she stayed out of the water and mostly inside, using the time introvertedly to write a complete novel and she had already written her first serious collection of songs at age 12, some of which were able to be reconfigured into her debut album at age 16 in 2006, such as *The Outside* which already was focusing on her being unable to fit into the world of her contemporaries (Benitez-Eves 2024). Taylor became so focused on the songwriting early on in her life that the songs became a solace to her and by never naming names (or at least full names) in her songs, they could eventually float out as universal experiences with which so many young women identified (Ta 2022).

These kinds of influences on her early life led to her learning to express her isolation and fantasies in her

FIGURE 6: Taylor Swift at the 2007 American Music Awards at the Nokia Theatre, Los Angeles. November 19, 2007 Los Angeles, CA Picture: Paul Smith / Featureflash.

musical compositions, much like the Surrealist painting of the Belgian artist Rene Magritte whose paintings take us into impossible combinations of things which live in his mind alone and who, despite coming from a rich family, was bullied as a child and his family harassed after his mother was found drowned, a possible suicide in Belgium's River Sambre, when he was 13. It is this unexpected illogical combining of imagery, perhaps triggered by the oppression and bullying of his youth, that is a hallmark of Magritte's unique style and made him so popular in the psychedelic later sixties which opened up the world of the mind to popular art such as rock and roll album covers and lyrics by The Beatles, Jefferson Airplane and Donovan, to name a few of the 1960s and early 1970s recording artists, and provided an escape from reality during the Vietnam War and Nixon years in America.

FIGURE 6: *Golconda* by René Magritte on postage stamp of the country of Mozambique.

I've already talked about *Anti-Hero* and how the video of it takes us to the very threshold of what is conceivable in real life and then pushes us beyond that point. To be sure Taylor has written many many songs about real events in her life (breakups, happy relationships, the joy, wonder and confusion of being young, and even revenge) but the thread of fantasy seems to be increasingly taking over her thoughts as she matures, especially as she moves more and more into video directing, expressing the lyrics of her songs in a more complex visual manner.

Taylor's Surrealism, her lyrics and visuals that float us to the edge of this world's possibilities, or to the very edge of another world and just beyond are not only the product of her early life fueled by social isolation. It is also fueled by her love of the use of metaphor which she would have learned about, we suspect, from her school teachers (LaCroix 2024) and especially at the SONY music school she attended at age 14 (Choudhury 2024) when she was beautifully mentored by tiny, sensitive Liz Rose with whom she collaborated on 17 early songs (Krewen 2024).

A metaphor is a figure of speech in which something is used to designate something else, or in other words one image is used to represent or further define another. A song such as *Red* is a great example. It shows how Taylor searches for special phrases that illuminate the feeling of a song or characterize her relationship with someone. She's attracted passionately to someone in the song but the relationship isn't easy. She often looks for key metaphors that she particularly loves and repeats them in her songs because she wants them to be the main phrase that makes the song stand out sharply in the listener's mind.

In *Red*, as I mentioned above, I particularly love the concept that "loving him is like driving a Maserati down a dead end street." It's a great line. It suggests a love affair with a man who is rich, wild and adventurous but when she tries to harness him in any way she cannot and the relationship goes nowhere. You could theoretically drive a Maserati known for its quick pickup and high performance down a dead end street but what would be the use. It's a line that expresses frustration, wildness, passion and is also something that defines something that is pointless and yet extremely flashy.

In fashioning her music Taylor is thinking all the time and listening for inspiration, not knowing when it will come as she lives her daily life or lies in her bed at night. As such it means that when someone talks to Taylor she is always a good listener for she has had an early lifetime of solitude and reverie and listening and at any minute she can take what is told to her and turn it into a hit song and from there she can create a total image of how her song might fly from her brain into becoming a visual on a tour or in a video.

FIGURE 7: 2020 Maserati Levante GranSport

Mike Mareen/Shutterstock.com

I am also struck by the fact that once a song gets fixed in her mind, that is how it remains and when she performs it it sounds amazingly like her recording, even to the breathing and the stuttery ah ahs or repeated sounds she commonly uses. And there is absolute precision and even breathing unity between herself and her super-rehearsed backup singers. Once in a while she will do an alternate version of a song, perhaps with another singer or for a change of pace, but in general the precision of everything she does comes through in the design of her shows, the way she uses a stage, the super coordination of her dance moves with her dancers and their movement across the big stage. In real life Taylor is known as a great supporter and listener and mentor (Chinman 2024), no doubt a conscious attempt to reverse behavior she experienced as a child from her peers.

Of course Taylor is not the only one who works in the manner we've been describing. In 1985 I was a guest at Oxford University along with 24 other so-called American Successor Generation Representatives and my bus mate, amazingly, was Lawrence Kasdan who had recently written the screenplay for *Raiders of the Lost Ark* and had directed and written *Body Heat*, among other successful films, his career having taken off after he wrote the comedy *Continental Divide* with John Belushi. Larry didn't talk much but kept a notepad with him into which he jotted down his everyday observances. He occasionally asked questions and was a very good listener but he was never "on" selling himself or displaying any ego. He was interested intently in whomever he was speaking to at the moment and he made you feel as if he really cared about you. I should imagine Taylor is the same way because everyone who meets her for the first time always talks about how nice she is and how "normal" and how she doesn't push her own accomplishments or display gratuitous ego but puts her interest and focus on the other person (*Beautiful Meme* 2023).

People with synethesia are generally "sensitives", individuals who are good listeners and listen particularly deeply into the conversation of others. This means that they can be particularly good on interviews and on talk shows. Pharell Williams is always caring, articulate and wonderful as a listener and a thoughtful responder to questions in his interviews. Taylor is amazing at interviewing and can do it seemingly effortlessly and even enjoys lightning rounds (extratv 2014). Taylor is a master at fielding rapid-fire questions, accepting Vogue's lightning round challenge to answer 73 questions within 10 minutes with charm, perception and wit (Ball 2016; Katz 2016)!

In the 1970s I was the host of a morning show entitled *Good Morning Missouri* for the ABC tv affiliate in Columbia, Missouri. On that show I learned what it took to have a good guest to interview. The answers from the guest should be relatively short, and the guest should bring to the discussion something to talk about in his or her life that he or she found to be significant or humorous. And the guest should be able to walk in and make an attractive stylish entrance, and he/she should listen carefully and respond to the actual questions without leaving a lot of gaps or grammatical errors. If you've ever seen Taylor make an entrance on an interview show it is something you'll remember for she walks as if she has just emerged from Vogue and one can imagine that during that brief walk-in every aspect of what she is wearing and how it moves with her is under serious study by thousands upon thousands of viewers.

Her 5 to 10 minute talking sessions on the old David Letterman Show are classic examples of how to do a talk show interview and one reason why Letterman himself is such an admirer and has described Taylor as "a glowing bright light of goodness in the world" (Letterman 2023). In her Letterman interviews she enters wearing the height of contemporary fashion, walks like a professional model to the interview location, and engages in charming repartee with the host. She has prepared stories to tell but can also be observed feeding letterman deft quips and listening to make sure that he gets his joke in and the audience has time to laugh. She is relaxed and poised as can be. It is a textbook example in how to do it and at the time she did it first she was only 19 years old (Letterman 2014)!

Although she continues to have myriads of detractors, it strikes me that anyone who can carry her interview segment on a popular comedic talk show, write hit after hit, co-produce or produce the song, design the basics of her tour and oversee every aspect of its production, envision and enable the greatest and most successful musical tour in the history of show business, design and even direct videos and oversee a multi billion dollar empire with regular staff meetings while serving as its chief executive officer and subject while still remaining an easy to talk to down to earth pleasant person and major level philanthropist certainly deserves a hell of a lot more kudos than brickbats. I find her to be a genuine savant as her early collaborator Liz Rose frequently suggests:

> "She's such a force. You remember the songs you write with Taylor, because the emotion that goes into them is so palpable….When she's writing something, she's already producing in her head. She hears it all (Leahy 2014)."

As to the argument often raised that Taylor Swift's music is for young girls and not worthy of serious study and contemplation and possibly harmful to them (Montgomery 2024;), let us quote a few individuals who are closer to my age. Barbara Eden, the 93 year old Swiftie and former film star and star of tv's *I Dream of Jeannie* sitcom has said it best when asked if Taylor Swift should be the next

FIGURE 8: Barbara Eden at the Barbara Eden Tribute Exhibition Opening Night at the Hollywood Museum on August 21, 2019 in Los Angeles, California

Jeannie: "You know I'm a Swiftie. Right now I think that that girl can do anything! She's a cutie!" (*OnTheRedCarpet* 2024).

Just recently 92 year old Michael Caine, one of the most successful and universally respected actors in the world wrote in his 2024 memoirs:

> "You can just tell how much hard work lies behind what she's achieved, too. It's no accident. She has really earned her success, and it hasn't come overnight. She's down-to-earth, which is almost always part of it. Not spoiled by all the accolades and money. That's impressive."

NOTES

Ahlgrim, Callie, "The mom whose story inspired Taylor Swift's 'Ronan' says it's 'unbearable to think about' anyone else owning the rights to the song," *Business Insider* 11-12-2021 https://www.businessinsider.com/taylor-swift-ronan-true-story-mom-maya-thompson-interview-2021-11?op=1

Ball, Tasha, "Taylor Swift Answers 73 Interview Questions in Under 10 Minutes," *Fab Fit Fun* 4-19-2016 https://fabfitfun.com/magazine/taylor-swift-vogue-73-questions/

Beautiful Meme 2023- "Is Taylor Swift Actually a Nice Person," *The Beautiful Meme* 11-23-2023 https://thebeautifulmeme.com/is-taylor-swift-actually-a-nice-person/

Benitez-Eves, Tina, "The Story Behind One of the First Songs Taylor Swift Wrote When She Felt Like an "Outcast" at Age 12", *American Songwriter* 6-19-2024 https://americansongwriter.com/the-story-behind-one-of-the-first-songs-taylor-swift-wrote-when-she-felt-like-an-outcast-at-age-12-the-outside/

Boot Staff, The 2014, "You Belong With Me: The Story Behind the Song," *The Boot* 11-21-2014 https://theboot.com/story-behind-the-song-you-belong-with-me-taylor-swift/

Brown, Jeffrey, "Pharrell Williams' musical evolution is reconstructed with Legos in 'Piece By Piece'," *PBS News Hour* 10-15-2024 https://www.pbs.org/newshour/show/pharrell-williams-musical-evolution-is-reconstructed-with-legos-in-piece-by-piece

Chinman, Luke, "How 'Unbelievable Artist, Friend and Mentor' Taylor Swift Inspired Gracie Abrams to Stick with 'Writing Daily'," *Y! Entertainment* 6-17-2024 https://people.com/how-taylor-swift-inspired-gracie-abrams-writing-daily-8663860

Choudhury, Meghdeepa, "The Lesser-Known Truth Of Taylor Swift's Childhood And Hometown," Nicki Swift 10-28-2024 https://www.nickiswift.com/1697399/taylor-swift-hometown-childhood-lesser-known-truth/

CLRN Team, "Was Taylor Swift Bullied in School?," *California Learning Research Network* 1-3-2025 https://www.clrn.org/was-taylor-swift-bullied-in-school/

Couric, Katie, "Taylor Swift on Katie The First Half," *Tayswiftruclub* 8-14-2013 https://www.youtube.com/watch?v=h6r-HsdmKdA

Cramer, Charles and Kim Grant, "Surrealist Techniques: Automatism," *Smart History* 2025 https://smarthistory.org/surrealist-techniques-automatism/

Dailey, Hannah, "Taylor Swift's Fifth Inspiration for 'Midnights' Is a Dark One," *Billboard* 10-20-2022 https://www.billboard.com/music/music-news/taylor-swift-midnights-inspiration-dark-one-1235158597/

extratv – Alecia Davis, " Taylor Swift Talks '1989,' Takes our Rapid-Fire Quiz on Her Favorite Things," *YouTube* 2014 https://www.youtube.com/watch?v=cXeytWRS1so

Hawkins, Autumn, "Michael Caine praises Taylor Swift's work ethic in new book," Clutchpoints 3-26-2025 https://clutchpoints.com/celebrity/michael-caine-praises-taylor-swifts-work-ethic-in-new-book

Katz, Jessie, "Watch Taylor Swift Answer 73 Awesome Questions in One Video," Billboard 4-19-2016 https://www.billboard.com/music/music-news/taylor-swift-vogue-video-73-questions-watch-7340656/

Krewen, Nick, "She was Taylor Swift's early secret weapon, who helped write some of the star's biggest songs. Meet Liz Rose," Toronto Star 11-25-2024 https://www.thestar.com/entertainment/music/she-was-taylor-swifts-early-secret-weapon-who-helped-write-some-of-the-stars-biggest/article_8edcb4ca-97cd-11ef-abd3-2b9d1f067267.html

LaCroix, Jane, "What Taylor Swift's Teachers Had to Say About Her As a Student," *Newsweek* 4-24-2024 https://www.newsweek.com/entertainment/celebrity-news/taylor-swifts-teachers-reveal-what-she-was-like-student-1893951

Leahy, Andrew, "Songwriter Spotlight: Liz Rose," *Rolling Stone* 10-24-2014 https://www.rollingstone.com/music/music-country/songwriter-spotlight-liz-rose-188704/

Letterman, David, "Taylor Swift Loves New York, Not Lousy Boyfriends," Letterman 10-28-14 https://www.youtube.com/watch?v=ozrrUio3AB0

Letterman, David, "Dave is Team Taylor," Letterman 2023 https://www.youtube.com/watch?v=2oPz6ckjlJ0

McGhlionn, John, "Taylor Swift Is Not a Good Role Model," *Newsweek* 7-2-2024 https://www.newsweek.com/taylor-swift-not-good-role-model-opinion-1916799

Montgomery, Amaya Grace (7-year-old Swiftie), "I'm a Seven Year Old Swiftie. Here's Why Taylor Swift Is a Role Model for Girls Like Me," *Newsweek* 7-1-2024 https://www.newsweek.com/im-seven-year-old-swiftie-heres-why-taylor-swift-role-model-girls-like-me-opinion-1919851

OnTheRedCarpet 2024, "Barbara Eden interview about "I Dream of Jeannie," Elvis Presley and Taylor Swift," *OnTheRedCarpet* 4-6-2024 https://www.youtube.com/watch?v=VhhEH9HCh_s

Popova, Maria, "Emily Dickinson's Electric Love Letters to Susan Gilbert," The *Marginalian* 12-10-2018 https://www.themarginalian.org/2018/12/10/emily-dickinson-love-letters-susan-gilbert/

Ta, Amy, "Why is Taylor Swift so popular? Young women relate to her vulnerability," *KCRW* 11-1-2022 https://www.kcrw.com/news/shows/press-play-with-madeleine-brand/mayor-la-climate-police-midnights/taylor-swift-billboard-top-10

Watson, Kathryn, "What is Synesthesia?", *Healthline* 10-24-2018 https://www.healthline.com/health/synesthesia

Watts, Marina, "61 Taylor Swift Lyrics About Midnights & The Nighttime From 2006 To Today," *Bustle* 10-21-2022 https://www.bustle.com/entertainment/taylor-swift-lyrics-about-midnights-night-am-songs-albums

12

Ten Songs I Really Like and Why In No Particular Order

By David Soren

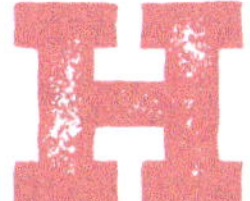ere are 10 of her songs that I love to play and watch again and again and which it seems to me are really extraordinary for various reasons.

WILL YOU LOVE ME TOMORROW

So far as I know the cover version of this song, written by Carole King and Gerry Goffin, was only performed by Taylor Swift one time, in front of Carole King at the ceremony honoring her for her induction into the Rock and Roll Hall of Fame in 2021 (Duncan and Balagtas 2021), despite the fact that it featured a new, more up-to-date arrangement, terrific singing by her backup group and a wonderful individualized presentation by Taylor. I'm old enough to remember when the song first came out in 1960 and was a huge hit for the early girl group The Shirelles and the raw earthy New Jersey accent of lead singer Shirley Owens. I loved it back then but hearing Taylor and her backup singers do this new slightly disco version of it takes it into another dimension for me. The emotional performance (and the speech that Taylor delivered along with it) and the driving beat and overall professionalism with her fabulous backup singers drove the audience absolutely wild, not to mention how much Carole King seemed to enjoy Taylor's presentation of it.

To my knowledge there is no issued recording of this but it is on YouTube (EAS 2021) and well worth a look. I believe this could be a hit record right now in the updated version. Taylor blew Carole a kiss and Carole blew it back. The two have had a long friendship where Carole has thought of Taylor as similar to her own daughter and Carole has also been active in the Swifties for Kamala Harris movement. Taylor also personally gave the induction speech for Carole (Zalewski 2021), making a 180 degree shift because Carole gave the speech honoring Swift as Artist of the Decade at the 2019 American Music Awards (Macke 2019).

COWBOY LIKE ME

Here is an often overlooked country song from Taylor's *Evermore* album of 12-11-2020 (Whitman 2022). It was recorded with background vocals by British/American folk star Marcus Mumford at whose Scarlet Pimpernel Studios in England it was originally record-ed during the heart of the pandemic. It was sung live in Las Vegas on the Eras Tour with Mumford playing guitar, singing and clowning on-stage with Taylor (Kreps 2023; Irenkoo 2023). It is one of Mumford's favorite country songs and it is my favorite (along with *Mean*) of Taylor's pure country efforts, being about two grifters who apparently fall deeply in love. It is full of wonderful lines such as "never wanted love, just a fancy car" and the all-time classic: "Forever is the sweetest con (Whitman 2022)."

At one point in the song her lover is said to be hanging from her lips like the Gardens of Babylon. The gardens themselves were supposedly real but no trace of them was ever found and over time they became a symbol of paradise-like luxury and beauty, a dream of a place you'd love to see and wander through, hence the use in this song (van Huyssteen 2023). The idea of "hanging" from my lips is a reference to the gardens which in English were termed the "hanging" gardens, which meant overhanging or luxuriant, coming from the word κρεμαστός in ancient Greek or *pensilis* in Latin which was used to describe the place. The term doesn't work as well in English since it likely referred to a garden made on terraces in the ancient Near Eastern tradition.

PETER

This little remembered classic from the Tortured Poets Department Anthology collection tells the sad story of mortal Wendy waiting for Peter Pan to return and now imagining him as being part of "closets like cedar", i.e. just a memory from childhood that was never to be fulfilled but tucked away. It is such a sad song it always makes me cry as one is forced to reflect on lost loves that might have been, meaningful promises of long ago that have long since been broken and someone you loved once who didn't turn out as you had expected. He made "promises oceans deep but never to keep." To me this song/poem is about how little we know about life and how we believe in things when we are young only to have these illusions shattered by cold reality and later reflection. It is beautiful, poignant and terrifying all at the same time. It makes me think of Taylor's own trajectory of romance but it could apply to everyone who has been in love or thought they had been. So many of her songs remind one of fairy tales as in her song of 2010 *Today Was a Fairytale*, complete with a prince and damsel in distress and she herself has said:

> "I am completely fascinated by the differences and comparisons between
> real life and fairy tales (Bombay 2021).

But this song from her latest album registers depression, sadness and despair and is like the difference between *London Boy* and *So Long London*. *Tortured Poets Department* has so much sadness and angst that I have to listen to it in stages in order to stay on a level emotional keel even though I can appreciate where it came from within her. I was happy when she finally issued her statement that she had gotten all of her rage and sadness out of her because I was hoping the next work she makes will have a more positive spin:

> "This period of the author's life is now over, the chapter closed and boarded up
> (Legardye 2024)."

FALSE GOD

I first heard this on *Saturday Night Live* where I was amazed that it had been written by Taylor Swift who is so often accused of using basic, simple chords and melodies such as

Shake It Off, but this song is more at home in a smoky jazz club with the likes of Nina Simone running through the lyrics that feel like someone is in the throes of a failing love affair, still moving blindly into it despite the aloofness of the object of veneration. The SNL performance is the best version to hear and view with the incredible Lenny Pickett handling a mind-blowing saxophone-blowing solo. Lenny was the director of the show's band but is also a go-to guy for famous musicians needing an innovative solo in their work. Pickett out-does himself here and exceeds the work done in the original recording while Taylor seems to groove out on it and delivers her part complete with spacy hand gestures that make you almost think you are in a Beatnik café in 1958 where everyone sits around stoned! It's really something different if you've never seen it.

WHEN EMMA FALLS IN LOVE

This is a song that isn't that well known but it has been one of the most enigmatic for Swifties. I really like the song itself which was intended for the album *Speak Now* back in 2010 but didn't make it until Taylor's Version came out 13 years later and she released it as a vault song!

The main speculation here is who is Emma and some think that it is a reference to Taylor's close friend, the actress Emma Stone but the problem is that not much about the Emma discussed within the song can be pinned on Emma Stone.

My theory is that "Emma" is one of those alter ego songs like *Anti-Hero* where it is Taylor herself who wants to be Emma at times but can't find it in herself to be that way so she admires the way that she could be. This is a theme of superego versus id that we discussed in the *Anti-Hero* chapter and I think this is an early version of it. Let me take a minute to plead my case.

First of all, who closes the blinds and locks the door as the lyrics say. Taylor would be a likely person to do just that back in high school when she got a crush on a student in her class named Drew Hardwick and wrote a song about him called *Teardrops on My Guitar*. After the song was released and Drew was mentioned as the first word in the song, he knew quickly of course that it was about him. It has been reported that several years later Taylor was in the process of exiting from her home near Reading, Pennsylvania and Drew showed up in her driveway and she was embarrassed to see him and the resulting direct confrontation was reportedly awkward (Allen 2023). Had she been inside her house it seems reasonable that she would have likely locked the door and pulled down the shades rather than go through with meeting him again after all that time. It's something we can imagine her doing because of her strong desire to avoid personal confrontation and after having been shunned and bullied in her youth as we have discussed earlier in this volume.

Also, who but Taylor back then would have asked her mom for advice about love and joked about how her many boyfriends might not work out. Taylor was also constantly concerned about continuing her success as if all the sunshine in her life could turn to rain and she, with her beautiful blonde hair, IS "little Miss Sunshine", not Emma Stone despite Stone's association with a film role with a connection to the song *Pocketful of Sunshine* by Natasha Bedingfield (Jeffrey 2023).

The Taylor of this song would like to be more of a take-charge person who could really make things happen but in 2010 she is still trying to be that person but hasn't reached the heights she would reach. However, she could admire a woman with the cleverness and imagination of Cleopatra. In fact she could be the Cleopatra in the small town if she could only be more like "Emma" but Emma Stone was not from a small town for she grew up in wealthy, exclusive Scottsdale in the Phoenix area. The joke told about Scottsdale in Tucson is that the town is so exclusive that even the police there have an unlisted number.

It's also a constant criticism of Taylor by her closest friends that she falls in love too quickly and too deeply and it can have a negative effect and harm the relationship (Greer 2012). This is also brought out in the song because when Emma falls in love it's for keeps and you can see it in her face and she won't walk away from it unless she absolutely has no other choice. But if the boys had the chance to really love her even bad boys would become good boys. Her attraction to bad boys that she has attempted to reform might be exemplified best on Tortured Poets by the song *But Daddy I Love Him* or her comments about Joe Jonas and their breakup on the Ellen Show and her subsequent assistance to Jonas' wife after their breakup (Wiswanath 2024; Perkins 2024). She admits to having difficulty being alone and handling the pain of failed love because she falls hard and deep and is in it for keeps.

In the song she admires the fact that Emma can put guys in their place and turn them around but she can't and Emma can switch her mood from L. A. to New York at will and she can put people who bother her in their place. She admits that she is learning from the way this Emma can handle things.

Emma is the person she wants to be and cannot quite except in her mind but she says in the song "I'm learning" and adds that "yeah between me and you sometimes I wish I was her."

But why the name Emma. Taylor loves to play word games and spell words backwards and forwards and highlight letters in caps in the middle of words, but Emma is an easy one to grasp because if you read the name forward it is Emma. Read it forward and then backwards and you get "Emma Am Me." I rest my case.

THIS LOVE

When Taylor was first learning about songwriting at the age of 14 she was taught about the importance of having an outstanding hook for each song (Taylor Swift Station 2019). This one has lyrical and musical hooks galore and there isn't a second of it that isn't fresh and innovative. It's as beautiful a ballad as one can write and just when you think it's said what it will say and expressed itself musically it cuts to a bridge that ascends into yet another heavenly melody. The links between the bridge and the diverse melodies in this song are also seamless and extraordinary.

The best way to view this is the beautifully produced clip for the 1989 World Tour from the end of 2015. For me this is the summation of her talent and has all of the characteristics: remarkable song, incredible vocal color and presentation, exquisite costume and overall look plus the typical Taylor stride up and down the stage as she chants the title of the song over and over and the background singers sing the melody and accompany her.

I can remember back to the Beatles and Elvis and even as far back as the second coming of Al Jolson in the Korean War and after but the quality of this work exceeds any of it in my opinion. It's good to hold on to the memories of the past superstars but to my mind it's okay to embrace something new when it is of this quality. Check it out (Swift Leaks 2.0).

CORNELIA STREET

Cornelia Street appeared on the *Lover* album in 2019 and is yet another song produced with Jack Antonoff. I've been on this street in Greenwich Village in New York and I remember having a female friend there who was torn between two lovers—a poor guy with no ambition who passionately loved her and a richer guy she'd known for years who was crazy about her but she didn't love him physically in the same way. I was told to choose for her because she couldn't make up her mind so I took her to lunch, deliberated and then picked the richer guy who could actually take care of her and give her a fabulous lifestyle as opposed to a guy who was never caring about anything but her and wouldn't be likely to be able to provide for her. The rich guy married her, then, and took her and her parents to a fabulous exotic beach where she promptly went out swimming, got caught in the undertow and drowned. Her father tried to swim out and rescue her and he drowned too. That is my memory of this area and I am haunted by the advice I gave her which inadvertently led to her death so Cornelia Street and Greenwich Village in general is kind of nostalgic for me but also filled with an air of tragedy.

This song seems to also convey a tragic feeling for me, that of passionate love that is not completely returned and a lover, Taylor, who has to decide whether to stay in the relationship or get out, reminding me of the choice I was to make for my co-worker and close close friend.

I wasn't that impressed with the song on the *Lover* album recording actually and there was no real *Lover* tour due to the pandemic but there was an acoustic performance of this song in Paris with just Taylor and her guitar and it's a knockout: the City of Love Paris Concert of 2020. When she sings of the agony and ebbing and flowing of her love and how painful it is living with, presumably, Joe Alwyn, it is gut-wrenching and so emotional.

Her phrasing and emotional delivery is incredibly intense and when she screams out that she will never walk Cornelia Street again it is preceded by a kind of falsetto followed by a sound that makes me think of a banshee in agony full blast. It's a tour de force performance of just the woman and her guitar and you can thankfully witness it and don't ever ever again let anyone tell you that this amazing songwriter can't sing (Taylor Swift 2020).

These are 10 songs I like for various reasons but the list could easily go to 100 or more. I love *Speak Now* for example because it is a throwback song that can evoke memories of the great Vesta Victoria, the English music hall star of the early 20th century who sang "Poor Me" songs such as *Waiting at the Church* in which the groom never shows up on her wedding day. Taylor's story-song is the modern successor for me of this old English music hall traditional song and I love the way she acts out all the words with her hands when she is singing it (Swift 2011).

And who can leave out *Mean*, an absolutely quintessential down-home country song which began as her response to an over-harsh critic who ultimately proved himself wrong, claiming that Taylor "cain't sing" (Corbett 2023). The song became an anthem for bullied children and gave thousands of kids hope for the future and courage to survive. I even know some of them!

I Know Places is another song I didn't mention. It starts out with just a few notes repeated again and again like the slow beginning of a fox hunt in England and sets up a jarring uneasy feeling that proceeds into something like the thrill of a foxhunt at full galop as if Taylor is the fox. It strikes me as one of her creepiest songs but fascinating in that she must no doubt play games avoiding the paparazzi and stealing off to exclusive places where she can hide. The music progresses with the suggestion of the thrill of the chase and all built around a few simple slightly discordant notes.

OMG, I just realized that I left off my list such songs as *All Too Well* which just surpassed a billion streams (Forward 2025). And there is also *Enchanted* and its *Cinderella* video. And the perky *Message in a Bottle* which is so much fun and which typifies the great songs that were kept "bottled up" for so many years, such as *Mr. Perfectly Fine*.

As to whole albums I find it hard to choose a favorite because her eras actually reflect different moods of mine at different times as I choose what to listen to. I suspect *1989* holds a special place in my heart because it's so full of fine songs and positive vibes but I have to admit that *Folklore* and *Evermore* are real works of art that seem to be visiting our planet from outer space due to their beauty and contemplative striking lyrics. And then there's *You Need to Calm Down* off the *Lover* album and its celebration of diversity and its assessment of two different Americas.

While I'm rambling, I love the crazy dance she does in *Delicate* that suggests she's all but invisible to the people around her and how she uses indelicate, weird dance steps, which at the same time are very graceful and fluid movements. Although not a dancer she has a natural ability at free-form dancing and does a spectacularly memorable full split on the hood of a car at the end. The video views like a spoof of modern jazz or interpretive dancing done by a nerd, reminiscent of the crazy self-deflating improv stuff in the wonderful *Shake It Off* video that inspired many people to take dance classes to release tension.

Another one I forgot is the beautiful children's song *Never Grow Up* which I have been told by many moms brings them to tears about how fast their kids grow up and how important it is to cherish and protect them and take lots of videos of them and it also instills an appreciation of family in children. It's a song with a beautiful purpose that has actually affected people's lives deeply.

One final omission from my list is *Here Where You Left Me*, one of the most stunningly devastating portraits of a woman utterly paralyzed by abandonment and loss. The woman seems to inhabit the garish world of despair of Vincent Van Gogh's *Night Café* and is the sort of person we might find sitting dazedly against a building wall on the dirty street and deep inside we wonder how they got there while we pretend not to notice them. The rollicking driving beat of the song seems almost to mock the victim. To me this is Taylor's terrifying horror movie, a side to her perhaps that she never wants anyone to see close up except for here.

But the above listed 10 "official"songs on my list are among those that I return to again and again and never fail to be amazed at with regard to their poetry, hooks and bridges, and visual presentation. Nobody else does it quite this way and affects an audience's emotion individually or collectively. Much has been written about how the secret of Taylor's success is that she wrote for teenage girls who liked country music and that, in business terms, this was a forgotten and underserved market and it catapulted her to the top of her profession because of the loyal following they served (Evers 2025). While this may be true it isn't the whole truth. As you have seen in this book, Taylor Swift's music is more universal than that. If one allows it, it can reach out to all ages and generations because it deals in basic human emotions and expresses them with an uncanny ability to cross over genders, age groups and even countries and cultures throughout the world.

And yet as I close out this volume I wonder why so many people even in my neighborhood actively either hate her or dismiss with a snarky laugh the decades-long achievements of this unique entertainer, including her desire for everyone to try to get along and to make the world more inclusive and harmonious. I can't really come up with an answer to all the negativity except that overwhelming sustained success (over 20 years now!) seems so often to breed unreasonable contempt and jealousy or, put another way, people throw rocks at things that shine.

NOTES

Allen, Erica, "All Taylor Swift Songs About Drew Hardwick," *Music Industry How To* 12-28-2023 https://www.musicindustryhowto.com/taylor-swift-songs-about-drew-hardwick/

Bombay, Brandon, "The Real Meaning Behind Taylor Swift's 'Today Was A Fairytale' (Taylor's Version)," *Nicki Swift* 4-8-2021 https://www.nickiswift.com/377882/the-real-meaning-behind-taylor-swifts-today-was-a-fairytale-taylors-version/

Corbett, Kelly, "Who Did Taylor Swift Write 'Mean' About? He Messed With the Wrong Queen," *Distractify* 7-10-2023 https://www.distractify.com/p/who-did-taylor-swift-write-mean-about

Duncan, Gabrielle and Tristan Balagtas, "Taylor Swift Performs Tribute to Carole King at Rock and Roll Hall of Fame Induction Ceremony," *People* 10-31-2021 https://people.com/music/taylor-swift-performs-tribute-carole-king-rock-roll-hall-fame-induction-ceremony/

EAS Music Channel, "Will You Still Love Me Tomorrow? - Taylor Swift • Rock & Roll Hall of Fame" 2021 https://www.youtube.com/watch?v=BABeGvfg1fA

Evers, Kevin, "How I came to understand Taylor Swift—and what she gets right about success," *Forbes* 4-3-2025 and see also his new book *There's Nothing Like This: The Strategic Genius of Taylor Swift* https://fortune.com/2025/04/03/taylor-swift-business-genius/

Evers, Kevin, "The Strategic Genius of Taylor Swift," *Harvard Business Review* March-April 2025 https://hbr.org/2025/03/the-strategic-genius-of-taylor-swift?ab=HP-magazine-text-2

Forward, Devon, "Taylor Swift Hits Yet Another Mind-Boggling Milestone," *Parade* 3-31-2025 https://parade.com/news/taylor-swift-all-too-well-spotify-milestone

Greer, Jane, "Taylor Swift: How Fast Is Too Fast?," Psychology Today 9-8-2012 https://www.psychologytoday.com/us/blog/shrink-wrap/201209/taylor-swift-how-fast-is-too-fast

Ibañez, Peter Thaddeus, "13 Fan-Favorite Bridges From Taylor Swift's Discography" *Village Pipol* 3-11-2023 https://villagepipol.com/13-fan-favorite-bridges-from-taylor-swifts-discography/

Irenkoo, "Taylor Swift - cowboy like me (The Eras Tour Guitar Version) featuring Marcus Mumford," *YouTube* 3-25-2023 https://www.youtube.com/watch?v=Usb3_S4eVvA

Jeffrey, Joyanne, "Is one of Taylor Swift's new songs about Emma Stone? Fans think so." Today 7-7-2023 https://www.today.com/popculture/music/taylor-swift-new-song-emma-stone-fan-reactions-rcna93028

Kreps, Daniel, "See Taylor Swift Bring Out Marcus Mumford to Perform 'Cowboy Like Me' at Las Vegas Show" Rolling Stone 3-26-2023 https://www.rollingstone.com/music/music-news/taylor-swift-marcus-mumford-cowboy-like-me-las-vegas-1234703883/

Legardye, Quinci, "Taylor Swift Says 'The Tortured Poets Department' Is the End of Her Fleeting and Fatalistic Era," Marie Claire 4-19-2024 https://www.marieclaire.com/celebrity/taylor-swift-tortured-poets-department-fleeting-fatalistic-era/

Macke, Johnny, "Taylor Swift Gives Emotional Speeches About 'Complicated' Year at American Music Awards 2019," Us 11-24-2019 https://www.usmagazine.com/entertainment/news/amas-2019-taylor-swifts-speech-for-artist-of-the-decade/

Perkins, Njera, "Sophie Turner Calls Taylor Swift Her 'Hero' After Joe Jonas Divorce Filing: She 'Provided Us with a Home,'" People 5-16-2024 https://people.com/sophie-turner-calls-taylor-swift-her-hero-after-joe-jonas-divorce-filing-8648868

Swift Leaks 2.0, "Taylor Swift - This Love (1989 World Tour)," Swift Leaks 2.0 1-28-2023 https://www.youtube.com/watch?v=JccC_l6ocQA

Taylor Swift, "Lyrics That Hook You," YouTube 2019 https://www.youtube.com/watch?v=a_W3DoGwP7o

Taylor Swift, "Speak Now (Live on Letterman)", YouTube 2011 https://www.youtube.com/watch?v=4wUPASp2hfY

Taylor Swift, "Cornelia Street (Live From Paris)," YouTube 6-22-2020 https://www.youtube.com/watch?v=Vgt1d3eAm7A

Van Huyssteen, Justin, "Hanging Gardens of Babylon – A Wonder of Ancient Engineering," Art in Context 5-23-2023 https://artincontext.org/hanging-gardens-of-babylon/

Whitman, Sara, "The Real Meaning Behind Taylor Swift's Cowboy Like Me Lyrics," Nicki Swift 5-11-2022 https://www.nickiswift.com/294057/the-real-meaning-behind-taylor-swifts-cowboy-like-me-lyrics/

Wiswanath, Jake, "Taylor Swift's "But Daddy I Love Him" Is An Ode To Bad Boys," Bustle 4-18-2024 https://www.bustle.com/entertainment/taylor-swift-but-daddy-i-love-him-lyrics-meaning

Zalewski, Anna, "Taylor Swift's Rock Hall of Fame Carole King Tribute Had the Woman Herself in Tears," Rolling Stone 10-30-2021 https://www.rollingstone.com/music/music-news/taylor-swift-rock-hall-carole-king-1250873/

TAYLOR SWIFT BOOK FRONT AND BACK COVER QUIZ ANSWERS

Readers are encouraged to try to guess the answers BEFORE reading the book and see how many you get. After reading the book try again and see how many you get then!

FRONT:

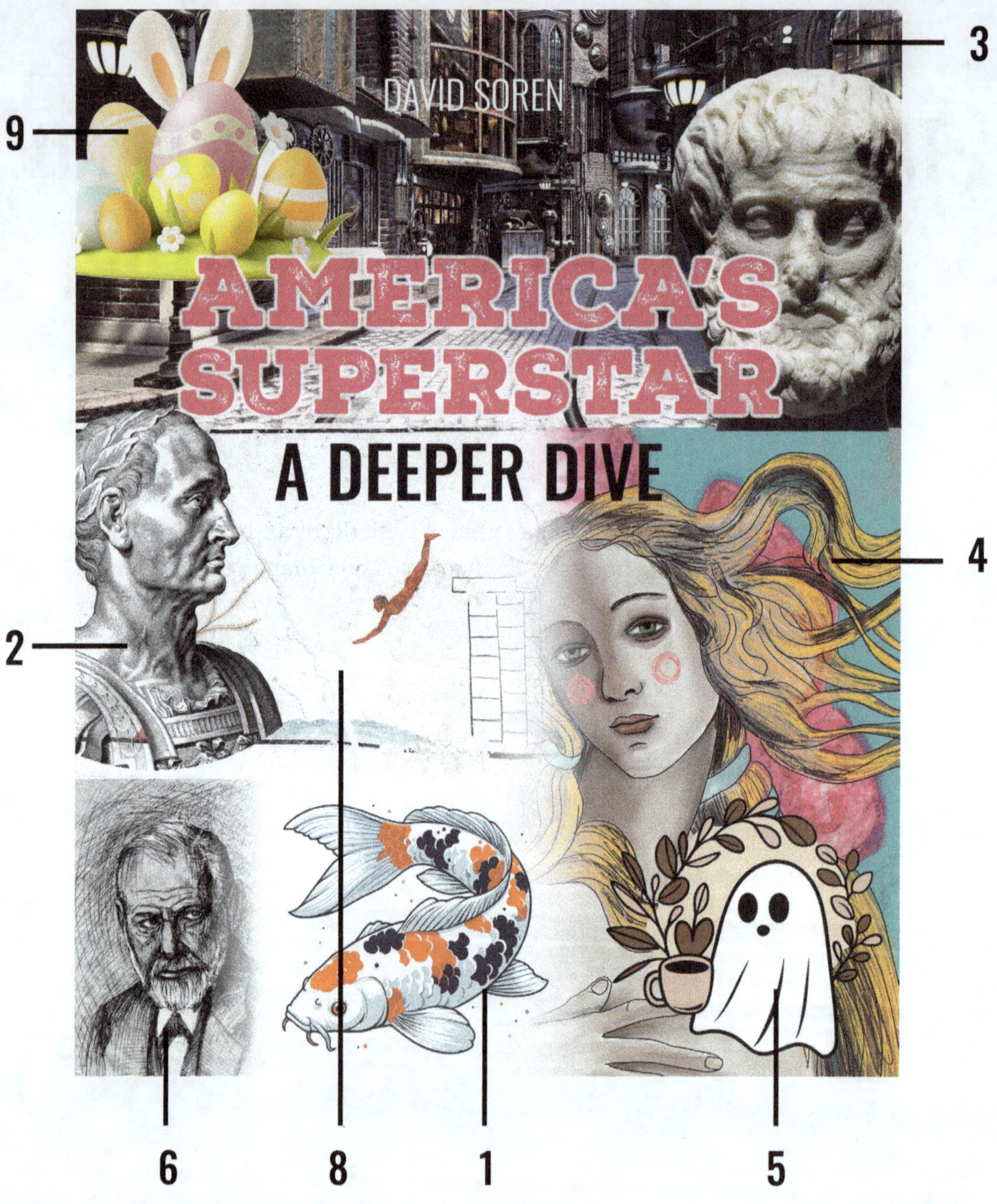

1. KOI FISH Japanese Koi Fish are symbols of luck, prosperity and good fortune and Taylor Swift used a Living Jewels brand koi decorated guitar in 2011 on the Speak Now Tour to perform *Last Kiss* and in 2022 for *Anti-Hero*. It was placed in the Country Music Hall of Fame but has appeared again used by her on the Eras Tour.

2. JULIUS CAESAR Julius Caesar was the powerful dictator of Rome and a famous military conqueror who was assassinated in 44 B.C. by senators including Brutus whom he thought was his friend. *Et tu brute* in Latin means "even you Brutus" and appears on her throne in the *Look What You Made Me Do* video on the *Reputation* album in Latin!! It is from Act 3 Scene 1 of William Shakespeare's play *Julius Caesar*. Taylor also has kept a pillow with this Latin phrase in at least one of her homes on her couch!

3. STEAMPUNKED CITY STREET- This refers to the steampunk-influenced video *Fortnight* which borrows heavily from concepts of the 1980s movement. Post Malone even described the video in that manner as he learned to use a manual typewriter. It refers to using steam power to generate a future world and is sometimes referred to as Retro-Futurism.

4. BOTTICELLI VENUS- Taylor admires film director Peter Weir and films such as *The Tortured Poets Society* with Robin Williams. Weir used this famous painting by Sandro Botticelli in his movie *Picnic at Hanging Rock* back in 1975. Furthermore, it stands for Neo-Platonism, an ancient Roman and Renaissance Florentine movement based on the literature of the Greek scholar Plato and Roman philosophers such as Plotinus. Taylor has apparently been studying the works of Plato's student Aristotle.

5. GHOST WITH LAUREL WREATH DRINKING COFFEE This refers to the coffee drinking ghosts who show up in Taylor's official video of *Anti-Hero* dressed in similar sheets. The laurel is a recurrent Taylor symbol.

6. SIGMUND FREUD- This is based on the id, ego and superego characterizations of Taylor developed in her video *Anti-Hero*. Sigmund Freud was the pioneer of modern psychoanalysis who first presented this understanding of the human psyche. In *Anti-Hero* Taylor appears to conduct her own Freudian analysis of…herself!

7. ARISTOTLE- The remarkable ancient Greek polymath who seems to have written about everything was the great pupil of Plato. Among the things he wrote was his *Poetics* which explained in detail how to communicate with an audience when you are creating theater and the critical things you have to know when affecting your audience dramatically. In the song *So High School* on the *Tortured Poets Directory* Taylor mysteriously proclaims "I know Aristotle" and by that she seems to mean that she studied *The Poetics*.

8. THE PAESTUM DIVER- This is a famous South Italian Greek fresco painting of around 470 B.C. from a tomb of an unknown but distinguished person of the area of the ancient Greek and Samnite town of Paestum, not far from Naples. The lid that seals the tomb features someone, perhaps the deceased, delighting in diving from a high platform into the water near his town. The dive has inspired scholars to think that the dead person loved these joys as a symbol of the wonder of life and of course Taylor used the deep dive from the stage into the "water" to astonish her audience in *The Eras Tour*.

9. EASTER EGGS- These are the symbols that Taylor uses to describe the hidden secrets that she buries within her work and invites you to decipher, sort of like what we are doing right now!

BACK COVER:

END
DAVID SOREN
AMERICA'S
SUPERSTAR
A DEEPER DIVE
innovativeink
PUBLISHING
A Division of Kendall Hunt

1. MELTING TIMEPIECE- Here is a melting timepiece indicative of Salvador Dali's famous Surrealist painting *Persistence of Memory*, from 1931. Songs such as Cardigan contain Surrealist imagery seemingly influenced by Dali such as the piano and water sequences. It also shows Taylor's frequent obsession with the passing of time as in songs such as *Timeless* in the vault of her *Fearless* album.

2. LAUREL WREATH- Taylor uses these quite a bit and they are symbols of a Nobel Prize Laureate of course but are also found on Julius Caesar and especially on the god Apollo who is the Greek god patron of the Muses who inspire mortals such as Taylor with so many gifts of the Humanities and…he is a snake killer which is a powerful symbol used by Taylor on the Reputation album in particular to face down her enemies.

3. 12 STRING ACOUSTIC GUITAR- This is the first kind of guitar that Taylor learned to play when she was just 12 and it is considered the easiest kind to learn on because the strings are under less tension. She still occasionally plays it for its distinctive rich full sound.

4. HANGING GARDENS OF BABYLON- This artist's conception of the famous lost palatial gardens built for King Nebuchadnezzar II in the first half of the sixth century B.C. in what is now Iraq and a perennial symbol for exoticism and pleasure. They are one of the wilder images described in Taylor's song *Cowboy Like Me*. If you missed them, they are located behind Romeo and Juliet.

5. SCOTTISH FOLD CAT is of course Meredith Grey named for the character in the tv show Grey's Anatomy. Meredith appears on Taylor's friend Ryan Reynolds t-shirt in the movie *Deadpool 2* and Taylor has even gone to Cat School to learn how to behave in a cat-like manner for the movie *Cats* in which she sang an original song.

6. PICKUP TRUCK. This is that old beat-up pickup truck that her would-be boyfriend would never let her drive, from the song *Picture to Burn* on her debut album. She was 14 years old when the alleged incident was supposed to have taken place!

7. ROMEO AND JULIET. This is from Taylor's international breakthrough hit *Love Story* from the album *Fearless* in which she is standing on a balcony and a young man comes along and says hello. It is of course based on the Shakespeare tragic play which she turns into a happy ending.

8. DEAD END STREET. This refers to the song *Red* from the album *Red* in which Taylor's complex romantic relationship is compared to driving a new Maserati car down a dead-end street. It's just something you wouldn't want to do and yet you can't stop yourself!

9. VINTAGE TYPEWRITER. This is reminiscent of the steampunked typewriters with mystical powers in the video *Fortnight*.